Edward Frossard

Catalogue of the large and valuable medallic collection of Isaac F. Wood

Part 2

Edward Frossard

Catalogue of the large and valuable medallic collection of Isaac F. Wood
Part 2

ISBN/EAN: 9783742818898

Manufactured in Europe, USA, Canada, Australia, Japa

Cover: Foto ©Thomas Meinert / pixelio.de

Manufactured and distributed by brebook publishing software
(www.brebook.com)

Edward Frossard

Catalogue of the large and valuable medallic collection of Isaac F. Wood

The Medallic Collection

OF

Isaac F. Wood,

Feb'y 25-29, 1884.

BANGS & CO.

Nos. 739-741 Broadway,

NEW YORK.

Bids for this Sale will be faithfully executed by

CATALOGUE

OF THE RARE AND VALUABLE

Medallic Collection

OF

ISAAC F. WOOD, A. B., of New York,

Formerly Librarian of the Am. Num. & Arch. Soc'y.

PART II.

Washington Coins and Medals,

AMERICAN MEDALS,

Revolutionary, Historical, Presidential, Political, Centennial,
Army and Navy, etc., etc.

ALSO

MEDALS OF PHYSICIANS, PHILOSOPHERS, ARTISTS,
AUTHORS, etc.,

AMERICAN AND FOREIGN COINS,

A VERY COMPLETE NUMISMATIC LIBRARY,

Coin Cabinets, etc., etc.,

TO BE SOLD AT AUCTION,

On FEBRUARY 25th, 26th, 27th, 28th and 29th, 1884,

BY

Messrs. Bangs & Co.,

Nos. 739 AND 741 BROADWAY NEW YORK CITY

☞ Sale begins each day at TWO o'clock in the Afternoon.

Catalogue by ED. FROSSARD,

IRVINGTON-ON-HUDSON, N. Y.

THIRTY-FOURTH SALE.

AMERICAN COIN SCALE.

NOTE.— A special edition of that part of the Catalogue comprising the Numismatic Library is issued. Copies can be had, on application only, from Messrs. Bangs & Co.

25 copies of the entire Catalogue, thick paper, are printed. Copies, neatly priced in ink, can be obtained at $1.25 each, immediately after the Sale, by addressing

ED. FROSSARD,

Irvington-on-Hudson, N. Y.

CATALOGUE.

— ·· —

FOREIGN COPPER COINS.

ANTIGUA. 1836. Farthing tokens. Slight variations in dies. Fine and scarce. 5 pcs

AUSTRALIA. 1855-1864. Penny tokens of different firms in the several colonies. An extremely fine lot. 21. 11 pcs

Montpelier Retreat Inn. Hobart Town. Uncirculated. 18.

Jno. Andrew & Co. Melbourne. 1862. Ostrich and Kangaroo halfpenny token. Nearly proof. 18.

John Pettigrew & Co. Ipswich, Queensland. 1865. Penny token. Fine. 20.

AUSTRIA. 1760-1816. Includes several large necessary coins, and Lombardo—Venice. Good to uncirculated. 17 pcs

BAHAMA. 1806. Halfpenny. Uncirculated.

Duplicate of last number. Fine.

BARBADOES. 1788. Penny. Bust of negro crowned with plumes. I SERVE. Rev. Pineapple. Thick planchet; proof obverse. Rare. 20.

Penny. 1788. Same type as last. Extremely fine.

1792. Penny. Bust of negro, crowned with plumes. Rev. George III. as Neptune. Bronze; proof obverse. Rare. 20.

1792. Pennies. Same type as last. Very good. 3 pcs

1792. Halfpenny. Same type. Bronze proof. Very rare. 16.

1792. Halfpenny. Copper, nearly proof. Very rare.

1792. Penny and halfpenny. Very good. 2 pcs

16 Moses Tolanto. Barbadoes. Penny token without date. Fine. 18.

17 The same. Penny and halfpenny. Fine but nicked. 2 pcs

18 Thomas Lawlor & Co. Barbadoes. Halfpenny token without date. Fine and scarce.

19 BERMUDA. 1793. Penny. Bust of George III. and ship. Bright red; uncirculated. Scarce. 20.

20 Duplicates of last No. Good and very good. 2 pcs

21 BELGIUM. 1861 and '62. 10 and 5 centimes. Nickel. Very good. 4 pcs

22 CANADA. Miscellaneous cents and tokens of various provinces. Includes the scarce Magdalen token. 1815, in fine condition. Good to bright red. 11 pcs

23 CHINA. Brass token of house of ill-fame. Obscene type. Fine. 18.

24 CEYLON. 1802. 48 stuber. Copper ; fire-gilt. Proof. 19.

25 CHINCHA, Island of. Brass token for ½ real of Jose Oliviera. Fine. 12. 2 pcs

26 COSVELDT. 1713. 8 groschen. Very fine. 16.

27 DANISH AMERICA. 1763. 24 skilling, struck in yellow copper. Uncirculated.

28 1760–1868. 24, 10 skilling, cents, etc. Fair to uncirculated. Several base silver. 12 pcs

29 DOMINICA. 1844 and '48. Quartillas. Copper and brass. Very good. 15. 3 pcs

30 ENGLAND. James II. Plantation piece. 24 part real. King on horseback and four shields of arms linked. In copper, much rarer than in tin. Fine. 17.

31 George III. 1790. Penny; edge inscribed, "Render unto Cesar," etc. Very good ; rare.

32 George III. 1799. Halfpenny, bright red. 20.

33 George III., William IV. and Victoria. Pennies, halfpence and farthing; includes Victoria Empress, quarter anna 1877. Fair to fine. 7 pcs

34 PENNY TOKENS. 1665. William Ferris, Colchester. Good. 10.

35 London penny token. Rev. View of Ironmongers Almshouse, erected 1713. Very fine. 21.

36 Penny token of David Hood, Cambridge. Sheaf of wheat. PEACE, PLENTY AND LIBERTY, etc. Nearly proof. 20.

37 HALFPENNY TOKENS. British flag. MAY IT BE
    DISPLAYED, etc. Rev. View of naval battle.
    CAPE ST. VINCENT, 1797. Very fair; rare.

38 Curiosity House. 1795. Grotesque figure of Sir
    Jeffery Dunstan, etc. Uncirculated.

39 Daniel Eccleston. Lancashire halfpenny. 1794.
    Bust; rev. AGRICULTURE, MANUFACTURE AND
    COMMERCE. Uncirculated.   2 pcs

40 Prince of Wales Masonic halfpenny token. SCHERT-
    LEY FECIT 1794 on edge. Fine.

41 Montrose halfpenny. 1799. Rev. View of the
    Lunatic Hospital. ERECTED BY SUBSCRIPTION
    1781. Very good; rare.

42 Isaac Newton halfpenny token. 1793. Uncircu-
    lated.

43 End of Pain. Man suspended from gibbet. Rev
    Open book, inscribed. THE WRONGS OF MAN. JANY.
    21, 1793. Thin planchet; very good and rare.
         2 pcs

44 Rhinoceros. SIR SAMUEL HANNAYS ORIGINAL, GEN-
    UINE, AND ONLY PREVENTATIVE, etc. *Medical*
    halfpenny token. Fine.

45 Miscellaneous. Includes two Scriptural halfpennies,
    etc. Extremely fine or uncirculated.   8 pcs

46 Other halfpenny tokens. Includes 1792 Cathedral
    token, Falmouth, rev. double-headed eagle, and
    Shakespeare, duplicate of one in following lot.
    Fair to very good; one pierced.   10 pcs

47 Shakespeare halfpenny tokens. Each with bust;
    all different. Very good.   4 pcs

48 Sarum Cathedral. 1796. Uncirculated.

49 Engraved halfpennies. "Nassau Hall." 1775; "Cap-
    tain James Phillips whipped at the carts' a"——
    Good.   2 pcs

50 Negro in chains. AM I NOT A MAN AND A BROTHER.
    Rev. Two hands joined. MAY SLAVERY AND OP-
    PRESSION CEASE THROUGHOUT THE WORLD. Proof
    surface; extremely fine.

51 Duplicate of last number. Very fine.

52 Similar obverse. *James* in exergue. Different
    reverses. Extremely fine and rare *farthing* tokens.
         3 pieces

53 Kneeling negress in chains impressed on square cop-
    per planchet. Extremely fine. 12x10.

54 T. SPENCE. Bust to left. 7 MONTHS IMPRISONED FOR HIGH TREASON. 1794. Rev. Highlander in full costume. Uncirculated and rare.

55 Same obverse. Rev. Heart on hand. HONOUR. Uncirculated and rare.

56 Same obverse. Rev. Men dancing under a tree. AFTER THE REVOLUTION. Uncirculated and rare.

57 Same obverse. Rev. Human and donkey heads joined. ODD FELLOWS. 1795. A GUINEA PIG, A MILLION HOGG. Uncirculated and rare.

58 Cain slaying Abel. THE BEGINNING OF OPPRESSION. Rev. A dog. MUCH GRATITUDE BRINGS SERVITUDE. SPENCE on edge. Uncir. and rare.

59 Same obverse. Rev. Press-gang officer dragging a man. BRITISH LIBERTY DISPLAYED. 1795. Nearly proof. Very rare halfpenny.

60 Same obverse. Rev. Four men dancing around liberty pole surmounted by grotesque head of George III. TREE OF LIBERTY. Uncirculated ; rare.

61 Heart on hand. Rev. BRITISH LIBERTY DISPLAYED, as before. Uncirculated.

62 Three grenadiers, facing. WHO KNOW THEIR RIGHTS and KNOWING DARE MAINTAIN. Rev. BRITISH LIBERTY DISPLAYED, as before. Uncirculated.

63 Shepherd reclining under a tree. 1790. Rev. Man chained in a dungeon. BEFORE THE REVOLUTION. Uncirculated ; rare.

64 Same obverse. Rev. Bonfire. THE END OF OPPRESSION. Fine and scarce.

65 Same obverse. Rev. J. SPENCE SLOP SELLER NEWCASTLE. Nearly proof ; scarce.

66 Same obverse. Rev. Cottage in ruins, church in the distance. ONE ONLY MASTER GRASPS THE WHOLE DOMAIN. Fine.

67 Britannia seated, a liberty cap falling from the staff in her hand. ROUSE BRITANNIA. Rev. Hog trampling on papal and kingly crowns. Uncirculated and rare.

68 Bust to right. RT. HᴮE. C. J. FOX. Rev. Indian with tomahawk and bow. IF RENTS I ONCE CONSENT TO PAY, MY LIBERTY IS PAST AWAY. Proof ; rare.

69 Bust to right. JOHN THELWALL. Rev. T. Spence's card as book and coin dealer. Nearly proof.

70 FARTHING TOKENS. "Am I not a woman and sister," pierced ; Isaac Newton ; Mont de Piété, Limerick, 1837 ; Truro, 1830. Fine. 4 pcs

71 ESSEQUEBO & DEMERARY, 1813. 1 and ¼ stiver. Uncirculated. 22 and 18. 2 pcs

72 Duplicates of last number. Very fine. 2 pcs

73 Duplicates. Stivers (2) ; half-stivers (6). Average fine. 8 pcs

74 FRANCE. Miscellaneous ; includes a denier tournois, 1649, Lille siege XXs, and several Colonial. Very good and fine. 19 pcs

75 1842, 2, 1846, 5, and 1851, 1 centimes. *Essais.* Uncirculated or proof. 3 pcs

76 1848. 5 francs, *essais.* Bronze ; different. 3 pcs

77 1848. 10 centimes, *essais.* Copper ; different and uncirculated. 3 pcs

78 Napoleon II. 1816. 5, 2, 1, and ½ francs ; 10 and 1 centimes. *Essais* in copper. Very fine or proof. 6 pcs

79 FRENCH COLONIAL. Island of France and Bourbon (3) ; Cayenne (5), inclusive of a rare necessity coin ; Guyanne (1) ; 1710, two L crowned, type of the Canada livre, and 1740, so-called Louisiana farthing. Average good ; copper or brass. A scarce lot. 11 pcs

80 GUAIANA. 1814-1817. Necessity tokens of ½ real. Lion and castle. Rude, but nearly all fine. 14. 12 pcs

81 HAYTI. Henry. 1812. Bust laureate to right. HENRICUS DEI GRATIA HAITI REX. Rev. Crowned phoenix DEUS CAESA ATQUE GLADIUS MEUS. *Essai.* Thick planchet, engrailed edge. Dull proof. Extremely rare. 18.

82 1828-1865. 1, 2, 6, 50 and 100 centimes. All different and fine. 9 to 28. 25 pcs

83 Duplicates of last number. Good ; 1 pierced. 28 pcs

84 Geffrard. 1863. 20, 10, and 5 centimes. Fine proofs. 3 pcs

85 20 and 10 centimes. Same as last. Proof. 2 pcs

86 1877. 20 centimes. *Essai.* Proof. 10.

87 HISPANIOLA. Head to left. TYRCVFELLERIVS ; rev. Female seated, and rising sun, fine ; another, AVCTORI PLEBIS and harp, fair. 17. 2 pcs

88 HAWAIA. Kamehameha. 1847. Cent. Bright red. 18.

89 Duplicate of last number. ~~Uncirculated.~~

90 The same. Fair and very good.   2 pcs

91 JAMAICA. 1869–1871. 1 and ½ pennies. *Nickel.* Fine.   5 pcs

92 George Brandon, Thomas Lunday & Co. 1844, M. Howard, William Smith Kingston, Jamaica, Tradesmen's tokens. Copper and brass. Good. 14–18.   4 pcs

93 Man and horse. Rev. Carriage. M. HOWARD, KINGSTON, JAMAICA. Very good. 18.

94 Arms, surmounted by an alligator. JAMAICA CUR-RENCY BY WILLIAM SMITH. Penny ; also ½ penny of the same. Fine.   2 pcs

95 JAPAN. 2, 1, ½ sen, 1 rin. Anglo-Japanese coinage. Bright red.   4 pcs

96 JAVA. 1810. ½ stuber. Fine ; bent. 17.

97 LIBERIA Colonisation Society tokens 1833. From different dies. Fine. 19.   3 pcs

98 1847. Two cents. Head of Liberty and palm tree. *Legend on raised border.* Fine bronze proof ; rare. 22.

99 Duplicate of last number. Fine.

100 1847. Two cents. Similar to last, but *the legend in the field.* Fine bronze proof. 22.

101 1862. One cent. Legend on border. Proof obverse. 18.

102 MAGDALEN ISLAND. 1815. Seal and cod fish. Penny token. Fine. 21.

103 Duplicate of last number. Equally fine.

104 MONACCO. Honoré V. 1837 and '38. 10 and 5 centimes. Good and fine.   , 2 pcs

105 Duplicates of last number. Fair to fine.   7 pcs

106 MISCELLANEOUS. Includes a few obscure coins or tokens. Poor to fine.   37 pcs

107 POLAND. 1794. 4 grossi. Good. 16.

108 PORTUGAL. 20 reis, 1795, 5, 1830 Azores ; 10, 1842, Madeira. Fine. 18 to 23.   3 pcs

109 PONDICHERRY. 1785. 1 and ½ dudu. Thick ; fine. 8 and 10.   2 pcs

110 SAN MARINO. 1869. 5 centesimi. ~~Fine.~~   2 pcs

111 SPAIN. Several early issues. Nearly all fine. 11 pcs

112 Barcelona. 1650, 1812, 1823. Fine and scarce. 14
to 20. 3 pcs

113 Catalina. 1841. 6 and 3 cuartillas. Fine. 16 and
20. 2 pcs

114 Rome. 1849. ½ baioccho, pontifical arms; 40, 20,
8 and 4 baiocchi, Republic, silvered. Fine. 15
to 22. 5 pcs

115 Santa Marta. 1809. Cuartilla; another F. 7
crowned. Rev. S. D. Fine and scarce. 14. 2 pcs

116 St. Helena. Solomon Dickson and Taylor. Halfpenny token. Fine. 18.

117 Sierra Leone. 1791. Penny. Prowling lion and
joined hands. Bronze ~~proof~~. Rare. 20,

118 1791. Cent. Same type as last. Bronze proof.
Rare. 18.

119 Sultana, Sumatra. 1804. One with date 1250
(Hegira) on rev. Very good and fine. 13. 4 pcs

120 South America, etc. Tradesmen tokens. White
metal (1), brass (1), copper (4). All different and
fine. 12 to 18. 6 pcs

121 Surinam. 1764. Coffee plant and inscription. Fine.
12. 3 pcs

122 Switzerland. Miscellaneous; includes a 4 sous
token of a Swiss society abroad. Very good. 10
to 18. 9 pcs

123 Sweden. 1852. 4 skilling banco. Very good. 24.

FOREIGN COINS—SILVER.

124 Austria. Francis I., 1833. Crown. Uncirculated.

125 1763-1814. 10, 20 and 60 Kreutzer. Fair to very
good. 4 pcs

126 1822. Half lira, very good. 1832: 3 Kreutzer (4).
Uncirculated. 5 pcs

127 1832 and 33. 20 Kreutzer. Uncirculated. 3 pcs

128 Bavaria. Maximilian. 1816. Crown. Bust and
crown between crossed swords. Fine.

129 Louis I. 1832. Crown. Bust and crown in wreath
of oak and olive. Uncirculated.

130 Brunswick. 1740. ⅓ Thaler. Bust of George I.
and crowned arms. Uncirculated.

/. 9 0 131 George II. 1756. Crown of the mine of the White
Swan. Fine and rare.

ſ- 132 CARACAS. 1819. 2 real. Good to uncirculated.
4 pcs

/0 133 COLOMBIA. 1821. Dollar; Indian head and pome-
granate. Pierced; doubtful.

/7 134 COB MONEY. 4, 2, 1 real. Round triangular, etc.
Four counterstamped, 5 pierced. Fair to good.
7 pcs

6 ſ- 135 CENTRAL AMERICA. 1846. 2 real. Cob money,
counterstamped on each side. Good; rare.

2 0 136 1831. 2 real; and 1843 ½ real. Fine.   2 pcs

6 ſ- 137 COSTA RICA, 1842. State; 1840, etc., Republic,
also Colombia (1833) and Bolivia. 2, 1, ½ real.
Very good; one pierced.   6 pcs

ſ0 138 CORDOBA (Province). 1848. 1 real. Thick, fine and
rare.

,ſ- 139 CURACAO. 1821 and 1822. Real (2) and stiver. Uncirculated.   3 pcs

ſ0 140 DENMARK. 1614. Christian IV. 1 mark. Very fair.

ſ 141 1677-1871. 1¼ to 16 skilling. Also 10, 25 ore, etc.
Average fine; quite a number base.   24 pcs

; 142 DANISH-AMERICA. 1740-67. 12 and 24 (1) skilling.
Fine.   6 pcs

/ʎ 143 1837-'62. 2, X, and XX skilling, Danish-America;
also 5, 10 and 20 cents. All very fine.   16 pcs

ſ 144 Duplicates of two last numbers, etc. Fair to good.
21 pcs

2 ſ- 145 DOMINICA. 1877. 2½ and 5 centavos. Uncirculated.   4 pcs

4ſ 146 ENGLAND. Edward III. Pennies, London Mint;
also Elizabeth, "Rosa sine spina" penny. Very
good.   3 pcs

.?. ʎ0 147 James I. and Charles I. Engraved medalet. Bust
on each side. "Give thy judgments, O God, unto
the King, and thy righteousness unto the King's
sons." Fine. 17.

ſ. /0 148 Jeton. Within a wreath of roses, fleurs-de-lis and
thistles. JACOBVS DVX EBOR NAT. 15 OCT. BAPTIZ
24 NOVE, 1633. Rev. Arms crowned. NON SIC
MILLE COHORTES. Fine and rare. 18.

ſ. ſʎ 149 Busts jugata. GVLIEMVS ET MARIA D. G. ANG. FRA
ET HIB REX ET REGINA, etc. Rev. Warrior on
altar. Fine Dutch medal; repoussé. 32.

150 Anne. 1703. Crown. VIGO under the bust. Rev. Four shields crowned, plain angles. Fine.

151 The same. 1703. Half-crown. VIGO. Fine.

152 The same. 1707. 2 shilling. E under the bust. Good.

153 The same. Vigo medalet. INCENS CLASSE OPES AMERIC INTERCEPT. 1702. Fine; brass. 16.

154 The same. 4, 3, 2, 1 pence. Maundy. Fine. 4 pcs

155 George II. 1746. Half-crown. LIMA under the bust. Rev. Four shields crowned; plain angles. Very fine.

156 The same. 4 and 1 pence. Maundy. Fine. 2 pcs

157 George III. 1787. Shilling and sixpence. Uncirculated. 2 pcs

158 George III. 1804. Bank of England dollar. ~~Nearly proof.~~

159 1811. Peterborough Bank token for 18 pence. Proof.

160 The same. 1811 and 1814. Bank tokens for three shillings. Fine. 2 pcs

161 The same. 1813. Bank tokens. 1s. 6d. Nearly proof.

162 The same. 1818. $\frac{1}{2}$ Ackey trade. Rev. Elephant over arms supported by Indian and naked man. FREE TRADE TO AFRICA BY ACT OF PARLIAMENT 1750. Uncirculated and rare. 16.

163 The same. 1809. 1, $\frac{1}{2}$ and $\frac{1}{4}$ stuber for Essequebo and Demarary. Average good. 6 pcs

164 1816. 1, $\frac{1}{2}$ and $\frac{1}{4}$ stuber, same colony. Good and uncirculated. 3 pcs

165 The same. 3, 2, and 1 pence. Maundy. Uncirculated. 4 pcs

166 George IV. 1822. Colonial currency, $\frac{1}{2}$, $\frac{1}{4}$, $\frac{1}{8}$, and $\frac{1}{16}$ crown. Rare set; fine. 4 pcs

167 Duplicates of last number. $\frac{1}{4}$, $\frac{1}{8}$, and $\frac{1}{16}$. Good. 6 pcs

168 The same. 1829. Shilling. Crowned lion on crown. Fine.

169 William IV. 1832 and '35. 1 (2) and $\frac{1}{2}$ guilder for Essequebo and Demarary. Good. 3 pcs

170 The same. British Guiana. 1836. 1 guilder; good and scarce.

.2 0 171 William IV. and Victoria. Shillings (4) and 6 pence
(2). Good to uncirculated.   6 pcs

§ 172 Geo. IV., William IV., and Victoria. 4, 3, and 1½
pence. Maundy. Good to uncirculated.   5 pcs

/ 0 173 Victoria. 1841. Two annas; also double fanam;
the latter only fair.   2 pcs

/ 2 /₂ 174 CANADA. 1858. 20 (2), 10 (2), and 5 cents. Very
good.   5 pcs

/ 3 175 1870. 50 (2), 10 (3), and 5 (3) cents. Fine.   8 pcs

/ / 176 1872 and '74. 25 cents; '71 and '74, 10 cents; '72 and
'74, 5 (4) cents. Fine.   8 pcs

/ 4 177 New Foundland. 1865. 20 cents; New Brunswick,
1862 and '64, 10 and 5 cents. Good and fine.   3 pcs

/. 2 5 178 SCOTLAND. Alexander 1. Penny. Very good and
scarce.

8. 0 0 179 James VI. 1567. Sword dollar. Crowned sword;
hand pointing to XXX and a counterstamped
thistle in the field. Rev., I. R. crowned, on each
side of a crowned shield. Very fine; rare.

2 0 180 FRANCE. Louis XV. Isles du Vent tokens. Good.
13.   2 pcs

6 181 Duplicates of last number. Fair and good.   4 pcs

7 182 Mauritius. 1779 and '81. 3 sols; also Cayenne, 2
sous and 10 cents. Fair to fine.   5 pcs

4 2 183 Treasury token for 50 sous. GOUV. DE MAURICE ET
DEP. Thick. Fine and scarce. 14.

4 4 184 Duplicate of last number. Good.

5 2 185 Pondicherry (1769–74). Double fanam. Five lilies,
and crown. Thick ; fine 9.

6 6 186 Token. 1781. "Maison philantropique de Paris."
Hand from heaven watering plants, three signs of
the zodiac to left. Very fine. 19.

8 187 Louis XIV., Napoleon I. and III., and the Republic. Minor silver coins, inclusive of a franc. Good
to fine.   9 pcs

2 8 188 HOLLAND. 1802 and 1854. ¼ guilder for Dutch
India. Fine.   2 pcs

7 8 189 HANNOVER. 1865. Waterloo Victory thaler. Uncirculated.

6 0 190 William IV. 1834. ⅔ thaler. Uncirculated.

191 GERMANY. Thaler struck to commemorate the
martyrdom of John Huss, first reformer. Bust to
right. Rev. Huss at the stake. JO . HVS . ANNO
. A . CHRISTO NATO. 1415, etc. Cast, as all these
thalers are, but the finest I have seen.

192 Marriage medal. Pair joining hands over an altar.
Rev. (German) "God said, it is not well for man
to be alone." Sharp and uncirculated. 27.

193 Another. Marriage ceremony. Rev. Lovers pray-
ing before an altar, the hymeneal couch in the
background. Sharp, uncir. and artistic medal of
the 17th century. 27.

194 Love, marriage and baptismal tokens, one with
busts jugata. Very fine. Average size 16. 4 pcs

195 HESSE. 1776. Blood-money half thaler; said to
have been struck from silver received for hire of
German troops against America. Uncirculated.

196 HAITI. 1800. Monnoie d'Haiti. Liberty with cap
and fasces. Rude. Good and rare. 10.

197 Year 10, 11, 12, 13, 14, 15, 18, 24 and 25. 6, 12, 25
and 50 centimes. All different. Fine to uncirculated. A rare lot. 8 to 16. 20 pcs

198 Year 18, 24, 25. 50 and 25 centimes. Fine to uncirculated. 7 pcs

199 Year 26. Boyer, president. 100, 50 and 25 centimes. Fine to uncirculated. 13 to 20. 3 pcs

200 Year 26 and 27. 100 centimes. Fine and uncirculated. 2 pcs

201 Year 27 to 30. Boyer, president. 100, 50 and 25
centimes. Fine and uncirculated. 6 pcs

202 Duplicates of preceding lots. 100 (2), 50 (3), 25 and
12 centimes. Good to uncirculated. 19 pcs

203 ITALY. Victor Emmanuel. 1871. 5 francs. Very
fine.

204 The same. 1863. Lire (2); Napoleon. 1808, and
Lucca, 1833, 10 soldi; Sicily, 1844, 5 grana. Good
to uncirculated. 5 pcs

205 MEXICO. 1783. Dollar, struck on irregular planchet. Very good; small hole near border.

206 1747 Pillar dollar. Mexico mint. Fine.

207 1792 and 98. Dollars. Mexico mint. Fine. 2 pcs

208 Augustinus. 1823. Dollar. Bust to right. Rev.
Crowned eagle on nopal. Very fine.

1. 18 209 Maximilian. 1867. Dollar. Mexico mint. Fine.

70 210 The same. 1866. Half-dollar. Mexico mint. Fine.

13 211 The same. 1866. Ten cent. Fine.

13 212 MANTUA. 1702; Monacco, 1687 and Charles V. for
Italy. Dime size ; good, base.   3 pcs

75 213 PRUSSIA. William and Augusta. 1861. Coronation thaler. Uncirculated.

25 214 War medalet. "To Prussian veterans," in Danish-
Prussian war. Very fine. 12.

13 215 PAPAL STATES. Clement XI. 1709 and '11, for
Ferrara. Bust and saint. Good and fine. Base.
12 and 15.   2 pcs

65 216 SAXONY. John V. 1867. Mining thaler. Uncirculated.

13 217 SOUTH AMERICA. ¼ dollar, 1 and ½ real, cuartillas
of several States, including 2 of Mexico, one
pierced. Fair to fine.   12 pcs

2. 20 218 SIERRA LEONE. 1791. Dollar. Prowling lion and
two hands joined. ~~Very fine~~; rare.

1. 85 219 1791. Half-dollar; same type. Fine and rare.

1. 00 220 1796. Ten cents; same type. Very fine and rare.

5. 20 221 SPAIN. Ferdinand VI. Proclamation half-dollar.
HISPAL IN EJVS PROCLAMATIONE. Barely fair.

P. 25 222 Ferdinand VI. and Charles IV. Proclamation
medalets, two with arms of Havana. Very rude
impression ; 2 pierced. 14 to 18.   3 pcs

1. 10 223 Charles IV. and Ferdinand VII. Proclamation
medalets. Madrid, San Salvador and Campeche.
Good to fine ; 2 pierced. 10 to 14.   4 pcs

1. 25 224 Charles IV. 1808. Dollar. Very fine.

10 225 Ferdinand VII. 1818. Dollar. Good. *counterfeit*

5 30 226 Isabella. Proclamation medalets Mallorca and
Minorissa. 1833. Very fine. 11 and 14.   2 pcs

75 227 The same. Guines and Havana. 1834. Uncirculated. 14.   2 pcs

1 50 228 The same. 1834. March 30. Guanabacoa. Reeded
and lettered edge. Uncirculated. 18.   2 pcs

1. 80 229 The same. 1834. Matanzas, Feb. 8, Jaruco, March
30. Uncirculated. 20.   2 pcs

25 230 1858 and '62. Birth medalets. Names of god-par-
ents, etc. Uncirculated. 11.   2 pcs

10 231 SWITZERLAND. Berne and Vaud. Cantonal 5 and 1
batzen. Uncirculated.   4 pcs

232 1876. 1 franc; new type. Helvetia standing. Uncirculated.

233 Miscellaneous. Half-dime to quarter-dollar size. Average fair; 1 pierced. 14 pcs

234 Miscellaneous. Germany, etc; chiefly base. Large and small. A fair lot. 52 pcs

WASHINGTON COINS.

235 1783. Military bust. Rev. UNITED STATES. Cents from different dies ; fine and very fine. 3 pcs

236 1783. Cents. Bust in toga. Rev. UNITED STATES. Good and fine. 2 pcs

237 1783. Cents. Bust in toga. Rev. UNITED STATES. Very fine.

238 Duplicate of last number. Very good.

239 Duplicates of preceding numbers. Good and fine ; one pierced. 3 pcs

240 Double-head cent. Very fine.

241 Duplicate. Fine.

242 Bust in toga. Rev. UNITED STATES. Cent, said to have been restruck in England about 1803. *Silver;* proof.

243 The same. Copper ; proof. 2 pcs

244 Another. Very fine.

245 1783. Cent. Bust to right. GEORGIUS TRIUMPHO. Rev. VOCE POPOLI. Very fine and scarce.

246 Another. Nearly as fine as last.

247 The same. Counterstamped G. W. before the face. Fine.

248 New York Washington cent. Bust to right, NON VI VIRTVTE VICI. Rev. Liberty seated with staff and scales, NEO-EBORACENCIS, 1786. Planchet slightly nicked on edge, the center of rev., as usual with these pieces, lightly struck. *One of the finest known and extremely rare.*

249 Military bust to left. Obv. WASHINGTON BORN VIRGINIA FEB. 11, 1732. Rev. GENERAL OF THE AMERICAN ARMIES, etc., in ten parallel lines, a star above. Copper ; extremely fine and rare. 10.

250 Duplicate of last number. Very good.

2.50 251 Washington cent. 1791. Large eagle rev. *Dr.* L. *Roper* stamped under the bust. Very fine.

3.00 252 Duplicate of last number. Unstamped. Fine.

9/.00 253 Bust laureate and draped to left GEORGIVS III. DEI GRATIA. Rev. The same as the rev. of the large eagle cent of 1791. Unique specimen, originally in the Clay collection. Bronzed copper; nearly proof. 20.

12.00 254 Liverpool halfpenny. 1791. Bust of Washington, etc., same as in No. 251. Rev. Ship sailing to right ; two branches of oak crossed, below. Fine; extremely rare.

6.75 255 Washington cent. 1791. Small eagle reverse. Extremely fine and rare. 18.

5.25 256 Duplicate of last number. Very fine.

12.00 257 Disme. 1792. Bust of Liberty to left. LIBERTY PARENT OF SCIENCE & INDUS. Rev. Flying eagle. UNITED STATES OF AMERICA. Copper ; milled edge. Very fine and rare. 14.

8.00 258 Martha Washington half dime. LIB. PAR. OF SCIENCE & INDUSTRY, 1792, etc. *Silver;* obv. fine, rev. good. Rare.

20.00 259 Naked bust cent. Bust laureate to right, WASHINGTON PRESIDENT 1792. Rev. Small eagle displayed, CENT above, edge inserted "United States of America." Has been circulated ; in fair condition and extremely rare. 18.

8.00 260 Cent. 1792. Military bust to left. WASHINGTON PRESIDENT 1792. Rev. Eagle displayed; 12 stars in curved line above, and one just over the head. Edge plain ; *fine and of extreme rarity.* 18.

5.50 261 Similar obverse. Rev. GENERAL OF THE AMERICAN ARMIES 1775, etc., in 10 parallel lines. *Very fine and rare.* 19.

20.00 262 Half-dollar Military bust to left. G. WASHINGTON PRESIDENT. I. 1792. Rev. Eagle displayed, 15 stars about the head. UNITED STATES OF AMERICA. Edge plain. *Copper ; very fine and rare.* 20

00 263 Duplicate of last number. Small nicks in the field, but *fine ; rare.*

1.60 264 Liverpool halfpenny. 1793. Obv. from the same die as small eagle cent of 1791. Rev. Ship sailing to right. HALFPENNY 1793. Very fine ; scarce.

19

265 Duplicate of last number. Quite as fine as last.

266 Military bust to left. GEORGE WASHINGTON. Rev.
Eagle over American shield. LIBERTY AND SECU-
RITY. Narrow milling on border. Edge inscribed.
"An asylum for the oppress'd of all nations."
Bronzed copper; uncirculated. 21.

267 The same. No milling on border. Copper: nearly
bright red. 21.

268 Another; duplicate of last number. Very fine. 21.

269 Military bust to right. Rev. LIBERTY AND SECU-
RITY 1795; edge inscribed "Birmingham Redruth
and Swansea." Copper. Very fine. 18.

270 Same as last, but edge inscribed "Payable at London, Liverpool, or Bristol." Cop.; thick and thin
planchet; very good. 18.   2 pcs

271 Another nicked; also rev. of this token combined
with "Irish halfpenny 1795." 18.   2 pcs

272 Washington Grate cent. Bust to right. Rev. A
grate. LONDON 1795. Copper: engrailed edge.
Uncirculated. 18.

273 Another; engrailed edge. Barely circulated. 18.

274 North Wales token. Military bust to left.
GEORGEIVS WASHINGTON. Rev. A harp. Cop-
per; very good or fine. 17.   2 pcs

275 Military bust to right. GEORGE WASHINGTON. Rev.
SUCCESS TO THE UNITED STATES. Silvered copper;
uncirc. 14 and 16.   2 pcs

276 Duplicates. Two of each size. Brass; fine.   4 pcs

277 1794 "Liberty and Commerce." Rev. "John
Howard," etc. Counterstamped on obverse with
hideous head of Washington (?). Very good.

278 Spanish ½ dollar counterstamped with head of Washington. Barely fair. *Silver*.

279 Incuse impression of the head of Washington on a
cent of 1803. Fair.

280 Cent of 1846 counterstamped with heads of Washington and Lafayette. Fine.

281 Cents of 1847 and 1822 counterstamped as in last
number. Fine.   2 pcs

282 Washington half and quarter dollars. 1872. Octagonal. *Gold*.   3 pcs

⁷ 𝒪 283 PATTERN PIECES. Bust of Washington to right.
GOD AND OUR COUNTRY 1863. Rev. UNITED
STATES OF AMERICA, and 2 CENTS in wreath of
wheat. *Nickel;* proof. 14.

𝟫 𝒰 284 The same. *Copper;* proof.

7 𝒪 285 Bust of Washington to right. UNITED STATES OF
AMERICA 1866. Rev. 5 in circle of 13 stars, CENTS,
and UNITED STATES OF AMERICA (sic) on edge,
Copper; very fine.

/. ⁶𝒪 286 Same obv. Rev. 5 CENTS in broad wreath. IN
GOD WE TRUST, above. *Nickel;* proof.

𝟫 𝒪 287 Same obv. Rev. Bust of Washington to right.
1866. IN GOD WE TRUST, above. *Nickel;* fine.
This and No. 285 I believe to be rare combinations struck at the mint, probably to oblige
some friendly collector

ᴠ⁻𝒪 288 Bust to right. 1866. IN GOD WE TRUST, above,
same as last rev. Rev. 5 in circle of stars and
rays. *Nickel;* very fine.

ᴠ⁻𝒪 289 Same obv. Rev. 5 in wreath. *Nickel;* proof.

7 𝒪 290 Same as last. *Copper;* proof.

.𝟫ˢ⁻ 291 Same obv. Rev. 5 in broad wreath. *Nickel;* proof.

𝟤. /𝒪 292 Bust of Washington to right. 1866. GOD AND OUR
COUNTRY, above. Rev. 5 in wreath. *Nickel;* proof.

/. ᴜ𝒪 293 Duplicates of two last numbers. *Nickel;* proof,
one spotted.   2 pcs

⁶. 𝟤 ᴊ⁻ 294 FUNERAL MEDALS. Military bust in wreath of
laurel to left. HE IS IN GLORY, THE WORLD IN
TEARS. Rev. Urn. B. F. 11., 1732. G. A. ARM.
75. R. '83. P. U. S. A. '89. R. 96. G. ARM. U. S. 98.
OB. D. 14. 1799, in two curving lines. *Silver;*
partly pierced; some letters engraved on rev.
Very fine and rare. 18.

𝟤. ᴜ𝒪 295 Obv. similar to last. Rev. The same. Tin,
pierced, fine.

ᴠ⁻𝒪 296 Another; from different dies. Tin or electrotype;
Bronzed.

7. 𝟤ᴊ⁻ 297 Military bust, etc., as in No. 295. Rev. Skull and
cross-bones; inscription in 4 curving lines, similar
to 294. *Silver;* pierced. Fine and rare. 18.

ᴊ 𝒪 298 The same. Silvered and electrotype. Both fine
and pierced.   2 pcs

ᴜ⁻ᴠ 299 COPIES, &c. Bust to left. 1789. Rev. Eagle.
Copper proof. 19.

300 Duplicate of last number. Copper proof. 19.

301 Half-dollar. 1792. Copper and brass proof. 21. 2 pcs

302 Obv. and rev. same as last, combined with Idler's card. Copper and brass; proof. 2 pcs

303 New York Washington cent. Merian's copy. *Silver*; nearly proof.

304 The same. Copper proof.

305 ELECTROTYPES. Cent. "G. Washington the Great." Rev. Links with names of States.

306 Washington. Jersey cent. Original sold for $600. Fine.

307 1791. Liverpool halfpenny. Extremely fine and deceiving.

308 1792. Varieties of half-dollar, cents, etc. All very fine. 6 pcs

309 1792. Cent. "Liberty. Parent of Science and Industry." Very fine. 21.

310 1792 Small cent.; 1793. Liverpool halfpenny; Liberty and Security. Fine. 3 pcs

311 Washington half cent. Fine.

312 Other electrotypes of Washington coins: several duplicates of preceding Nos. A fine lot. 11 pcs

WASHINGTON MEDALS.

The finest and most complete collection of Washington medals ever offered at public or private sale, containing beside all the rare but well known Washington medals, a large number, unpublished or excessively rare, besides very many duplicates of medals generally conceded to be of great rarity. In the multiplicity of the combinations of dies, the lack of positive information, in many instances, of the exact number struck, the compiler finds it simply impossible always to convey exact and accurate information, and for this reason statements of rarity, etc., are usually omitted. Special information on the subject may be found in Mr. Wm. S. Appleton's "Description of the Medals of Washington," published in the *American Journal of Numismatics*, and afterwards separately reprinted, also in many Coin Catalogues, notably that of the "Holland Sale," sold by W. E. Woodward, Esq., in 1878.

NOTE.—THE MEDALS IN THIS SERIES ARE GENERALLY ARRANGED BY SIZE; the term "*very fine*," or "*perfect*," applied to a medal denotes that it is a perfect impression, of fine color and unimpaired.

313 Naked bust of Washington to left. Legend WASHINGTON in parallel perpendicular lines on each side of bust. *C. C. Wright d. & f.* Rev. View of the signing of the Declaration of Independence, from Trumbull's painting. Bronze. Very fine and extremely rare. 56.

1. 5 0 314 The same medal. Fine electrotype.

6 0 0 315 Large bust in armor to right. GEORGE WASHING-
TON, INSCRIBED TO HIS MEMORY BY D. ECCLESTON.
LANCASTER, MDCCCV. Rev. Indian with bow
and arrow. THE LAND WAS OURS, inscription
around this in three lines. Bronze ; very fine.
48.

4. 1 0 316 The same medal with solid raised border, making
the diameter 4½ inch. Bronze cast ; very fine,
probably unique. _cast_

1. 2 5 317 Washington before Boston, by Duvivier. Bust to
right. Rev. Evacuation of Boston by the British,
1776. *Silver ;* very fine. 42.

1. 7 5 318 The same. Thick planchet. Bronze ; very fine.

1. 7 5 319 The same. Thinner planchet. Yellow bronze ; very
fine.

7 5 320 Another. Stamped BRONZE on edge. Very fine.

9. 5 0 321 Naked bust to left. GEORGE WASHINGTON. *C. C.
W. f.* under the shoulder. Rev. BORN IN VIRGINIA
FEB. 22, 1732. DIED IN VIRGINIA DEC. 14, 1799,
in heavy wreath of oak. *Silver ;* nearly proof.
A superb medal, and rare. 40.

1. 8 0 322 The same. White metal. Nearly proof. 40.

1 9 0 323 Naked bust to left. GEORGE WASHINGTON. *F.
B. Smith & Hartmann, N. Y.,* under the shoulder.
Rev. A tomb, Fame with a trumpet above. TOMB
OF WASHINGTON, MOUNT VERNON, VIRGINIA.
Bronze ; very fine and rare. 40.

1. 0 0 324 The same obverse. Rev. THIS MEDAL IS STRUCK TO
PERPETUATE THE MEMORY OF WASHINGTON, AND
IN HONOR OF THE PATRONS WHO ATTEND OUR
CENTENNIAL EXHIBITION AT PHILADELPHIA, PA.,
U. S., 1776-1876. White metal ; proof, rare. 40.

1. 1 0 325 Bust in Roman toga to left. GEORGE WASHINGTON.
F. B. Smith & Horst, N. Y., under the bust.
Rev. View of Mount Vernon. RESIDENCE OF
WASHINGTON, MOUNT VERNON, VIRGINIA. White
metal ; proof and rare. 40.

1. 5 0 226 The same obverse. Rev. Entrance of tomb, five
persons before it. TOMB OF WASHINGTON, MOUNT
VERNON, VIRGINIA. White metal ; proof and
rare. 40.

6 0 327 Duplicate of last number. White metal ; proof. 40.

328 The same obverse. Rev. THIS MEDAL IS STRUCK, etc.; same as rev. of No. 324. White metal: proof. 40.

329 View of Mount Vernon and of tomb, combining reverses of Nos. 325 and of 326. White metal; nearly proof. 40.

330 View of Mount Vernon and inscription; combining reverses of Nos. 324 and 325. White metal; proof. 40.

331 Entrance of tomb, and inscription; combining reverses of Nos. 324 and 326. White metal; proof. 40.

332 Large head in high relief to left. G. WASHINGTON. Fine and perfect copper shell. Diameter 4½ in.

333 Large bust nearly facing. Fine placque; Berlin iron. 4½ in.

334 Bust to right. GEORGE WASHINGTON. *A. Demarest, sc., N. Y.* THE GREAT FATHER: FIRST IN WAR, etc. Rev. Two hands joined: tomahawk and hatchet crossed above. PEACE AND FRIENDSHIP. Two copper shells soldered, and with loops. Very fine. Diameter nearly 4 in. *Electrotype*

335 Naked bust to right. GEORGE WASHINGTON. *J. CRUTCHETT, MT. VERNON FACTORY. A. Demarest, sc., N. Y.* Rev. View of entrance of tomb: two persons before it. Raised ornamental border. White metal gilt. Very fine and rare. 48. *duct*

336 Copper shells of the obverse and reverse of last medal. Very fine.

337 Another shell, nickel-plated, in frame made of wood grown at Mount Vernon, as per printed certificate pasted on back.

338 Small head laureate to right. METROPOLITAN CARNIVAL, FEBRUARY 20 & 21, 1871. Rev. View of the Capitol at Washington, and inscription. Trial impression in lead; fine and rare. 46.

339 Duplicate of last number. Lead; good.

340 Small bust to right. PREMIUM AWARDED TO JABOR VAN HORN FOR THE BEST RYE WHISKEY. VIRGINIA. 1824. Brass shell; very fine and rare. Diameter, 3½ in.

341 Bust to right, and inscription, same as No. 317; plaque. Berlin iron. Diameter nearly 3½ in.

342 Bust to left. WASHINGTON, and 13 stars; rudely stamped on tin disk. 3½ in.

7 0 343 Bust of Washington on ornamental pedestal, guarded by Pallas, and an Indian. GEN. WASH- INGTON PRESI. OF THE UNIT. STA. In exergue, BORN FEB. 1732, DIED DEC. 1799. Shell, *silver*. Very fine. 40.

3 0 344 Pocket looking-glass. Tin cover, impressed with head and name of Washington. Perfect. 3 in.

1. 0 -0 345 Washington on horseback to left, surrounded by a heavy wreath of maize, wheat, etc.; near the bor- der THE CONFEDERATE STATES OF AMERICA, 22 FEBRUARY, 1862. Very fine, copper shell, 3¾ in. in diameter, glass cover and square velvet frame. Extremely rare.

7 0 346 Draped bust to left ; GRAYS, beneath. Soldiers' belt-plate. Brass. Very fine. Oval. 3x2 in.

6 5 347 The same. Lozenge shaped. Brass. Extremely fine.

2. 0 -0 348 Engraved urn. WASHINGTON, WARREN, MONTGOM- ERY, WOOSTER, MERCER. Oval brass breast plate of the N. Y. Fusileers, worn in the war of 1812-14 2½x3¼ in.

1. 3 0 349 Bust of Washington to left. Oval copper shell, filled. 3¼x2½ in.

3. 0 -0 350 Bust of Washington in uniform to left. Oval cop- per shell ; very fine. 3x2¼ in.

1. 0 -0 351 Portrait of Washington and view of Mount Vernon, in frame of Mount Vernon wood. Perfect. 3¼ in.

1. 1 0 352 Glass paper press. Head of Washington. Perfect. 3 in.

2. 0 -0 353 Full figure of Washington in military uniform. Brass shell ; perfect. Length 7 in.

4 354 Bust of Washington nearly facing. Copper shell ; perfect. 3½x3¼ in.

4 355 Another. Tin : fine. 2¾x2¼ in.

2 356 Another. Bust to right. Copper shell, 2¼x2 in.

5 0 357 Bust of Washington to left. Rev. The Cherry tree scene. Issued during the Philadelphia Centennial celebration. *Compressed wood;* dark brown. 36.

5 5 - 358 Duplicates. Red and white wood. 2 pcs

5 0 359 Duplicates. Yellow and light brown. 2 pcs

2 5 - 360 Large bust to right. Rev. GREAT INTERNATIONAL EXHIBITION, etc. Compressed walnut. 36.

2 5 - 361 Smaller head to right. Same rev. Compressed walnut. 36.

362 Naked bust to right by *Paquet.* The United States
Mint cabinet medal. Bronze; very fine. 36.

363 The same. White metal; silvered. Very fine.

364 Copper shells of the obv. and rev. of last-described
medal. Very fine

365 Military bust facing left, surrounded by a wreath.
GEORGE WASHINGTON. Rev. Tomb surmounted
by an urn, military emblems, weeping figures, etc.,
HE IS IN GLORY, THE WORLD IN TEARS. The large
funeral medal by Perkins. Tin; fine for this
medal. 55.

366 Duplicate of last number. Tin; barely fair,
possibly cast. 36.

367 Military bust with aged features, to left; GEORGE
WASHINGTON; *J. A. Bolen* under the bust.
Rev. I HOPE THAT LIBERAL ALLOWANCES,
etc., extract of his letter to Hamilton, in eleven
lines. Silver; dull proof; rare. 37.

368 The same. The die cracked on obverse from shoulder
to border. Fire gilt. A beautiful medal. 37

369 Naked bust to left. GEORGE WASHINGTON, PRESI-
DENT OF THE U. S. A. Rev. Blank. Trial impression in lead by *Wright.* Fine. 35.

370 Military bust to left. GENERAL WASHINGTON.
Brass shell of early period. Loop; fine; scarce. 34.

371 Electrotype of last number. Fine.

372 Naked bust to right. GEORGIUS WASHINGTON PRÆS.
PRIM. REP. CONF AMER. MDCCLXXXIX. *Lovett,
Phila.* under the bust. Rev. TO THE JAPANESE
EMBASSY FROM BAILEY & CO., JEWELLERS, PHILA-
DELPHIA, 1860, in wreath. Bronze proof; 33.

373 The same obverse. Rev. Minerva seated to left
with wreath. NATUS FEB. XII. ETC., MDCCCLX.
Bronze; very fine. 33.

374 Duplicate of last number. Yellow bronze; very fine. 33.

375 The same obverse. Rev. TO COMMEMORATE THE
HUNDREDTH ANNIVERSARY OF AMERICAN INDE-
PENDENCE, etc., 1876. Bronze; very fine. 33.

376 Medallion bust of Washington to left, a cupid on
each side and an eagle below. FIRST IN WAR,
FIRST IN PEACE, FIRST IN THE HEARTS OF HIS
COUNTRYMEN MDCCLXXVI Rev. Columbia
distributing gifts to four females. The Copenhagen
Centennial medal. Philadelphia, 1876. Bronze
proof. 32.

377 Duplicate of last number. Copper gilt; proof. 32.

378 The same. White and black rubber. 30 and 32.
2 pcs

379 The same, except legend LET US HAVE PEACE. 1776. THE CENTENNIAL YEAR OF THE UNITED STATES OF AMERICA, 1876. Bronze; proof. 32.

380 Bust jugata of Washington, Koskiusko and Lafayette. TO THE HERO'S, etc. Rev. Inscriptions between wreaths. Bronze; very fine. 32.

381 The same. Fine electrotype.

382 The same. Copper shell of obverse. Fine.

383 Within an ornamental circle, the naked bust of Washington to left. A. C. M. under the shoulder. GEORGE WASHIGTON, UNITED STATES OF AMERICA. Eagle grasping the American flag above, and ornamental wreath near border. Rev. Ground floor of Masonic temple. NON NOBIS SOLUM SED TOTO MUNDI NATI. MDCCCLIX. Bronze; extremely fine. 32.

384 The same obverse. Rev. View of the Crystal Palace, NEW YORK 1853, and inscription in exergue. Silver; very fine, 32.

385 The same. Bronze; very fine. 32.

386 Naked bust to left, by *Laubenheimer.* FIRST IN WAR, etc. Square and compasses below. Rev. The cherry tree scene. 1876. Bronze; extremely fine. 31.

387 The same medal. Brass; proof.

388 Short bust in inner circle, to right. GEORGE WASHINGTON, G. H. L., under the neck; around this a broad border, ornamented with eagle, flying mottoes, stars, and trophy of arms. Rev. View of equestrian statue. WASHINGTON STATUE UNION SQUARE N. Y. MDCCCLXI. Bronze; extremely fine. 32.

389 Duplicate: White metal; silvered. Extremely fine. 32.

390 The same obverse. Rev. Ground floor of Masonic temple. MDCCCLIX. Bronze; extremely fine. 32.

391 The same. Brass proof. 32.

392 Another. White metal proof. 32.

393 The same obverse. Rev. Blank. White metal proof. 32.

394 The same obverse. Rev. Bust of Kane over a view of Arctic scenery. Trial piece; unique combination. White metal; fine. 32.

395 Military bust to left and names of presidents to 1834. Rev. Eagle and shield, etc. 1834. Fine. 32.

396 Electrotype copy of last-described medal. Fine.

397 Bust to left. Rev. View of Stony Point. 1779. Electrotype. 31.

398 Busts jugate of Washington and Lafayette to right. CENTENNIAL YORKTOWN VA. 1881. Rev. View of the surrender of Cornwallis. OCT. 19. 1781. Bronze, proof. 32.

399 Naked bust to left. A C M. under the shoulder. GEORGE WASHINGTON, THE GREAT AND GOOD. Rev. Cornucopia from which wreaths issue. White metal; proof. 30.

400 MANLY MEDALS. Military bust with aged features to left; S. B. F. under the shoulder. GEO. WASHINGTON NATUS VIRGINIA BP WM. C; in exergue, 11 FEB. O. S. 1732. Rev. GENERAL OF THE AMERICAN ARMIES, 1775. RESIGNED, 1783. PRESIDENT OF THE UNITED STATES 1789. J. MANLY & C 1790. Silver; extremely fine and rare. 30.

401 Another. Bronze; extremely fine. 30.

402 Bust to left similar to last. GEO. WASHINGTON BORN VIRGINIA. Brooks f under the shoulder, and FEB. 11, 1732. in exergue. Rev. The same inscription as last. Silver; extremely fine; rare. 30.

403 Another. Yellow bronze; very fine. 30.

404 Another. Bronze; fine. 30.

405 Another. Obverse very good; rev. poor. 30.

406 HALLIDAY MEDALS. Long bust to right; HALLIDAY S. under the shoulder. GEORGE WASHINGTON PRESIDENT OF THE UNITED STATES. Rev. Sword, fasces, and wreath upon an altar; COMMISSION RESIGNED; PRESIDENCY RELINQUISHED 1797. Tin; extremely fine and rare. 34.

407 The same. Electrotype; fine. 34.

408 Another electrotype; silvered; fair.

409 Bust to right, similar to last described. G. WASHINGTON PRES. UNIT. STA. Rev. Altar, etc., as before. Bronze proof. 29.

410 Duplicate of last number. Dark bronze; extremely fine. 29.

411 Another. Bronze; very fine. 29.

412 Another. Thick planchet. White metal silvered. Fine. 29.

413 The same medal. White metal; proof. 29.

414 Duplicate of last number. White metal; proof. 29.

415 Bust to right, similar to preceding. G. WASHINGTON PRES. UNIT. STA. R under the shoulder. Rev. Altar with sword, fasces, and wreath; inscription and date as in the larger medals. *Silver*; proof, and an undoubted original. 26.

416 Exact duplicate of last number. Original, from the Holland sale. *Silver;* about same condition. 26.

417 The same. Bronze; extremely fine. 26.

418 The same. Bronze; fine. 26.

419 The same. Thicker planchet. Bronze; very fine. 26.

420 The same. One tin; another electrotype.   2 pcs

421 The same medal. Thick planchet. Possibly a restrike. Bronze; extremely fine. 26.

422 Duplicate of last number. Thinner planchet. Same metal and condition as last. 26.

423 SEASON MEDALS. Cow and calf before a cabin; a shepherd and sheep in the distance. C. H. Küchler f. U. S. A. in exergue. Rev. SECOND PRESIDENCY OF GEO. WASHINGTON MDCCXCVI. Original loop. Bronze; very fine and rare. 30.

424 Duplicate of last number. Nicked in the field; loop removed. Bronze; fine and rare. 30.

425 Women spinning; child and baby in cradle to left; otherwise same as last number. Bronze; loop removed. A little nicked, but fine and rare. 30.

426 A sower to left; a plougher and cabin in the distance. U. S. A., etc., as before. Bronze; a little nicked, but fine and rare. Loop removed. 30.

427 Eagle grasping olive branch and arrows; an American shield on his breast and scroll in his beak. WASHINGTON BORN FEBY. 22, 1732. Trieste FEBY. 22, 1841. Rev. LIBERTY PRESENTED TO ANDREW CANEL BY THE AMERICANS FOR HIS GENTLEMANLY HOSPITALITY ON THE FOREGOING OCCASION; 26 stars near the border. *Silver;* nearly proof, and a rare medal. 29.

428 Duplicate of last number. Bronze; nearly proof.
29.

429 Small bust of Washington, surrounded by the busts
of seven following presidents, each in a slightly
depressed circle. Rev. Their names within deli-
cate wreaths of flowers. Bronze; thick planchet.
Very fine. 29.

430 Duplicate of last number. White metal proof. 29.

431 The same obverse. Rev. Small bust of Washington
to left; *Key* under the bust. THE UNION MUST AND
SHALL BE PRESERVED, etc. 1856. Bronze; very
fine. 29.

432 The same obverse. Rev. A stag and cannon surrounded by 32 stars. (BUCHANAN) AND BRECKIN-
RIDGE 1856. Bronze; extremely fine. 29.

433 Bust of Washington. Rev. Stag and cannon, as
before. Bronze; very fine. 29.

434 Duplicate of last number. White metal; proof. 29.

435 Private soldier and veteran saluting the bust of
Washington on pedestal inscribed 1776-1876.
JULY 4TH PHILADELPHIA. Near border, IN COM-
MEMORATION OF THE VISIT OF THE SEVENTH REGI-
MENT AND THE VETERAN CORPS, N. G. S. N. Y., etc.
Rev. Arms of the regiment in trophy, etc. *Sil-
ver* medal by *Demarest*; loop, guard, and original
ribbon. Extremely fine. 28.

436 Duplicate, with guard and ribbon. Bronze; perfect.

437 William Washington; for Cowpens. Battle-scene
and inscription. Stamped BRONZE on edge. Very
fine. 29.

438 Duplicate; thicker planchet, stamped COPPER on
edge. Very fine. 29.

439 Large head to left. GEORGE WASHINGTON *W. H*
under the bust. Rev. BORN FEB. 22D, 1732, etc.,
in 6 lines; wreath of oak near border. Bronze;
very fine. 28.

440 Electrotype copy of last number. 28.

441 The same obverse. Rev. Blank. W. M. Very
fine. 28.

442 Naked bust to left. *Laubenheimer* in the field,
below. A CENTURY ADDS LUSTRE TO HIS FAME,
etc. 1776-1876. Rev. America pointing the
Exhibition buildings to a visiting sister. SEE HOW
WE PROSPER. Bronze; extremely fine. 28.

28   *Washington Medals.*

443 The same. White metal; proof. 28.

444 Naked bust to right, by Key. Lancaster Co. Agricultural and Mechanical Society. Award medal *for case of Indian relics*, 1860. Copper; proof. 28.

445 Another, without name of recipient. *Silver;* nearly proof. 28.

446 Military bust to left. GENL. GEORGE WASHINGTON. Rev. BORN FEB. 22D, 1732, DIED DECR. 14, 1799, in broad wreath of oak. Tin; pierced above, very good. 28.

447 Duplicate. Tin; pierced, fair. 28.

448 Another. Tin; pierced. Poor. 28.

449 Small bust of Washington to left, similar to obverse of 1791 cent, surrounded by eight representations of Granby, Connecticut, Fugio, and other Colonial coins. Rev. NEW HAVEN NUMISMATIC SOCIETY, FOUNDED NOV. 25TH, 1862; small wreath of oak. White metal; fine and rare. 28.

450 Full figures of Washington and Grant; between them a large American shield surmounted by an eagle; twenty-five stars near border. 1776-1876. In exergue CENTENNIAL and *Koehler* below. Rev. Wreath of laurel, within which DEDICATED TO THE PEOPLE OF THE UNITED STATES AS A MEMORIAL OF THE FIRST CENTURY OF LIBERTY, in eight lines. *Silver; proof.* 26.

451 The same medal. Bronze; extremely fine. 26.

452 Another. White metal; proof. 26.

453 Duplicate. White metal proof; pierced. 26.

454 Military bust facing right. GEORGE WASHINGTON; *Westwood* under the shoulder. Heavy wreath of oak near border. Convex *silver* shell. Fine; probably unique. 28.

455 Naked bust to right, *Lovett* under the bust. WASHINGTON TEMPERANCE SOCIETY. Rev. HOUSE OF TEMPERANCE. Tarnished proof. Brass. 26.

456 Duplicate. Bronze; very fine. 26.

457 The same obverse. Rev. WE AGREE TO ABSTAIN FROM ALL INTOXICATING LIQUORS, ETC. Brass; nearly proof. 26.

458 The same obverse. Rev. Bust of Franklin. MECHANICS LITERARY ASSOCIATION ROCHESTER. White metal; fine. 26.

459 The same obverse. Rev. AWARDED TO. White metal ; fine. 26.

460 Large bust to left. *Vivier f.* Series Numismatica. Bronze ; fine. 26.

461 Large bust to right. BACON SCULPT. Series Numismatica. Bronze ; proof. 26.

462 Duplicate of last number. Slightly spotted proof ; Bronze. 26.

463 Electrotype of obverse of 459. Fine. 26.

464 Large bust to left. GEORGE WASHINGTON. *u. s. m. co.* under the bust. Rev. IN COMMEMORATION OF THE 100TH ANNIVERSARY OF AMERICAN INDEPENDENCE, 1876, etc. White metal, gilt. Extremely fine. 26.

465 Duplicate of last number. White metal ; proof. 26.

466 Liberty crowning a bust. WASHINGTON BENEVOLENT SOCIETY. 1808. Rev. Benevolence relieving distress. NEW YORK. *Silver ;* loop. Extremely fine. 26.

467 Duplicate of last number ; loop removed. Extremely fine. 26.

468 Bust of Washington, nearly facing. Wide border of curving lines. Tin shell ; very fine. 27

469 Bust nearly facing. 1776–1876 ; 13 stars in curving line below, and laurel wreath near border. Rev. View of Art Gallery, Phila. A GOVERNMENT OF THE PEOPLE, etc. White metal ; very fine, pierced. 26.

470 Duplicate of last number. Same metal and condition. 26.

471 The WESTWOOD Medal. Bust to right. *Westwood f.* under the shoulder. GEORGE WASHINGTON, ESQR., LATE PRESIDENT OF THE UNITED STATES OF AMERICA. Rev. MADE COMMANDER IN CHIEF OF THE AMERICAN FORCES, etc. Copper ; fire-gilt. Very fine obituary medal. 26.

472 Duplicate of last number. Bronze ; extremely fine. 26.

473 Another. Bronze ; fine. 26.

474 Naked bust to right. THE FATHER OF HIS COUNTRY. In exergue, BORN FEB. 22, 1732. Rev. View of monument. NATIONAL MONUMENT. JULY 4, 1848. *Silver ;* extremely fine and rare. 25.

475 Duplicate of last number. *Silver ;* very fine. 27.

ᘒ 476 Another. Tin. Very fine ; pierced. 25.

ᘒ 477 Another. Tin ; possibly cast or electro. 25.

, Ɔ. 2 ᘔ 478 Military bust to left. G. WASHINGTON, C. C. A. U. S.
Rev. Eagle, grasping flames from which lightning
issues, an olive branch in his beak, hovers over
section of sphere inscribed UNITED STATES. 1783
above. *Silver ;* in perfect condition, a very beautiful and rare medal. 25.

1. ᘒᘔ 479 Busts jugata to left of Washington and Franklin.
Rev. Same as last reverse. Bronze ; extremely
fine and rare. 25.

1. ᘒᘔ 480 Same obverse as last. Rev. A beaver gnawing the
trunk of an oak tree. 1776. Bronze : extremely
fine and rare. 25.

1. 8 0 481 THE VOLTAIRE MEDAL. Bust to right. Gᴱ. WASH-
INGTON ER. GENERAL OF THE CONTINL. ARMY IN
AMERICA. Rev. Trophy of arms. WASHIN.
RÉUNIT PAR UN RARE ASSEMBLAGE, etc. Bronze ;
fine. 24.

2. ᘒᘔ 482 Duplicate of last number. Thicker planchet.
Bronze ; fine. 24.

1. 7 ᘔ 483 Naked bust to right. *Barber* under the shoulder.
GEORGE WASHINGTON*COMMANDER IN CHIEF.*
Rev. IN COMMEMORATION OF THE DEPARTURE OF
THE CONTINENTAL ARMY, JUNE 19. VALLEY FORGE
CENTENNIAL. 1778-1878. *Silver ;* dull proof.
rare. 26.

ᘒ 0 484 The same. Bronze proof. 26.

1. 1 0 485 California. 1876. Centennial medal. Medallion
bust of Washington over landscape, a mail coach
in the foreground and ship in the distance. Rev.
Arms of California ; same landscape with train of
cars and steamer, etc. *Silver ;* proof, loop. 25.

2 ⸜ 486 The same medal ; struck in tin. Loop. Proof. 25.

6. ᘔᘒ 487 FAME MEDAL. Bust with aged features, facing right.
H under the shoulder. WASHINGTON BORN FEB-
RUARY 11, 1732, DIED DECEMBER 21, 1799. Rev.
Fame with wreath and trumpet, flying over land
and sea ; the sun rising over the ocean, a ship in
the distance. WISDOM, VIRTVE & PATRIOTISM
MDCCCIII Bronze ; very fine and rare. 24.

ᘒᘔ 488 Duplicate of last number. Bronze ; about same
condition.

* The occurrence in this cabinet of a duplicate of this extremely
rare medal is good evidence of its wealth in rarities.

489 Bust with aged features, resembling that on the Fame medal. GEORGE WASHINGTON. OB 14 DECR 1799 Æ. 68. Rev. THE HERO OF FREEDOM, THE PRIDE OF HIS COUNTRY AND ORNAMENT OF HUMAN NATURE 1800, in wreath of oak and laurel, dotted with stars. Extremely fine funeral medal. Bronze; fire gilt, and nearly proof. 24.

490 The same. Bronze; nearly proof. 24.

491 Another. Same metal and condition as last. 24.

492 Another. Copper; fine. 24.

493 Another. Yellow copper; barely fair. 24.

494 Another. Tin or cast; good. 24.

495 Electrotype of obverse of this medal. Good. 24

496 Bust to right. TO COMMEMORATE THE 100TH anniversary of the DECLARATION OF INDEPENDENCE. Panels with infantry and cavalry on border. Rev. View of the Declaration of Independence. *Silver*; proof. 26.

497 The same. W. M. proof. 2 pcs

498 Same obverse. Rev. Similar to last. *Demarest* in exergue. Thick planchet, bronze, very fine. 26.

499 Duplicates of last number. Bronze; very fine. 3 pcs

500 The same. Brass proof. Rare.

501 The same. W. m. proof. 2 pcs

502 Same obverse. Rev. *John Hancock's* signature. THERE! JOHN BELL CAN READ THAT NAME WITHOUT SPECTACLES, etc. *Silver*; nearly proof. 26.

503 The same. Bronze; very fine. 26.

504 The same. Bronze, brass and w. m. proof. 3 pcs

505 Duplicate set. 3 pcs

506 Declaration of Independence, same as 498. Rev. John Hancock's signature, as before. *Silver*; nearly proof. Rare combination of dies. 26.

507 Same obverse. Rev. H. G. SAMPSON. DEALER IN RARE AMERICAN AND FOREIGN COINS, etc. CENTENNIAL LINEN MARKER; 1876. *Silver*; nearly proof. 26.

508 Duplicate of last number. *Silver*; proof. 26.

509 The same. Copper; proof. 26.

510 The same. Brass; proof. 26.

511 The same. W. m.; proof. 26.

512 The same. Copper, brass, and w. m.; proof. 26.

3 pcs

513 Declaration of Independence, as in No. 496. Rev.
Sampson's card as before. W. m. proof; a rare
combination of dies. 26.

514 Obv. same as last. Rev. IN COMMEMORATION OF
THE CENTENNIAL OF COLONIAL INDEPENDENCE,
1876, etc. Bronze; nearly proof. 26.

515 Duplicate. Bronze; nearly proof. 26.

516 Bust to right as before, but in a semicircle of 13
stars. TO COMMEMORATE the 100TH ANNIVERSARY,
etc. Rev. Hands joined. INTERNATIONAL EXHI-
BITION AT PHILADELPHIA, 1876, etc. Bronze,
fine. 25.

517 The same. Brass; proof. 25.

518 Same obv. Rev. Arms of the Sheldon family.
H. L. S. 1821. H. A. S. 1870. Thick pl.; bronze,
nearly proof. 25.

519 The same. Bronze and w. m.; proof. 2 pcs

520 Duplicates of last number. 2 pcs

521 Bust to right, same as last. 1775—100 YEARS—1875.
I. F. W. des. G. H. L. fec. THE LOVER OF PEACE,
etc. Rev. THE WASHINGTON ELM, etc. 1875.
Isaac F. Wood's series "C" No. 4. Bronze;
very fine. 25.

522 Duplicate. Bronze; very fine. 25.

523 The same. Bronze; copper and w. m.; very fine.

3 pcs

524 Bust to right, as before, FIRST IN WAR AND IN
PEACE LAST IN SECURING. Rev. A MONUMENT.
View of unfinished monument at Washington,
smooth surface. *Wood's series "C" No. 3. Silver;* nearly proof. 25.

525 Duplicate. *Silver;* nearly proof. 25

526 The same. Thick pl.; copper proof. 35.

527 The same. Bronze (2) and w. m.; very fine. 25.

3 pcs

528 The same, but stone of monument or rev. squared.
Thick pl.; *silver,* nearly proof. 25.

529 The same. Bronze; very fine. 25.

530 The same. Bronze, brass and w. m.; very fine.

3 pcs

531 Duplicate set. 3 pcs

55 532 Large head to left. *Mitchell f.* under the neck.
Rev. PRESENTED BY THE METROPOLITAN MECHAN-
ICS INSTITUTE ; name of recipient engraved.
Silver ; fine. 25.

533 The same. Other name engraved on rev. (1857).
Brass ; fine.

534 Bust with aged features to right. Rev. Wreath of
oak. Tin ; good and very rare. 24.

3 535 Bust to right. N. and G. TAYLOR, PHILADELPHIA,
1862. Rev. TIN PLATE, etc. From different
dies ; Gothic letters. Brass ; fine. 24. 2 pcs

3 536 N. G. Taylor's card as before. Without date and
Roman letters ; also duplicates of last. Brass and
white metal ; fine. 24. 3 pcs

4 537 Bust nearly facing. *I. B. C.* under the shoulder.
GEORGE WASHINGTON BORN FEBY 22, 1732 ; DIED
DECR 14, 1799. Rev. A MAN HE WAS TO ALL HIS
COUNTRY DEAR, in wreath of olive ; All-seeing eye
above. Copper ; proof. 24.

538 Fame to left, inscribing the word WASHINGTON on a
cloud. *R. L. Phila.* below. VIRTUE AND VALOR
W. L. I. Rev. W. L. I. CAPT. SIMONTON 144 MEN
4th JULY, 1860, under a palmetto tree and encircled
by a scroll bearing names of soldiers. Copper ;
fine and rare. 24.

539 Military bust to right. *Key* under the breast. NOR-
WALK CONN MEMORIAL BOUGHT OF THE NORWAKE
INDIANS, etc. *C. No. I. I. F. Wood's own series.*
Silver ; proof. 24.

540 Duplicate. Silver ; proof. 24.

541 The same. Copper ; proof. 24.

542 The same. Dark bronze, red bronze and w. m. ;
proof. 3 pcs

543 Military bust to right by *Key.* GEORGE WASHING-
TON. In exergue, on label, BORN FEB 22 1732,
DIED DEC 14 1799. Rev. INDEPENDENCE HALL
1776—1876. *Silver ;* proof. 24.

544 The same. Bronze ; very fine. 24.

545 Same obverse. Rev. Large cracked bell. PROCLAIM
LIBERTY, etc. 1776—1876. Copper ; nearly
proof. 24.

546 Same obverse. Rev. REWARD OF MERIT, on scroll.
Brass ; proof. 24.

7 *0* 547 Large bust to right. GENERAL WASHINGTON 1776.
Rev. AMERICAN COLONIES 1776. Fire-gilt. Proof.
24.

2 5 548 Same obverse. Rev. FREE AND UNITED STATES.
Fire-gilt. Proof. 24.

2 5 549 Same obverse. Rev. BIRTH PLACE OF AMERICAN
INDEPENDENCE 1776. Copper and fire-gilt. Proof.
24. 2 pcs

/5 550 Same obverse. Rev. CENTENNIAL FOUNTAIN. 1876.
Copper ; proof. 24.

9 0 551 Same obverse. Rev. Blank. Border of arabesque
ornaments. *Silver*; proof. 24.

95 552 Bust to left. UNITED STATES OF AMERICA 1876.
Rev. CENTENNIAL MEMORIAL BUILDING 1876
PHILADELPHIA. Brass ; fine, pierced. 23.

3 0 553 Bust to left. WASHINGTON. CACHOU and CARDA-
MON AROMATISE. Brass shell by Key. Fine. 24.

/ 0 554 Bust to left. GEORGE WASHINGTON. Rev. GENE-
RAL OF THE AMERICAN ARMIES, etc. Tin; poor
but very rare. 24. 2 pcs

/. 5 0 555 Sailor leaning against an anchor on which is perched
an American eagle ; a ship in the distance. Rev.
U. S. N. WASHINGTON TEMPERANCE SOCIETY
SOC. 1842. *Silver* proof medal by *Stimpson*; rare.
23.

5 0 556 The same. Copper ; very fine. 23.

/5 557 Washington temperance pledge. WE PLEDGE, etc.
Rev. VINCIT QUI DEVINCIT. *True.* Tin, pierced;
fine. 22.

/5 558 Bust to right. *True* under the shoulder. GEORGE
WASHINGTON BORN, etc. Rev. Calender. Tin;
fine. 23.

0 0 559 Full figure of Washington, a battle horse behind
him. BORN, etc. Rev. Coat of Arms of Pennsylvania. POPULATION, etc. 1855. Brass ; fine
and rare. 22.

6 0 560 Same obverse. Rev. Coat of arms of New York.
Brass ; fine and rare. 22.

5 0 561 Same obv. Rev. Coat of arms of Ohio. Brass ;
fine and rare. 22.

05 562 Same obv. Rev. Coat of arms of Illinois. Brass ;
fine and rare. 22.

5 563 Same obv. Rev. Calender. Good. 22. 2 pcs

564 Military bust to left. G. WASHINGTON, PRESIDENT,
1797. Rev. Ground floor of Masonic temple.
AMOR, HONOR ET JUSTITIA G. W G. G. M. Brass;
fair and very rare. (See Marvin, 264.) 22.

565 Naked bust to right. BETHANY SABBATH SCHOOL
PHILA. Rev. PRESENTED, etc. 1883. Bronze
and w. m.; proof. 22. 2 pcs

566 Bust of Washington to left; 13 stars near border.
Rev. Advertising cards. *Brass shells*, line.
1 duplicate in the lot. 24. 8 pcs

567 Military bust to right; *Twigg* under the shoulder.
Rev. GENERAL OF THE AMERICAN ARMIES, etc.
Copper and tin. Fine. 22 2 pcs

568 Bust to right; 34 stars around it. THE CENTENNIAL
YEAR, etc. Rev. Names of engagements fought
in 1776, No. 1 to 8. Complete set. Bronze; very
fine. 21. 8 pcs

569 Duplicate of No. 1. Battle of Moore's Creek. *Silver*;
proof. 21.

570 Small bust in wreath of laurel and oak to left. 100th
ANNIVERSARY OF THE DECLARATION, etc. Names
of engagements as before on rev. Bronze; very
fine and rare. 21. 8 pcs

571 Obverses of two preceding nos. combined. *Silver*;
proof, very rare, if not unique in this metal. 21.

572 The same. Copper; proof. 21.

573 Small bust to left as before. Rev. DEDICATED TO
THE PUPILS OF THE DELPHOS UNION SCHOOL, and
another. White metal. Proof. 21. 3 pcs

574 The same obverse. Rev. DEDICATED TO THE CHIL-
DREN OF AMERICA. 1876. Copper; proof. 21.

575 Military bust to left. GEORGE WASHINGTON, FIRST
IN WAR, FIRST IN PEACE. Rev. Within a wreath
of leaves and flowers, in curving and straight lines,
BORN, FEB. 11. 1732. GENERAL AMERICAN
ARMIES, 1775, etc. Copper and brass. Brilliant
proof. 21. 2 pcs

576 Naked bust to right. THE MONMOUTH BATTLE
MONUMENT ASSOCIATION 1878. Rev. Inscription. Copper; fine, pierced. 22.

577 The same bust. HISTORICAL & FORESTRY SOCIETY
OF ROCKLAND COUNTY 1878. Rev. Washington's
Headquarters, Tappan. Bronze; very fine. 21.
2 pcs

60 578 Bust in toga to right. Rev. Washington's residence. Bronze ; extremely fine. 22.

30 579 The same bust, in wreath of oak leaves. Rev. Blank. W. m. proof. 22.

1.75 580 Small bust to left in square and compasses. COMMANDER-IN-CHIEF, etc. Rev. SOLOMON'S-LODGE, NO. 1 PO'KEEPSIE. *Wood's series "C" No. 2.* Silver ; proof. 22.

17 581 The same. Bronze, copper, brass, and w. m. proof. 22.   4 pcs

30 582 Bust to right. *Wyon* under the shoulder. GEORGE WASHINGTON 1796. Rev. GENL OF THE AMERICAN ARMIES, etc., in three circular lines. Bronze; very fine. 21.

20 583 Duplicate. Fine. 21.

14 584 The same bust. BORN FEB 11 1732 DIED DC 21 1799. Rev. Same as last. Bronze and white metal ; fine. 21.   2 pcs

1.5-0 585 Bust to right by *Barber.* Rev. YEAR ONE HUNDRED OF AMERICAN INDEPENDENCE. 1776. ANNUAL ESSAY 1876. Bronze proof mint medal. 21.

1.5-0 586 The same. Copper proof. 21.

30 587 Bust nearly facing. 1732–1799. Rev. Square and compasses ; *Harzfeld's series.* Copper, gilt; proof. 21.

31 588 Same obv. Rev. Coat of arms of Washington. Copper gilt ; proof. 21.

35- 589 The same. Bronze ; proof. 21.

60 590 The same bust, but broad ornamental border of olive branches. Rev. 1781–1881. SOUVENIR. CENTENNIAL OF THE SURRENDER OF YORKTOWN, VA. Bronze, proof. 20.

70 591 Busts of Washington, Lafayette, de Grasse, in circles. Rev. View of the monument at Yorktown, IN COMMEMORATION, etc. 1781–1881. Bronze, proof. 20.

30 592 Bust nearly facing. UNITY OF GOVERNMENT IS THE MAIN PILLAR OF INDEPENDENCE. Rev. "Religion our safeguard," etc., "HE IS A FREEMAN" etc., Log cabin, bust of Harrison, and blank. A rare lot, all very fine. Bronze, nickel and w. m. 21. 5 pcs.

2.20 593 Washington on horseback, dates of birth and death on each side in the field. Rev. Female with clock; TIME IS MONEY and S. J. Bettor's, Philadelphia, card. *Silver;* very fine and rare. 21.

5 594 Same obverse. Rev. Calender. Brass; uncirculated.
21.

3 O 595 Busts of Washington, THE FATHER, and of Lincoln,
THE SAVIOUR OF HIS COUNTRY. Rev. Bust of Lin-
coln to left. BORN FEB. 12, 1809, ASSASSINATED
APR. 14, 1865. White metal; fine. 21.

6 596 Long bust nearly facing. THE FATHER OF OUR COUN-
TRY. Rev. Columbia, seated, feeding the American eagle; LIBERTY AND INDEPENDENCE; silver;
nearly proof; rare. 21.

7 O 597 Same obverse. Rev. REWARD OF MERIT; 2) UNITED
WE STAND, etc.; 3) same as last rev. White
metal; fine, pierced. 21. 3 pcs

6 O 698 Bust in toga to right. Merr under the neck; THE
FATHER, etc. Rev. Bust of Lincoln; THE PRESERVER.
White metal; fine. 20.

2 599 Small bust to right. WASHINGTON stamped above.
Lead. 21.

6 O 600 Small bust to right surrounded by a wreath in a
keystone. Rev. FIT KEYSTONE, etc. 1776–1886.
I. F. W. des.; G. H. L. fec. Silver; proof. 20.

15 601 The same. Bronze and white metal. 20. 2 pcs
10 602 The same. White metal; proof. 2 pcs
7 603 Bust to right. I. F. W.—G. H. L. under the bust.
TRUE AND WISE AND MERCIFUL AND JUST. Rev.
MOUNT VERNON CHAPTER NO. 228 R. A.; M.;
N. Y. Silver; proof. 20.

12 604 The same. Bronze and white metal. Proof. 20.
2 pcs

3 605 Duplicates of last No. Bronze and w. m. Proof.
2 pcs

12 606 Naked bust of Washington over two palm branches
crossed; 13 stars in curving line above. I. F. W.
des. N. Y. Medal Club series No. 1, G. H. L. fec.
Rev. Bust of Lafayette to right. GENERAL LAFA-
YETTE. Silver; proof. Rare. 20.

2 607 The same. Bronze; fine. 20.

4 608 Long bust to left. GEORGE WASHINGTON, THE CIN-
CINNATUS OF AMERICA, etc. Rev. "The Union
must and shall be preserved"; "Industry pro-
duces wealth"; and John K. Curtis card. Reeded
edge; copper; nearly proof. 20. 3 pcs

4 609 The same. Copper and brass, one with smooth edge.
Good, fine and proof. 3 pcs

ꜱ‑0 610 Bust to right by Paquet. U. S. Mint Oath of Allegiance medal. 1861. *Silver;* proof. 19.

/ꜱ‑ 611 The same. Bronze; very fine. 19.

2 2 612 The same obverse. Rev. Heavy wreath of laurel. Copper; nearly proof. 19.

2 6 613 Bust to right in wreath of laurel and palm. Rev. Headquarters at Valley Forge, Tappan, Newburgh, and view of Mount Vernon. Copper; nearly proof; rare. 20. 4 pcs

// 614 Same obverse. Rev. WASHINGTON in blazing star, surrounded by thirteen stars in ornamental tressure. Copper and white metal. Proof. 20. 2 pcs

/ꜱ‑ 615 Small bust in oval to right; eagle above. PATRIÆ PATER on label. Rev. STRUCK & DISTRIBUTED IN CIVIC PROCESSION FEBY. 22D, 1832, etc. Copper and brass proof. 20. 2 pcs

ꜱ 616 Dickeson's coin safe, combined with this rev.; also, same rev. with H's Washington coat of arms. w. m.; very fine. 2 pcs

/2 617 Bust of Washington to right. UNION and 34 stars near border. Rev. 3 with —— co —— REG —— VOLVNTEERS ENTERED SERVICE —— 186 , the blank spaces filled up with stamped names, dates; one with blank rev., one with EMANCIPATION BILL PASSED, etc. Brass; very good and fine and a rare lot. Pierced. 20. 6 pcs

6 618 Bust to left; palm and laurel branches, crossed, below. WASHINGTON 100TH YEAR OF OUR NATIONAL INDEPENDENCE. 1776, 1876. Rev. Ground floor of Masonic temple. Brass; proof. 20.

3 619 Same obv. Rev. 47TH ANNIVERSARY OF THE BROOKLYN SUNDAY SCHOOL UNION MAY 1876. Copper and brass proof. 20. 2 pcs

1‑ 620 Small bust of Washington in blazing star. FREEDOM TO ALL MEN. Rev. Large bust of Lincoln to right. LINCOLN & JOHNSON UNION CANDIDATES. Copper and brass proof. 20. 2 pcs

3 0 621 Draped bust to right. GEORGE WASHINGTON. Rev. Washington on horseback; Pro patria, and monument at Baltimore. *Silver;* very fine. 3 pcs

6 622 Duplicates of last number. Bronze and copper; nearly proof. 3 pcs

4 623 Naked bust to right. *R. L.* under the bust.
GEORGE WASHINGTON SECURITY Rev. Washington on horseback; coin safe; Pro patria, and
ship as on rev. of Hog Island shilling. Bronze,
copper and nickel. Very fine or proof. 20. 5 pcs

50 624 Naked bust to right. GEORGE WASHINGTON. Rev.
BORN FEB. 22, 1732 ; DIED DEC. 14, 1799 in wreath
Silver; nearly proof. 20.

9 625 Duplicates of last number; thick and thin planchet;
also one with Edward Cogan's card on rev. Copper and bronze proof. 3 pcs

7 626 Sage's Historical tokens. No. 7, 8, 9, 10, 11. Copper; proof. 19. 5 pcs

7 627 Duplicates. Bronze, copper and brass; proof. 8 pcs

2 628 The old Hasbrook house. Rev. The Home of
Washington. W. M.; thick pl. Rare combination.

17 629 Washington on horseback to right. Rev Mount
Vernon, Headquarters at Valley Forge, Tappan
and Newburg. Copper and brass proof. 20. 4 pcs

8 630 Washington on horseback to left. Rev. SIEGE OF
BOSTON. Bronze, copper and brass proof. 20.
3 pcs

6 631 Same obv. Rev. R. Lovett, Jr.'s card and blank;
also duplicates of last numbers. Copper and
brass proof. 20 5 pcs

6 632 Naked bust to right by *Merriam.* GEORGE WASH-
INGTON BORN, etc. Rev. Bust of Everett; bust
of Franklin, Tomb, Oration at Boston, July 4,
1860, Boston Masonic Temple and blank. Bronze,
copper, and white m. Very fine; 3 duplicates.
19. 9 pcs

4 633 Same obv. Rev. Stamped names of soldiers in
Penn. and N. Y. Volunteers. White metal.
Pierced; good and rare. 19. 2 pcs

42 634 Similar obverse, without *Merriam.* Rev. Bust of
Everett, different from preceding, also Tomb.
Copper and w. m. Nearly proof. 19. 2 pcs

29 635 Washington medal, from *Brichaut's* series. Bronze
proof. 19.

95 636 Naked bust to left by *Paquet.* UNITED STATES
MILITARY ACADEMY. Rev. ACADEMIC MERIT.
Bronze proof. 48

98 637 Bust to right. M. A. ABRAHAMS, WHITON, WIS. Store
card. Brass; very fine. 18.

638 Bust nearly facing. GEORGE WASHINGTON. Rev.
EXHIBITION PHILADELPHIA CENTENIAL 1876. Two
varieties; brass. pierced and uncirculated.   3 pcs

639 Small bust to left. GEORGE WASHINGTON. *J. A.
Bolen* under the shoulder. Rev. AVOID THE
EXTREMITIES OF PARTY SPIRIT in broad wreath of
oak. Golden bronze; fine proof. 18.

640 Duplicate. Golden bronze; fine proof. 18.

641 Head of Washington. Brass spiel-marks. 3 varieties; uncirculated. 18.   4 pcs

642 Small military bust, surrounded by 13 stars, in
oval. 1775. JUNE 3. 1875. *I. F. W G. H L.*
Rev. Pens and swords crossed. HE ASSUMED
COMMAND, ETC. Silver, bronze, gilt and W. M.
Proof. 18.   4 pcs

643 Duplicates. Copper-gilt, bronze and w. m. Proof.
                                               5 pcs

644 Naked bust to left in arch ; *Key* under the shoulder.
PATRLÆ PATER 1732. Rev. ORNAMENTAL MEDAL
AND SEAL DIE SINKERS 329 ARCH ST. PHILA.
Silver ; nearly proof. 18.

645 Same obv. Rev. "Not transferable," "dedicated
to coin and medal colectors, 1860 ;" "We all have
our hobbies ;" "Woodgate & Co.'s N. Y. card ;"
"E. Hill's N. Y. card ;" bust of Forest ; bust of
Webster ; Mobile Jockey Club. Brass and white
metal ; nearly proof. 18.   9 pcs

646 Same obv., without arch. Rev. "Virtue Liberty
and Independence." "Cupid on dolphin 1861"
and "Providence left him childless," etc. Copper
and w. m., proof. 18.   5 pcs

647 Military bust to left by *Bolen.* The FATHER OF OUR
COUNTRY. Rev. "Bust of Abraham Lincoln ;"
"R. Chamberlaine, Norfolk ;" "Apollo gardens,
good for 6 cents ;" "Soldiers' fair, Springfield,
Mass., 1864 ;" "He lived for his country." 4
copper, 1 w. m. Nearly proof. 18.   5 pcs

648 Same bust as last but WASHINGTON above. Rev.
Same as last obverse ; "Bust of Lincoln ;"
"Appollo gardens ;" "Springfield, Mass., Soldiers' fair ;" "He lived for his country." 4 copper, 1 w. m. Nearly proof. 18.   5 pcs

649 Same obverse. Rev. MADE FROM COPPER TAKEN
FROM THE RUINS OF THE TURPENTINE WORKS,
NEWBERN, N. C., etc. Nearly proof. 18.

650 Duplicates of Nos. 647 and 648. Cop., br., and w.
  m. Nearly proof. 5 pcs

651 Bust to right. Rev. TIME INCREASES HIS FAME.
  Bronze; very fine. 18.

652 Military bust to left. TO AID ST. JOHN'S GUILD—
  FLOATING HOSPITAL. (*Wood's series* "C" *No. 5*).
  Rev. Bust of Martha Washington to left. CEN-
  TENNIAL RECEPTION, BALL AND TEA PARTY, etc.
  N. Y. FEBY 22d, 1876. *Silver*; nearly proof,
  extremely rare. 18.

653 The same. Copper proof. Unique in this metal. 18.

654 The same. Tin proof. Very rare. 18.

655 Naked bust to right in semicircle of 13 stars. Inscription and rev. same as last. *Silver*; nearly
  proof. 18.

656 The same. Bronze, copper and w. m. Very fine
  and proof. 18. 3 pcs

657 Draped bust to right. GEORGE WASHINGTON. Rev.
  Liberty cap in a glory of rays; 26 eagles and stars
  on border. WASHINGTON NATUS, 1732 OBIT 1799.
  Copper; proof. 18. 9 pcs

658 Naked bust to right. GEORGE WASHINGTON; G. H.
  L. in the field. Rev. Smaller bust to right. FIRST
  IN WAR, FIRST IN PEACE, etc. Copper and w. m.
  Proof. 18. 2 pcs

659 Same obv. Rev. LAKE CITY LODGE NO 27, LAKE
  CITY, FLA. Copper and w. m. Proof. 18. 2 pcs

660 Same obv. Rev. Square and compass. INST'D. IN
  FREDERICKSBURGH LODGE, MD. NOV 4 1752.
  Copper; proof. Rare. 18.

661 The same. Brass proof. 18.

662 Same obv. Rev. Similar to last, but error in State
  corrected. FREDERICKSBURGH LODGE NO 4
  VIRGINIA. Brass proof. 18.

663 Same obv. Rev., All-seeing eye over Masonic implements. Copper proof; spotted. 18.

664 The same. White metal proof. 18.

665 Same obv. Rev. BOYS AND GIRLS OF AMERICA 1876.
  Copper (2) and w. m. proof. 18. 3 pcs

666 Same obv. Rev. Coat of arms. EDWARD—WELLS
  PARSONS OF FLUSHING, N. Y. Marriage medalet.
  Copper and w. m. proof. 18. 2 pcs

2 0 667 Same obv. Rev. Bust of Martha Washington. THE 100TH YEAR OF OUR INDEPENDENCE. 1876. Copper and w. m. proof. 18. 2 pcs

1 0 668 Same obv. Rev. St. Patrick's Cathedral, New York. Copper and w. m. proof. 18. 3 pcs

1 0 669 Same obv. Rev. Bust of Grant to right. Copper and w. m. proof. 18. 2 pcs

6 670 Bust in wreath of laurel to left. WASHINGTON THE FATHER OF OUR COUNTRY. Rev. BOYS AND GIRLS OF AMERICA 1876. Copper and brass proof. 18. 2 pcs

9 0 671 Same obv. Rev. Coat of arms as in No. 666. Copper and w. m. proof. 18. 2 pcs

2 0 672 Same obv. Rev. Masonic emblems as in 663. Copper and brass proof. 18. 2 pcs

7 0 673 Same obv. Rev. same as rev. of 658 and 667. W. m. proof. 18. 2 pcs

1 4 0 674 Same obv. Rev. 21 ANNIVERSARY OF THE JERSEY CITY SUNDAY SCHOOLS MAY 22 1876 (corrected date). Bronze; fine. 18.

1 5 675 Bust of Martha Washington as before. Rev. same as last. Bronze; fine. 18.

3 0 676 Naked bust to right. G. W. in monogram below 1775–100 years–1875. Rev. *I. F. W des. G H L. F* Same as obv. No. 658. Copper proof. 18.

9 677 Same obv. Rev. same as rev. of No. 658. Copper proof. 18.

4 0 678 Same obv. Rev. Masonic emblems as in No. 663. Copper proof. 18.

9 0 679 Same obv. Rev. St. Patrick's Cathedral. Copper proof. 18.

1. 1 0 680 Small bust to right. FIRST IN WAR, etc. (Rev., No. 658). Rev. Bust of Lincoln to left. REVERSE LINCOLN and 12 stars near border. *Silver;* nearly proof; very rare. 18.

1 2 681 Same obv. Rev. "Reverse Lincoln," "Boys and girls," "Coat of arms." W. m. proof. 18. 3 pcs

2 5 682 Naked bust to left. Rev. Liberty cap in circle of stars and eagles, etc. (657). Copper proof. 18.

2 0 683 Same obv. Rev. Coat of arms of Washington. Copper proof. 18.

5 684 Same obv. Rev. Equestrian statue of Washington, N. Y. Copper proof. 18.

685 Same obv. Rev. Statue of Washington at Richmond, Va. Copper proof. 18.

686 Same obv. Rev. Amer. shield ; BORN 1732 DIED 1799. Copper proof. 18.

687 Same obv. Rev. Washington's tomb. Copper proof. 18.

688 Washington's statue, New York (684). Rev. Statue in Richmond (685). Copper proof. 18.

689 Same obv. Rev. Same as rev. of No. 686. Copper proof. 18.

690 Same obv. Rev. Same as rev. of No. 687. Copper proof. 18.

691 Washington's statue, Richmond. Same as rev. of No. 685. Rev. Liberty cap in circle of stars and eagles, same as rev. of No. 657. Copper proof. 18.

692 Same obv. Rev. Tomb, as in No. 687. Copper proof. 18.

693 Same obv. Rev. BORN, etc., as rev. of No. 686. Copper proof. 18.

694 American shield. BORN, etc. Rev. Tomb, as before. Copper proof. 18.

695 Naked bust to right. Rev. WASHINGTON BORN, 1732, DIED 1799 ; shield below, star above. *Silver* ; nearly proof. 18.

696 Same obv. Rev. Inscription as in last rev., without the shield and star. Copper proof. 18.

697 Naked bust to right, similar to last. Rev. PHILADELPHIA RIFLE CLUB. Bronze ; extremely fine. 18.

698 Naked bust to left. THE PATTERN OF PATRIOTISM, INDUSTRY, AND PROGRESS. Rev. 21ST ANNIVERSARY OF THE JERSEY CITY SUNDAY SCHOOLS, MAY 22 (corrected date), 1876. *Silver* ; proof. 18.

699 The same. Bronze and white metal, the latter proof and pierced. 2 pcs

700 Cloaked bust to left, P under the shoulder. IN GOD WE TRUST, 1776 CENTENNIAL 1876. Rev. Same as last. *Silver* ; proof. 18.

701 Bust of Martha Washington to left. ONE HUNDREDTH YEAR OF OUR INDEPENDENCE 1876. Rev. MARTHA WASHINGTON MEMORIAL MEDAL, on four angular lines. Copper and brass ; proof. 18. 2 pcs

702 Washington on horseback to right. GEORGE WASH-
INGTON. Rev. Andrew Jackson on horseback to
left. *Silver ;* proof.

703 Same obv. Rev. Draped bust of Henry Clay to
right. *Silver ;* proof. 18.

704 Same obv. Rev. Bust of Harrison to left over
semicircle of 23 stars. Brass ; proof. 18.

705 Same obv. Rev. BORN FEB. 22D, 1732, PRESIDENT
1789 TO 1796, DIED 1799. Border of 26 stars
and liberty caps. Copper and brass ; proof. 18.
2 pcs

706 Military bust to left, ornamental border of 13 stars.
Rev. View of military headquarters. No. 1 to
10, complete. Copper proof. 18.   10 pcs

707 Same obv. Rev. Same as rev. of 695, also naked
bust to right. Copper proof. 18.   2 pcs

708 Military bust to left, without buttons to coat, and
in other respects differing from last ; broad ornamental border. Rev. Headquarters, as in No.
706. Nos. 1, 5, 6, 7, 8, 9 and 10. *Silver;* proof.
18.   7 pcs

709 Same obv., combined with obv. 706. Copper proof.
18.

710 Same obv. Rev. Bust of Franklin to left. B.
FRANKLIN; a label below inscribed ERIPUIT COELO,
etc. Copper proof. 18.

711 Small naked bust to right. CHAS: K. WARNER,
DEALER, etc. Phila. Rev. Busts of Seymour,
Victora and Albert, Lincoln to right and left (3
varieties). Grant, McClellan (2 varieties). Lyle,
small head of Washington in trophy, "the Con-
stitution and the Union," "Monitor," "Cedar
Mountain to Ream's Station," "Surrender of
Gen. Lee"; all different reverses, and a rare lot.
Copper (5) and brass proof. 18.   14 pcs

712 Small head of Washington to right, in a trophy of
flags and over a star-dotted cloud. THE UNION MUST
AND SHALL BE PRESERVED. Rev. Busts of Lincoln (2 varieties). Grant (2 varieties), McClellan (2
varieties), "Monitor," "Surrender of Gen. Lee,"
and Key's card ; all different reverses. Rare ;
copper, brass, and w. m. proof. 18.   9 pcs

713 Same obv. Rev. Small head of Washington to
right ; no inscription. W. m. proof ; *unique* (?)
18.

‹ ᴐ 714 Busts facing front of Washington and Franklin by
Bale. Rev. PAR NOBILE FRATRUM. *Silver;* very
fine. 18.

ᴈᏳ 715 Same obverse. Rev. Small busts of Washington
and Lafayette in wreath, facing *W. & B.* below.
Copper and brass ; proof. 18. 2 pcs

Ꮪ 716 Small busts facing as in last reverse. *W. & B.*
below. Rev. PAR NOBILE FRATRUM, as before.
Copper and nickel proof. 18. 2 pcs

ᴣᴅ 717 Bust in broad wreath of laurel to right. ᴍ below.
Rev. MADE FROM COPPER TAKEN FROM THE RUINS
OF THE TURPENTINE WORKS, etc. Copper; very
fine. 17.

Ꭶ 718 Same obv. Rev. THE HERO OF AMERICAN INDE-
PENDENCE, etc. Copper and brass proof. 17. 2 pcs

Ꝑ 719 Same obv. Rev. Jos. H. Merriam's card, Boston.
Copper proof. 17.

› Ꞩ 720 Same obv. Rev. R. CHAMBERLAINE NORFOLK. W.
m.; very fine. 17.

ᴣᴐ 721 Same obv. Rev. C. F. TUTTLE, 130 WASHINGTON
ST. Amount due stamped in centre, etc. W. m.;
good. 17 3 pcs

Ꝇ 722 Bust to right. GEORGE WASHINGTON. Rev. Arms
of New York. *Davis* W. m. Pierced ; fine and
rare. 16.

ᴇᴅ 723 Bust of Washington in oval. C. WOLFE SPIES &
CLARKE NEW YORK, HARDWARE AND MILITARY
STORE. Rev. Bust to left. GEORGE IV. KING OF
GREAT BRITAIN. Brass, silvered ; fine and scarce.
16.

ᴀᴇ 724 Same obv. Rev. Bust in oval of Jackson. CUT-
LERY, PLATED WARE, GUNS, etc., 193 PEARL ST
N. Y. Brass, silvered. Plugged near border,
otherwise fine ; scarce. 16.

Ᏸ 725 No inscription on rev., except JACKSON over bust ;
otherwise same as last. Brass ; fair and scarce. 16.

ᴄᴅ 726 Same obv. Rev. Bust of Harrison in square.
PRESIDENT. Brass ; fine and scarce. 16.

ᴄᴅ 727 Duplicate of last No. Pierced and planchet cracked.
Good.

Ꝺ 728 Full figure in high relief of Washington facing.
THE FOUNDER OF OUR UNION, 1776. Rev. A
DECISIVE WAR ONLY CAN RESTORE PEACE AND
PROSPERITY. Tin ; thick pl. Uncir. and rare.
16.

1.30 729 Naked bust to right. EXPORTED SOLELY BY W.
GREAVES & SONS' SHEAF WORKS. Brass ; very
thick and fine. 16.

7.70 730 Horseman to right. GEORGE WASHINGTON. *Bale
& Smith, N. Y.*, in exergue. Rev. BALE AND
SMITH ENGRAVERS AND DIE CUTTERS 68 NASSAU
ST etc. N. Y. Copper ; uncir. and rare. 16.

4.20 731 Same obv. Rev. CARRY ME TO ATWOOD'S RAIL-
ROAD HOTEL 243 BOWERY AND MY FACE IS GOOD
FOR 3 CENTS. Copper ; uncir. and rare. 16.

3.90 732 Duplicate of last number. Copper ; very fine. 16.

1.20 733 Obverse of this token struck on a planchet size 13 ;
blank rev. Brass ; fine.

70 734 Another impression, same as last. Copper ; fine. 12.

15 735 Draped bust to right by *Bolen*. Rev. " The Union
is the main prop," etc., and head of Jefferson.
Cop., brass and w. m.   Proof ; one pierced. 16.
                                                   3 pcs

1.50 736 Same obv. Rev. Head of Liberty. LIBERTAS AME-
RICANA 4 JUIL. 1776. Thick planchet ; *silver ;*
very fine. 16.

10 737 Draped bust to right by *R. Lovett ;* FIRST PRES U.
S. 1789. Rev. E. Ivins, Phila., card. Nickel ;
very fine. 16.

2.7 738 Same obv. Rev. Arm with hammer in square and
compasses ; O U A M., etc.   Bronze, copper and
brass gilt.   Fine and proof. 16.   3 pcs

8 739 Small bust to right. N & G. TAYLOR CO PHILA., etc
Bronze and copper. Uncirculated. 16.   2 pcs

8 740 Naked bust to left. WASHINGTON. UNITED STATES
OF AMERICA. Rev. TO THE CAUSE OF TEMPERANCE
TEN DOLLARS, etc. Brass ; uncirculated. 16. 2 pcs

8 741 Female bust to left. MARTHA WASHINGTON BALTO
FEB 22 1875. Rev. Ship. PEGGY STEWART AN-
NAPOLIS OCTOBER 19 1774. Brass ; uncirculated.
15.

12 742 Naked bust to right. GEO. WASHINGTON PRESIDENT
and 8 stars near border. Rev. GREAT FAIR U. S.
SANITARY COMMISSION NANTUCKET MASS. AUGUST,
1864, etc. Copper. Uncirculated. 14.

5 743 Same obv. Rev. GREAT FAIR, SANITARY COMMIS-
SION NEW YORK MAY 1864 ; also, duplicate of
last number. Copper. Uncirculated. 14. 2 pcs

744 Same obv. Rev. T. BRIMELOW, DRUGGIST, etc. N. Y.
1863. Two reverses and variety of metals, including *silver*. All uncirculated. 14. 8 pcs

745 Bust to left. GEO. WASHINGTON PRESIDENT; 13 stars.
Rev. Brimelow's card, one with "2" in wreath.
Copper and brass; uncirculated. 14. 3 pcs

746 Small bust of Washington in wreath of olive to right.
MEMBER'S BADGE. Rev. WASHINGTON MARKET
CHOWDER CLUB 1848. *Silver*; very fine and ex-
tremely rare. 14.

747 Draped bust to right. GEO. WASHINGTON. FATHER
OF HIS COUNTRY. Rev. Military trophy. ONE
COUNTRY, etc. Brass; loop. Uncirculated. 14.
2 pcs.

748 Bust to right. WASHINGTON TEMPERANCE BENEV-
OLENT SOC. Rev. Fountain. W. m. Very good.
14.

749 Draped bust to left. Rev. PRO PATRIA, etc. Cop.
and brass; proof. 13. 2 pcs

750 Brass spiel marks, one with GEO DOLL & CO'S PHILA
card. Average very fine. 12 to 17. 21 pcs

751 Draped bust to left. PATER PATRIÆ. Rev. Bust of
Grant (2 varieties). Copper and brass proof. 13
5 pcs

752 Same obv. Rev. Bust of Washington to left; Mc-
Pherson, and two varieties of A. B. Sage's card.
Cop. and brass pr. 13. 4 pcs

753 Bust to right. PATER PATRIÆ. Mint cabinet medalet.
1859. *Silver* and bronze proof. 14. 2 pcs

754 Bust to right, etc. Rev. MONUMENT AT BALTIMORE.
Silver, cop. and brass. Very fine and proof. 14.
3 pcs

755 Bust of Washington nearly facing; *Rale* below.
Rev. Bust of Franklin. *Silver* and w. m. proof.
13. - 2 pcs.

756 Arm with hammer in square and compasses. G. F.
A. M. Rev. PUT NONE BUT AMERICANS ON GUARD
TO-NIGHT WASHINGTON. One *silver*, with loop,
good; the others bronze and w m. proof. 13.
3 pcs

757 Bust of Washington to left. MT HOLLY PAPER CO
MT HOLLY SPRINGS PA. Rev "1800" in wreath.
Copper and w. m. proof. 13. 2 pcs

758 The same. Tin; fine. 13.

759 Draped bust of Washington to left. Rev. View of the tomb at Mount Vernon. *Gold;* proof, *unique.* 12.

760 The same. *Silver;* very fine.

761 Bust facing of Martha Washington. 1876. Rev. IN HONOR OF WOMEN OF THE 1776 REVOLUTION. *Silver;* proof ; *rare.* 12.

762 Bust of Washington to right. Rev. Bust of Martha, w. m.; also rev. struck on thin copper planchet. Fine. 13. 3 pcs

763 Bust of Washington to right. Rev. T. Brimelow's card. One struck on nickel cent, copper and w. m. Very fine. 4 pcs

764 Small head to right, *Bale* under it. WASHINGTON TEMPERANCE, etc. Rev. WE SERVE THE TYRANT ALCOHOL NO LONGER. 4 pellets near border. *Silver;* pierced. Uncir. 13.

765 Similar obv., *Bale* under the wreath. Rev. Same legend, two pellets only near border. *Silver* and cop. Very fine, pierced. 13. 2 pcs

766 Small head of Washington in wreath of oak to right. Rev. WRIGHT & BALE, NEW YORK, etc., in 11 lines. Copper. Uncir. 12.

767 Duplicates; also obverse of this token struck on large w. m. planchet. Fine. 3 pcs

768 Bust of Washington to right in star of seven points ; *Schmidl* under the bust, HONOR TEMPERANCE around it. Rev. IN HOC SIGNO VINCES and wreath in star. *Foun ded* 22 *Feb* 1844. Silver ; very fine. 12.

769 Plough to right. G. W. in the field, eagle above, and ornamental border. Rev. Blank. Nickel, fine. 11.

770 Washington Schuetzen Park token for 5 cents, copper, rare ; also spiel-mark engraved in honor of Washington. 12. 2 pcs

771 Naked bust of Washington to right, with and without P' under neck. Rev. Heads of Jackson, Lincoln, Grant. etc. No duplicates. *Silver;* nearly proof. 12. 9 pcs

772 Smaller bust in civilian dress to right. Rev. Jackson, "Born," etc., also duplicates of last No. *Silver;* nearly proof. 12. 5 pcs

773 Naked bust of Washington to right, from 5 slightly
different dies. Rev. Heads of Jackson, Lincoln,
Grant, square and compasses on Bible, Children's
Centennial party, Pottsville, Pa., 1876, "Perse-
verance 5," Independence Hall, and blank. Cop.,
brass and w. m.; one pierced. Proof. 12. 15 pcs

774 Smaller bust as in No. 772. Various reverses, as
before; also 2 duplicates of last number. Bronze,
cop., brass and w. m. Uncir. or proof, one pierced.
12. 9 pcs

775 Bust nearly facing. BORN FEB. 22 1722, DIED DEC.
14 1799. Rev. Busts of Franklin, Lincoln, Grant,
"Gen. of the American Armies," "Progress,"
Indian head, 1864, Trophy, 1864, Mason and Co.,
also Stoner & Schroyer's cards. Cop., nickel,
brass and w. m.; one struck on very thick planchet. Uncir. or proof. 12. 13 pcs

776 Bust to left. REPRESENTED BY WM. LEGGETT BRAM-
HALL. Rev. Robbin, Royce & Hard's, N. Y.,
card. Cop., nickel and brass. Uncir. 12. 4 pcs

777 Bust to right. Rev. GREAT CENTRAL FAIR PHILA
1864. Silver, cop. and brass. Uncir. 11. 3 pcs

778 Naked bust to left. GEORGE WASHINGTON. Rev.
Naked bust to right. GENERAL LAFAYETTE. 1824.
Silver; uncirculated and very rare. 10.

779 Duplicate. Pierced above the head. Silver; fine.
10.

780 Same obv. Rev Blank. Silver; uncirculated. 9.

781 Naked bust to right. Rev. Twelve stars. Copper,
uncirculated. 9.

782 Duplicate of last No. Copper, uncirculated. 9.
2 pcs

783 Naked bust of Washington to left. Rev. Radiant
star. Silver; uncirculated and rare. 7.

784 Duplicate of last No. Silver; uncirculated. 7.

785 Military bust to right; 18 stars near edge. Rev.
G. Washington Natus 1732 Obiit 1799; engraved. Silver; uncirculated. 8.

786 Naked bust of Washington to right. Rev. Masonic
implements. Gold; proof. 6.

787 Duplicate of last No. Gold; proof. 6.

788 The same. Silver, copper, brass and w. m. Proof.
6. 5 pcs

789 Same obv Rev. Blank. Gold; proof. 6. 2 pcs

9 790 The same. *Silver*, copper and brass. Proof. 6.
4 pcs

50 791 WAR TOKENS, or Copperhead. Bust of Washington, etc. All different; two struck over dimes. *Silver;* uncirculated and a rare lot. 12.   9 pcs

13 792 Bust to right. THE WASHINGTON TOKEN 1863. No duplicates of metal. Nickel, copper, brass and w. m. Uncirculated. 12.   19 pcs

8 793 Washington War tokens, or copperheads. Very few duplicates in the same metal. Copper, nickel, brass and white metal. Uncirculated.   117 pcs

1.25 794 BUTTONS, ETC. G W. in monogram, around which LONG LIVE THE PRESIDENT, and 13 links with names of States. Copper; perfect. 22.

50 795 Another. G. W. in Roman text, and without names of States. Perfect. 21.

55 796 G. W. in monogram, and "Long live the President." Brass. 22.

20 797 Eagle displayed ; one with "Memorable March the fourth, 1789." Brass. 22.   2 pcs

15 798 Duplicates of last No. Brass. 22.   2 pcs

16 799 Electrotypes of Washington buttons ; also tin disks impressed with busts of Washington.   5 pcs

60 800 BADGES, ETC. Draped bust to right ; raised border. *Silver;* very fine. 12x15.

35 801 Naked bust to left. *Silver;* a shell, fine. 8x10.

1.00 802 Diamond shaped copper planchet, the angles cut, impressed with a Maltese cross bearing in the centre an eagle, supporting the American shield. KTS ST JONATHAN. OUR COUNTRY FEB 22 1832. Trial piece of Society badge. Perfect and probably unique. 19x21.

40 803 Silver pin, cross-shaped, with bust of Washington embossed in centre. Perfect. 25.

55 804 Bust of Washington. Cross-shaped badge of the Ladies Loyal League. *Silver;* perfect. 15.

75 805 Bust of Washington to right, 1776. Rev. Agricultural trophy, 1876. Centennial badge with pin. 19.

5 806 Maltese cross. View of Art Gallery ; head of Washington below, 1876. C. A G. E. Brass, fine. 32.

807 Gold mounted Watch charms; pins with head of
  Washington, hatchet, also impressions of Washington's head on lead planchets, etc. All very fine.
  20 pcs

808 Enameled breast pins, sleeve buttons, etc., all with
  busts of Washington and chiefly of French manu-
  facture for the 1876 Centennial. An extremely
  fine lot. 19 to 26. 10 pcs

809 Brass box with portraits of Presidents, Washington
  to Grant. Perfect. 28.

810 Medallion portrait of Washington and wife. Brass
  mounted with pins. 30. 2 pcs

811 Melanotypes of Washington; framed photos; also
  Centennial match box, with bust of Washington.
  5 pcs

812 Encased postage stamps, bust of Washington, 3,
  10 and 12 cents. Rev. Various cards. A fine
  and very rare lot. 12 pcs

813 Brass buttons, fire-gilt. Bust of Washington. Rev.
  "Presented to General Lafayette by L. H. &
  Scovill, Waterbury, Con." etc. Perfect. 13.
  2 pcs

814 Hatchet with pin, on ornamented pen-wiper. Red,
  white and blue.

815 Electrotype copies of Washington medals, etc., includes a tin planchet impressed with obverse of
  Bale and Smith's card. A good lot. 10 pcs

816 Washington silk and satin badges; one with metalic
  hatchet. Large and small; all fine. 6 pcs

PRESIDENTIAL AND POLITICAL MEDALS.

The term "perfect" and "very fine" denote that the medal is perfectly
struck, of fine color and entirely uninjured by circulation or handling.

JOHN ADAMS.

817 Bust to right. JOHN ADAMS PRES. I S. Rev.
  Hands clasped; PEACE AND FRIENDSHIP. W. m.,
  possibly cast; good. 37.

818 Bust to right. JOHN ADAMS PRESIDENT OF THE U. S.
  1797. Rev. PEACE AND FRIENDSHIP. Bronze;
  perfect. 32.

819 Bust, same as last. Trial impression in tin.

820 Bust to right. Rev. Residence. Bronze; perfect. 22.

821 Eagle displayed. Rev. JOHN ADAMS. 1797. *Brichaut's* series. Bronze; proof. 20.

THOMAS JEFFERSON.

822 Bust to left. Rev. PEACE AND FRIENDSHIP. *Electrotype;* perfect. 64.

823 Bust to left. Same design. Bronze ; perfect. 48.

824 Bust to left. TH. JEFFERSON PRESIDENT OF THE U. S. A. D 1801. Rev. PEACE AND FRIENDSHIP. *Silver* shells, solid edge. Fine, and undoubted original; very rare. 34.

825 Same design as last. Bronze; perfect. 32.

826 The same. Tin ; cast.

827 Bust to left. TH. JEFFERSON PRESIDENT OF THE U. S. 4 MARCH 1801. Rev. Minerva deposits a chart " declar independence" on a rock, inscribed CONSTITUTION. TO COMMEMORATE JULY 4 1776, etc. *Silver;* pierced. In good condition, and extremely rare. 28.

828 The same. Copper ; *cast.*

829 Bust to right. Rev. Residence. Bronze ; perfect. 28.

830 Eagle displayed. *Brichaut's* series. Bronze; proof. 20.

831 Bust to right by *Bolen.* Rev. Inscription. Bronze; proof. 16.

832 Bust to left. Rev. Shield. TO COMMEMORATE, etc. *Silver;* proof. 12.

833 The declaration of Independence, "Jefferson was its honored author," etc. Copper ; fine. 12.

JAMES MADISON.

834 Bust to left. 1809. Rev. PEACE AND FRIENDSHIP. Bronze ; perfect. 48.

835 Bust to left. A. D. 1809. Rev. PEACE AND FRIENDSHIP. Slightly pierced above. *Silver;* in very good condition and an undoubted original. 40.

836 The same. Bronze ; perfect. 40.

837 Same design. Bronze ; perfect. 32.

838 Bust to right by *Furst.* JAMES MADISON PRESIDENT OF THE U S. from 1809 to 1817. Rev. Eagle grasping implements of agriculture and a wreath. INDUSTRY BRINGS PLENTY, etc. Tin; nearly proof. 40.

3 0 839 The same. Struck on a tin planchet ⅞ in. in diameter. Fine.

1 0 840 Bust, same as last. Trial impression on oval tin planchet. Fine.

⁴ 0 841 Bust to right. Rev. Residence. Bronze; perfect. 22.

⁷ 8 842 Eagle displayed. *Brichaut's* series. Bronze; proof. 20.

JAMES MONROE.

2 0 843 Bust to right by *Furst.* 1817. Rev. PEACE AND FRIENDSHIP. Bronze; perfect. 48.

7 0 844 Same design. Bronze; slightly tarnished. 40.

7 5 845 Peace medal. Same design as preceding. *Silver;* pierced. Original; very fine and rare. 32.

8 0 846 Another. Bronze; perfect. 32.

2 5 847 Bust to right. Rev. Residence. Bronze; perfect. 22.

3 0 848 Eagle displayed. *Brichaut's* series. Bronze; proof. 20.

JOHN QUINCY ADAMS.

    849 Bust to right. 1825. The largest Peace Medal. Usual reverse. Bronze; perfect. 48.

    850 Same design. Bronze; perfect. 40.

    851 Another. Bronze; perfect. 32.

    852 Bust to right. MARCH 4, 1825, in exergue. Rev. Warrior presenting an olive branch to Indian seated on cornucopia, eagle in the background. SCIENCE GIVES PEACE AND AMERICA PLENTY. Tin; silvered (?) and burnished. Very fine and extremely medal by Furst. 32.

8 0 853 The same. Tin; perfect. Cost $9.00 in the Holland sale.

2 6 854 Heraldic eagle, bearing the U. S. shield, surrounded by a circle of 26 stars. Rev. HIS EXCELLENCY JOHN QUINCY ADAMS PRESIDENT OF THE UNITED STATES OF AMERICA. 1828. Early campaign medal, silvered tin, slightly pierced and in extra fine condition. Extremely rare. 28. (Holland sale, $11.00.)

2 5 855 Bust to right. Rev. Residence. Bronze; very fine. 22.

    856 Eagle displayed. *Brichaut's* series. Bronze; proof. 20.

ANDREW JACKSON.

857 Bust to right by *Furst.* Rev. PEACE AND FRIEND-
SHIP. Perfect. 50.

858 Military bust to right by *Furst.* Rev. Victory writing ORLEANS on a tablet, Peace behind her. RESO-
LUTION OF CONGRESS, etc. Bronze ; perfect. 40.

859 Bust to right by *Furst.* Rev. PEACE AND FRIEND-
SHIP. Bronze ; perfect. 32.

860 Bust at three-quarter face. GEN. ANDREW JACKSON.
Rev. Star and double wreath, between which
UNITED STATES OF AMERICA. Tin ; fine. 28.

861 Same obv. Rev. Another bust of Jackson, same
inscription. Copper ; good. Not in the Holland
sale. 26.

862 Eagle displayed, a circle of stars on border. Rev.
THE GALLANT AND SUCCESSFUL DEFENDER, etc.
Tin, pierced ; poor but rare. 28.

863 Bust nearly facing. AND. JACKSON, etc. 1829. Rev.
THE GALLANT & SUCCESSFUL DEFENDER OF N OR-
LEANS 1815, in wreath of olive. Tin, pierced.
Fine and very rare. Not in Holland catalogue. 24.

864 Eagle in a circle of stars. Rev. THE GALLANT AND
SUCCESSFUL DEFENDER, etc. W. m., pierced ; fine.
24.

865 Jackson on horseback. Rev. THE ADVOCATE, etc.
W. m., fine. 24.

866 Nashville Centennial Exposition. 1880. W. m.;
proof. 25.

867 Two heads of Jackson, name above, in oval panels,
impressed on English penny. Good ; unique. 24.

868 Head to right. Rev. Residence. Bronze; very fine. 22.

869 Bust to right ; OLD HICKORY, etc. Rev. Inscription.
Bronze ; very fine. 22.

870 Bust to right. Rev. View of battle of New Orleans. Tin ; silvered. Very good ; extremely rare.
22. *cast*

871 Eagle displayed. 1829. *Brichaut's* series. Bronze
proof. 20.

872 Jackson on horseback. Rev. THE UNION MUST AND
SHALL BE PRESERVED, etc. *Silver*; proof. 18. *Braut*

873 Bust facing in wreath of oak. AND. JACKSON PRE-
SIDENT OF THE UNITED STATES, 1835. Rev. Eagle
in wreath. THE GALLANT, etc. Brass ; fine. Very
rare. 16.

4 874 Jackson on horseback, "the Nation's pride," "We
commemorate the glorious victories," etc. Copper
and brass. Very fine. 12 to 18. 7 pcs

875 Bust to right by *Bolen.* THE STERN OLD SOLDIER,
etc. Bronze proof. 16.

876 Inauguration medalets (2); equestrian statue. Silver ; very fine. 12. 3 pcs

877 Brass button. Liberty cap. "Whigs of '76 & '34."
Fine ; rare. 8.

MARTIN VAN BUREN.

878 Bust to right by *Furst.* 1837. Large Peace medal,
usual design. Silver : pierced. Original ; fine and
very rare. 48.

879 The same. Bronze ; perfect. 48.

880 Another. Bronze ; perfect. 40.

881 Bust to right. Rev. INAUGURATED MARCH 4TH A. D.
1837, in wreath of oak and wheat. Bronze ; perfect. 40.

882 Peace medal. Bronze ; perfect. 32.

883 Bust facing left. MARTIN VAN BUREN & DEMOCRA-
CY. Rev. Temple of Liberty. A UNIFORM AND
SOUND CURRENCY. Tin ; pierced, very fair. 24.

884 Similar obv. Rev. Eagle with scales. "Federal"
"democr," etc. Tin, pierced. Very fine. 24.

885 Bust to left. THE ADVOCATE OF EQUAL RIGHTS.
Rev. Eagle on safe ; SAFE BIND SAFE FIND. Tin,
pierced. Fine. 24

886 Bust to left in wreath by *Smith.* Rev. Large eagle
on a small safe (?) THE COUNTRY DEMANDS HIS
RE-ELECTION. Tin, pierced. Very fine. Not in
Holland's sale. 24.

887 Bust to right, a wreath in exergue and 26 stars near
border. Rev. Temple of Liberty, bales of goods
and agricultural implements around its base.
DEMOCRACY AND OUR COUNTRY Tin; fine, pierced
Not in Holland's sale. 24.

888 Bust to right. Rev. Residence. Bronze; very
fine. 32.

§ 889 Medalets, each with bust. Rev. "Born 1782," "Our next president," "Justice and equality," "Democracy and our country," "Independent Treasury," "VIII president of the United States" "Sub-Treasury and Democracy," "Weighed in the balance and found wanting." A rare lot. Copper (3), brass (3), w. m. (2). 5 pierced; good to uncirculated. 14 to 22. 8 pcs

2 0 890 Eagle displayed. 1837. *Brichaut's* series. Bronze proof. 20.

2 5 891 Bust to right. 1849. Rev. FREE SOIL, FREE LABOR, FREE SPEECH. Brass shells; thick and good. 16.

6 892 Bust nearly facing. Rev. "National Union league." "long may it wave," and Chas. K. Warner's card. Copper and brass. Uncirculated. 16. 3 pcs

, v—o 893 Enameled bust to left, white on black ground; a square campaign pin, gold setting. 16x18.

WILLIAM HENRY HARRISON.

/. o v— 894 Military bust to right by *Furst*. Rev. Battle of the Thames. Bronze; perfect. 40.

v—v— 895 Large bust, facing. Rev. Log cabin; flag to right, inscribed TIP. NINTH PRESIDENT OF THE UNITED STATES. Tin; fine. 28.

v. o—o 896 Log cabin. TO LET. POSSESSION GIVEN IN 1841 ; circle of stars on raised border. Rev. THE YOUNG MEN'S HARRISON CONVENTION MAY 4 1880. Tin, pierced ; good, extremely rare. 28.

v o 897 Bust to left by *Mitchell*. Harrison Jubilee medal, Bunker Hill, 1840. Bronze; very fine original. 27.

v—o 898 Draped bust, the head turned to right. WILLIAM H. HARRISON; 26 stars near the border. Rev. Eagle in circle of 24 stars. Copper; nearly proof and very rare. 24.

/ o 899 Military bust to right. HONOR WHERE HONOR'S DUE. Rev. Bust of Clay, Bunker Hill monument, etc. Bronze, copper, and brass. Fine. 24. 3 pcs

/ o 900 Same obverse. Rev. HENRY CLAY OF KENTUCKY, etc. Type metal, also electro. of this obverse. 24. 2 pcs.

/. 7 o 901 Military bust to left over semi-circle of 26 stars. Rev. Log cabin, flag and nine soldiers to left, small cider barrel on right ; THE HERO OF TIPPECANOE. Tin, silvered ; very fine and rare. 23.

902 Similar : six soldiers to left on rev Tin ; fine, pierced. 23.

903 Military bust to left, under it, BORN FEB 9 1773, Rev. Log cabin, flag in centre, to right, tree and cider barrel on the left, and same inscription in exergue as before. Tin, gilt ; very fine, pierced. 24.

904 Same obv. Rev. Very similar to last, but flag flies to left. Tin, pierced ; very fine.

905 Similar obverse. Rev. Log cabin, flag to left, a tree on the right, a cider barrel on the left, same inscription. Tin ; good, pierced. 24.

906 Similar obverse. Rev. Log cabin, an eagle above it, flag and four soldiers to left, cider barrel on the right same inscription. Tin, silvered ; fine, pierced. 22.

907 Duplicate of last No. Tin ; very fine. 22.

908 Similar obv. Rev. Log cabin, flag in centre, flying to right, a small cider barrel on left, tree on each side. Tin ; pierced, fair. 24.

909 Military bust to left ; BORN FEB. 9, 1773, below it. Rev. Log cabin, "Sabbath School Jubilee, 1842," "He is a freeman," etc. Copper and bronze ; very fine. 22.   3 pcs.

910 Same obverse. Rev. Blank. *Silver* ; very fine and rare. 22.

911 Log cabin as before. Rev. OX IS A FREEMAN, etc. *Silver* ; very fine and rare. 22.

912 Log cabin. Rev. "Sabbath School jubilee." blank. Nickel and brass, very fine ; lead, good. 22.
                                                          3 pcs

913 Military bust to left, 1840 below it. Rev. Log cabin, flag on right, flying to left, cider barrel to left. W. m., very fine. 23.

914 Cloaked bust, nearly facing by *Davis*, GENERAL HARRISON PRESIDENT. Rev. Liberty with shield and cap, American eagle to left. LIBERTY AND INDEPENDENCE. Brass ; thick pl., very fine. 24.

915 The same. White metal ; very fine. 24.

916 Bust to right. Rev Residence. Bronze; very fine. 22.

917 Eagle displayed. 1841. *Brichaut's series*. Bronze, proof. 20.

918 Military bust to right. Rev. RESOLUTION OF CON-
GRESS, APRIL 4, 1818. Copper; fine and scarce. 20.

919 Head to right over semi-circle of thirteen stars. TIP-
PECANOE above. Rev. Log cabin, THE PEOPLE'S
above, CHOICE below. Copper; very rude design
and impression, but fine; struck over a coin. Extremely rare political token. 18.

920 Military bust to left. Rev. HE LEAVES THE PLOUGH
TO SAVE HIS COUNTRY. Varieties ; brass, one
pierced. Very good and scarce. 18.   2 pcs

921 Bust to left. Rev. Log cabin. 2 varieties. brass.
18.   4 pcs

922 Bust to left. Rev. Log cabin, bust of Clay. Copper and brass, proof. 17.   2 pcs

923 Bust to left. Rev. Eagle. GO IT. TIP; COME IT,
TYLER. Slight varieties ; brass, pierced ; fine.
16.   2 pcs

924 Bust to left, one nearly facing. Rev. Five varieties
of log cabins, scale, steamboat, Van Buren, Eagle
with label inscribed Tippecanoe, view of battle.
Brass, all but one pierced, and that is the rarest.
An interesting, fine and desirable lot. 14.   10 pcs

925 Bust with large projecting chest, ornamented with a
medal, to left. MAJ. GEN. W. H. HARRISON. Rev.
Log cabin and barrel of cider to right, a cannon
to left, and a few soldiers in the distance. Crow-
like eagle above, holding a scale inscribed LOCO
WHIGS; near the edge, WEIGHED IN THE BALANCE
AND FOUND WANTING. Brass, fine, pierced (Holland sale $6.00). 16.

926 Miscellaneous. 16 and 18.   3 pcs

927 Brass buttons; log cabins.   3 pcs

928 Campaign pins. Solid gilt setting. Fine and perfect. 16 and 18.   2 pcs

929 Military bust to left, white enamel (?) on black
ground. Rev. A log cabin, same materials. ''The
people's choice, the hero of Tippecanoe." In
glass, set in the form of a locket. Cost $17.00,
Holland sale (1139). Size 26.

JOHN TYLER.

930 Bust to left. 1841. Rev. PEACE AND FRIENDSHIP.
Bronze ; fine. 48.

931 Another peace medal. Bronze ; perfect. 36.

932 Another. Bronze; perfect. 32.

933 Same obv. as 931. Rev. APRIL IV. MDCCCXLI., in
wreath of oak. Copper nickel-plated. Perfect. 36.

934 Bust to right. Rev. Residence. Bronze; perfect.
22.

935 Eagle displayed. 1841. *Bricharal.* Bronze; proof.
20.

JAMES KNOX POLK.

936 Bust to left. 1845. Rev. PEACE AND FRIENDSHIP.
Bronze; perfect. 48.

937 Peace medal, same as last. Bronze; perfect. 36.

938 Another. Smallest size. Bronze; perfect. 32.

939 Bust to right. Rev. Residence. Bronze; perfect.
22.

940 Eagle displayed. 1845. *Bricharal's* series. Br.
proof. 20.

941 Bust to right ; brass shell, gilt. 16.

942 Miscellaneous. "Young Hickory," etc. W. m. and
electros., 2 pierced. 17 to 28. 4 pcs

943 Bust of Dallas to left. Rev. Bust of Polk. "Our
country, right or wrong." wreath. One pierced.
Cop. and w. m. Very fine. 26. 3 pcs

HENRY CLAY.

944 Head to left. Rev. CLAY within a wreath of maize
and tobacco. Cast iron, of the period, probably
unique. 66.

945 Naked bust to left by *Wright.* Rev. Inscription in
eighteen lines, within a heavy wreath of maize,
wheat, etc. Bronze; perfect. *A rare medal.* 36.

946 Trial impression of reverse of this medal. Copper
shell ; very fine.

947 Electrotype of the same medal. Fine. 66.

948 Bust to left. Rev. Hand on a rock inscribed "Constitution." Wright's smaller medal. Bronze;
perfect. 48.

949 Duplicate. Bronze; perfect. 48.

950 Silvered electro. of obverse of this medal. Perfect.

951 Head to left. Rev. Factories, a ship, etc. THE
PEOPLE'S CHOICE. 1844. Copper; thick pl.;
perfect. 32.

7.5- 952 Same obv. Rev. Ship sailing; varieties. Tin, pierced, good. 32. 2 pcs

1.60 953 Draped bust to left by *Mitchell*. Rev. THE FLAG WE WEAR AT OUR MASTHEAD, etc. Brass; fine and rare. 27.

60 954 The same, without artist's name. W. m. gilt; pierced; fine. 27.

2.0 955 Same obv. Rev. Angel inscribing dates of Clay's birth and death on a monument. W. m.: very fine. 27.

4.0 956 Head to left, by *Leonard*. Rev. Factories, a ship, etc. THE WEALTH OF A NATION, etc. Copper; very fine. 26.

2.6 957 Male figure with *torn* American flag. OUR FLAG TRAMPLED UPON. Rev. NATIVES BEWARE, etc. 1844. W. m., pierced; very fine and rare. 26.

1.50 958 Silver dollar, obverse removed and replaced by the inscription "Presented to Harry Clay Molan by Henry Clay of Ashland, March 6 1848". Interesting and unique memento, in fine condition.

7.& 959 Bust to left in heavy wreath of oak. THE FARMER OF ASHLAND, etc. Rev. Inscription, Bunker Hill monument, blank. Brass (3) and w. m.; very fine; all different. 24. 5 pcs

5.0 960 Large bust to right. HENRY CLAY. Rev. View of monument. IN COMMEMORATION OF THE GREAT CONVENTION HELD AT BALTIMORE May, 1844. Copper; fine; rare. 24.

4 961 Miscellaneous. All different; copper and brass, 6 pierced. An interesting lot. 15 to 20. 10 pcs

4 962 Miscellaneous. A few dupl. of preceding nos., but all different. Copper (1); w. m. (3), cast, etc. (3), 4 pierced. 15 to 27. 12 pcs

4 963 Draped bust to right. Rev. Jackson on horseback, inscription. Copper and brass; proof. 18. 2 pcs

'5- 964 Bust to left. ELECTED PRESIDENT A. D. 1844. Rev. INAUGURATED MARCH 4TH 1845. One of the lying tokens; brass, pierced, fine. 16.

// 965 Bust in wreath of oak. HENRY CLAY, PRESIDENT, 1845. Rev. Eagle. Tin; proof 14. Also dupl. of last no. 2 pcs

6 966 Large head to right. HENRY CLAY. Rev. A TARIFF FOR PROTECTION Yellow bronze. 12. Another, same obv., rev. blank. Copper. 15. Both very fine. 2 pcs

967 Naked bust to left in border of oak branches. Rev.
Blank. Yellow bronze ; 11x14. Very fine and
rare.

968 Brass-gilt campaign badges. Hollow shells, pins,
a rare lot, etc. A rare lot. 11 pcs

ZACHARY TAYLOR.

969 Bust to right. Resolution of Congress, May 9,
1848. Rev. Battle of Buena Vista. Bronze ;
perfect. 50.

970 Same obv. Rev. Bust of Scott (?). Trial impression in lead. Fair. 50.

971 View of battle of Buena Vista. Rev. State arms of
Louisiana. The Pelican medal, presented to
Taylor by the State of Louisiana. Bronze ; per-
fect. 48.

972 Bust to right. The Palo Alto medal, presented
by Congress, July 16th, 1846. Bronze ; perfect.
40.

973 Same obverse. The Monterey medal, presented by
Congress, March 2d, 1847. Bronze ; perfect. 40.

974 Bust to left. 1849. Rev. PEACE AND FRIENDSHIP.
Bronze ; perfect. 48.

975 Peace medal. Same design. Bronze ; perfect. 40.

976 Peace medal. Smallest size. Bronze ; perfect. 32.

977 Naked bust to right by *Wright*. Rev. Inscription
in 10 lines, ending with DIED JULY 9, 1850.
Bronze ; fine. 36.

978 Miscellaneous. 3 duplicates, 1 pierced. White
metal ; all fine. 19 to 26. 9 pcs

979 Bust to left. NEVER SURRENDERS. Rev. Trophy ;
I ASK NO FAVORS, etc. Copper proof. 26.

980 Bust to right. Rev. Residence. Bronze ; perfect.
32.

981 Naked bust to right by *Wright*. Rev. A LITTLE
MORE GRAPE, CAPTAIN BRAGG, etc. Copper proof.
26.

982 Eagle displayed. 1849. *Brichaut's series*. Bronze
proof. 26.

983 Miscellaneous. Copper and brass. One duplicate
of 988. 16 to 20. 4 pcs

984 Button, hollow shell, etc. Fine. 3 pcs

1.00   985 Cameo head of Taylor to right, set in gold as a pin.
Oval. 14x17. No. 1223, Holland sale, cost $2.50.

2.00   986 Military bust to right. Cameo, white on chocolate-
colored ground, set as a pin. Cost $14.25. Hol-
land sale, 1224. 23x28.

LEWIS CASS.

30   987 Bust to left. Rev. THE SUB-TREASURY AND THE
TARIFF OF '46 in wreath of roses. Copper proof. 26.

60   988 Bust to right. WHILE I AM ABLE, etc. Rev. Bust to
left. THE FREEDOM OF THE SEAS, etc. Copper ;
rude, rare. 18.

12   989 Bust to left. 1848. Rev. Female seated. Brass ;
pierced. 18.

MILLARD FILLMORE.

1.05   990 Bust to right by *Ellis.* 1850. Rev. Pioneer and
Indian before an American flag. Bronze ; perfect.
40.

5   991 Bust to right by *Odling.* Rev. Inscription in 10
lines ; THE UNION in double circle of stars.
Bronze and w. m. Very fine. 24.   2 pcs

//   992 Bust to right by Smith & Hartman. Rev. Bust of
John C. Fremont, and inscription in wreath.
Bronze ; very fine. 22.   2 pcs

22   993 Bust to right. Rev. Residence. Bronze ; v. fine. 22.

16   994 Eagle displayed. 1849. *Brichaut's* series. Bronze
proof. 20.

4   995 Bust to right and eagle. Varieties ; brass, one
pierced. 17.   2 pcs

FRANKLIN PIERCE.

125   996 Bust to left by *Ellis.* 1853. Rev. Pioneer and Indian
before American flag. Bronze ; perfect. 48.

900   997 Same obv. Rev. PEACE AND FRIENDSHIP. Bronze ;
perfect. 48.

20   998 Bust to left by *Leonard.* Rev. Trophy, and
UNITED WE STAND. Copper ; very fine. 26.

25   999 Bust to right. Rev. Residence. Bronze ; very
fine. 22.

18   1000 Eagle displayed. 1853. *Brichaut's* series. Bronze,
proof. 20.

1001 Miscellaneous. Brass ; fine, 1 pierced. 16 to 18.
3 pcs

1002 Looking-glass ; tin frame with bust. 4s.

WINFIELD SCOTT.

1003 Naked bust to left by *Wright*. Rev. The City of
Mexico in the centre, surrounded by views of 6
battles in chain of wreaths. Resolution of Congress March 9 1848. Bronze ; perfect. 56.

1004 Draped bust on square tablet inscribed THE COM-
MONWEALTH OF VIRGINIA, etc. Rev. Column
bearing the names of battles in heavy wreath of
oak. A beautiful medal by *Wright*, presented to
Scott by the State of Virginia. Bronze ; perfect.
56.

1005 Bust to right by *Furst*. Resolution of Congress
Nov. 8, 1814. Bronze ; perfect. 40.

1006 Naked bust to left ; *C. G. Guilfeldt & J. Lehr-
ton* under the shoulder. Rev. Shield. APRIL 19
1861, ONE FLAG, ONE COUNTRY, etc. W. m., very
fine. 40.

1007 Bust to left by *Leonard*. Rev. Trophy of flags ;
wreath. Copper ; very fine. 26.   2 pcs

1008 Bust to left in wreath of oak. Rev. NOMINATED
BY THE BALTIMORE CONVENTION 1852, etc. Cop.,
very fine. 22.

1009 Miscellaneous. Cop., br. and w. m. Two pierced ;
very fine. 16 to 20.   7 pcs

1010 Metallic calendar, enclosing photo., etc.   2 pcs

JOHN C. FREMONT.

1011 Bust to left by *Paquet*. Rev. THE PEOPLE'S
CHOICE FOR 1856, etc., in wreath. Bronze ; perfect. 38.

1012 Bust to right. Rev. Surveying scene. Tin, v. fine.
27.

1013 Bust nearly facing. Rev. Inscription in 18 lines.
Cop., very fine. 25.

1014 Bust nearly facing. Rev. FREMONT AND COCH-
RANE. Copper ; very fine. 22.

1015 Bust to right by *Smith & Hartman*. Rev. FRE-
MONT, etc., and inscription in wreath. Bronze and
w. m. ; very fine. 22.   2 pcs

1016 Bust nearly facing. FREMONT FOR PRESIDENT, 1864, etc. Brass and w. m. Very fine. 19. 2 pcs

1017 Miscellaneous. Cop., br. and w. m. Very fine, 2 pierced. 14 to 18. 7 pcs

1018 Melanotypes or encased photos. 3 pcs

JAMES BUCHANAN.

1019 Bust to right by *Ellis.* 1853. Rev. Pioneer and Indian before an American flag. Bronze ; perfect. 48.

1020 Same obv. Rev. Western scene ; Indian scalping an enemy on wide border, etc. Bronze : perfect. 48.

1021 The same, silvered ; also copper shell of this obv. *Electrotypes.* 2 pcs

1022 Bust to right by *Paquet.* Rev. TO DR. FREDERICK ROSE, ASSISTANT SURGEON, etc. Bronze ; perfect. 48.

1023 Same obv. Rev. FIRST EMBASSY FROM JAPAN, etc. 1860. Bronze ; perfect, 48.

1024 Bust nearly facing by *Paquet.* Rev. Eagle in a glory of rays, bearing the names of States, etc. Tin, bronzed ; very fine. 38.

1025 Bust to left ; trial piece in cop. Unique. 23.

1026 Bust to right. Rev. Residence. Bronze : very fine. 22.

1027 Eagle displayed, 1857. *Brichaut's* series. Bronze, proof. 20.

1028 Miscellaneous. Copper and brass. All different and very fine. 17 to 21. 5 pcs

STEPHEN A. DOUGLASS.

1029 Bust at full face. Rev. DEMOCRATIC CANDIDATE in heavy wreath ; inscription in 4 lines. Copper and brass ; very fine. 25. 2 pcs

1030 Bust to left. Rev. Eagle. Copper, fine. 24.

1031 Miscellaneous. All different ; one pierced, fine. W. m. 22 to 24. 6 pcs

1032 Bust to left. FOR PRESIDENT, etc. Rev. " Presidents house," " the wealth of the South," " No submission to the North," etc. All different ; a rare and fine set. Copper (10) and w. m. 14. 11 pcs

1083 Miscellaneous. One pierced, two duplicates. Copper, nickel and brass. Very fine. 12 to 20.   13 pcs

1084 Melanotypes of Douglass & Johnson in silvered metallic frames. All fine and large.   5 pcs

1085 Another lot; brass frames, etc., one rubber. 20 pcs

JOHN BELL.

1036 Bust to left. Rev. Eagle. Copper, very fine. 24.

1037 Miscellaneous. All different. Copper, brass and tin; 2 pierced. 14 to 24.   10 pcs

1038 Melanotypes, etc., metallic frames.   9 pcs

1039 Bust of Everett. Rev. Boston oration, July 4, 1860. Copper, very fine. 19.

JOHN C. BRECKENRIDGE.

1040 Bust to left. Rev. Eagle. Copper, very fine. 24.

1041 Miscellaneous. All different. German silver, brass centre, copper and tin. One pierced; fine. 14 to 24.   4 pcs

1042 Melanotypes; metallic frames. Fine.   7 pcs

ABRAHAM LINCOLN.

1043 Cloaked bust to right by *Ellis*, 1862. Rev. Western scene; Indians on broad border. Bronze; perfect. 48.

1044 Similar medal. Bronze; perfect. 40.

1045 Naked bust to right by *Paquet*. Rev. SOUTH WESTERN SANITARY FAIR. 1865. Bronze; perfect. 36.

1046 Bust in high relief to right by *Story*. SALVATOR PATRIÆ. Rev. IN MEMORY OF THE LIFE ACTS AND DEATH OF ABRAHAM LINCOLN, etc., in heavy wreath of laurel. Published by the *American Numismatic and Archæological Society of New York*. Very beautiful and rare medal in morocco case. Bronze; perfect. 52.

1047 The same. Thick planchet; white metal proof. 52.

1048 Large head to left. DÉDIÉ PAR LA DÉMOCRATIE FRANCAISE À LINCOLN, etc. Rev. Angel placing a crown on a monument, around which freedmen are gathered. LINCOLN, HONNÊTE HOMME, etc. A superb medal, paid for by penny subscription in France, struck in Switzerland. Bronze; perfect and very rare. 52.

1. ?.s - 1049 Bust to right by *Bovy.* Rev. ABOLITION OF SLAVERY PROCLAIMED SEPTEMBER 22nd 1862 ; WITH MALICE TOWARDS NONE, etc. 4th MARCH 1865. Bronze ; perfect, rare. 38.

s·v 1050 Bust to right by *Key.* Rev. Broken column. HE IS IN GLORY, etc. Bronze; perfect, rare. 32.

s-o 1051 Head to right by *Barber.* The Emancipation medal; *mint series.* Bronze ; perfect. 29.

o's- 1052 Head to left. Rev. THE RAILSPLITTER OF 1830. W. m., fine. 26.

/s- 1053 Busts facing of Lincoln and Johnson. Rev. REPUB-LICAN CANDIDATES 1864, etc. Tin ; bronzed. Very fine. 26.

/o 1054 Bust to right. *Henning & Hymann, N. Y.* Rev. REPUBLICAN CANDIDATE, etc. Bronze ; perfect. 25.

/s- 1055 Same obv. Rev. THOU ART THE MAN. 1861. Yellow bronze ; perfect. 25.

/s- 1056 Same obv. Rev. CENTENNIAL OF AMERICAN INDE-PENDENCE, 1876, etc. Bronze; perfect. 25.

/s- 1057 Head to right. 1860. Rev. PROGRESS, 1830. Bronze; perfect. 24.

/s- 1058 Bust to right by *Key.* Rev. Rails crossed ; LIN-COLN & HAMLIN, THE PEOPLES CHOICE 1860. Brass ; very fine. 24.

2 s- 1059 Profile bust to right. FOR PRESIDENT, etc. Rev. Eagle. Copper ; very fine. 24.

s-o 1060 Bust to right. SALVATOR PATRIE. Rev. IN ME-MORY, etc. The same as 1046, but reduced to size 22. Bronze proof.

// 1061 The same. W. m. proof.   2 pcs

/c 1062 Bust to left in circle of stars. Rev. Octagonal cir-cle of rails with roosting fowls. Bronze ; perfect. 22.

7o 1063 Bust to right. Rev. Residence. Bronze ; very fine. 22.

-.?o 1064 Busts jugata of Lincoln & Hamlin. Rev. REPUB-LICAN CANDIDATES, etc. 1860. W m.; fine. 22.

2o 1065 Same busts in wreath of palm. Rev. THE FALL OF FORT SUMTER WILL BE AVENGED, etc., in 12 lines. Bronze ; very fine. 22.

-/o 1066 Bust to right in wreath of oak by *Smith.* Rev. IF I AM ELECTED, etc., in wreath of laurel. Bronze ; perfect. 22.

1067 Bust to left. Rev. THE RIGHT MAN, etc. 1864.
Bronze ; perfect. 24.

1068 Bust to right, semicircle of stars above. HONEST
OLD ABE. Rev. UNION CANDIDATE 1864. W. m.,
one pierced. Very fine. 22. 2 pcs

1069 Bust to right by *Lovett.* ABRAHAM LINCOLN RE-
PUBLICAN CANDIDATE FOR PRESIDENT 1860. Rev.
"Our next president," "United we stand," "The
Union must" etc., "Free territory," "Born Feb.
12, 1809" etc., (varieties) "In memory." Copper,
brass, and w. m., proof. 20. 7 pcs

1070 Same obverse. Rev. "Sine fuco et falacia homo."
DIED APRIL 15 1865. Copper proof ; scarce. 20.

1071 Bust to left. ABM LINCOLN THE MARTYR PRESIDENT.
Rev. "Born Feb 12 1809," etc., (varieties) "In
memory," etc. Cop. and w. m. proof. 20. 3 pcs

1072 Bust to left. 1864 and 8 stars below. Rev. "The
peoples choice" (varieties). head of McClellan
(varieties) "resurgam." A scarce lot. Cop., brass
and w. m., 1 pierced. Fine to proof. 20. 5 pcs

1073 Reward of merit. Rev. LINCOLN SCHOOL. Brass ;
proof. 20.

1074 Bust to right over branches of oak and laurel
crossed, ABM LINCOLN. Rev. "May the Union
flourish" etc., "Sine fuco et falacia" etc. W.
m. Fine, pierced. 20. 2 pcs

1075 Bust to right. "Born Feb. 12 1809." Rev. NO
MORE SLAVE TERRITORY, etc., 1860. Copper ; very
fine. 20.

1076 Bust to right. 1864. Rev. Eagle over shield and
trophy. German silver ; very fine. 19.

1077 Bust to right. "War of 1861." Rev. Blank.
Brass ; proof. 19.

1078 Bust to right. HON. ABRAM LINCOLN, 1860. Rev.
THE MAN THAT CAN SPLIT RAILS, etc. Cop., very
fine. 19.

1079 Eagle displayed. 1861. *Brichauf's* series. Bronze ;
proof. 19.

1080 "In memory of Abm Lincoln, died, April 15,
1865," under drooping branches. Rev. Star of 24
points. *Silver;* pierced, good. 19.

1081 Spielmark. Bust of Lincoln. Brass ; good and
rare.

1082 Two men splitting rails. THE RAIL SPLITTER OF THE WEST. Rev. A. C. Yates card, Syracuse, N. Y. "The old man with specs." Nickel ; fine and very rare. 18.

1083 Same obv. Rev. Eagle, perched on a mortar, bear_ing label inscribed ESTABLISHED A. D. 1825. Cop per ; fine. 18.

1084 Large bust to left by *Key*. 1864. Rev. "Republican candidate," "Monitor," "Born Feb. 12 1809," etc. W. m. proof. 18. 3 pcs

1085 Same obv. Rev. SURRENDER OF GEN. LEE, etc. Bronze proof. 18.

1086 Same obv. Rev. "C. K. Warner," etc. "F. C. Key & Sons," etc. (varieties). Nickel, brass, and w. m. proof. 18. 3 pcs

1087 Smaller bust to left by *Key*. 1864, stars near border. Rev. Same as in 3 preceding nos. Nickel, cop., brass, and w. m. proof. 18. 7 pcs

1088 Long bust to right by *Ellis*. 1860. Rev. "The rail splitter of the West" and "Eagle." Copper : very fine, one silvered. 18. 2 pcs

1089 Bust to right by *Lovett*. 1860. Rev. Bust of Bell, "Free homes for free men" (varieties). "The constitution and the Union" (2), Key's card. Cop., brass, and w. m., proof. 17. 6 pcs

1090 Bust to right by *Merriam*. Rev. "Republican candidate," "He lived for his country," "Soldiers' fair, Springfield, Mass.," "Apollo," "R. Chamberlaine's" card. Copper, proof. 17. 5 pcs

1091 Bust to right. REPUBLICAN CANDIDATE, 1860. Rev. Eagle. LIBERTY UNION AND EQUALITY. Brass ; fine and scarce. 18.

1092 Abm Lincoln President of the U. S. DIED APRIL 15 1865 BY THE HANDS OF A REBEL ASSASSIN. Rev. A SIGH THE ABSENT CLAIM, THE DEAD A TEAR. W. m. proof. 18.

1093 Bust to right. 1860. Rev. FREEDOM NATIONAL, etc. Brass ; proof. 16.

1094 Bust to right. 1864. Rev. "Long may it wave," "Union Campaign Club," "National Union League." Cop. and w. m., the latter pierced. Proof. 3 pcs

1095 Same obv. Rev. "James E. Wolff, Petersburg, Va." German silver ; very fine and rare. 16.

1096 Bust to right; *J. A. Bolen.* Rev. WITH MALICE. etc. Copper. proof. 16.

1097 Bust to right by *Bolen.* Rev. "Emancipation the great event," "Franklin & Co.," "Jefferson Ins. Co." Bronze, cop., and w. m., proof. 16. 3 pcs

1098 Small bust to right. ABRAHAM LINCOLN, IN GOD WE TRUST; 25 (cents) under the bust. Rev. Eagle displayed; UNITED STATES OF AMERICA FOR EVER INSEPARABLE 1864. W m., gilt. Fine and rare. 15.

1099 Naked bust to right. 1860. Rev. OUR POLICY IS EXPRESSLY, etc. Brass; fine. 16.

1100 Bust to right. ABRAHAM LINCOLN. DIED APR. 15 1865. Rev. Roll in wreath in centre; EMANCIPA TION PROCLAIMED, etc. Brass, pierced; fair, rare. 15.

1101 Head to right by *Key.* PRESIDENT 1861-1865. Rev. "Shall be then, thenceforward, and forever free." Brass, proof. 14.

1102 Bust facing. ABRAM LINCOLN, FREE LAND, FREE SPEECH AND FREE MEN. Rev. Eagle displayed over 9 stars. UNION OF THE STATES. *Silver*; rare; uncir. 14.

1103 The same; brass, uncir. 14.

1104 Bust to right. 1864. Rev. "Born Feb. 12 1809" etc. (2). "Our country and our flag." Penny-packer Sibley, Indian head. All very scarce and uncirculated or proof. Cop. and brass. 11.
　　　　　　　　　　　5 pcs

1105 Bust to left. FOR PRESIDENT ABRAHAM LINCOLN. Rev. Bust of Douglass, bust of Breckenridge, "President's house." and blank. All rare and fine. German silver, cop., and brass. 14. 4 pcs

1106 Bust to left. FOR PRESIDENT. Rev. Star in wreath, trophy. German silver, pierced, and brass. Very fine. 14. 2 pcs

1107 Bust to right. Rev. Column MARTYR FOR LIB ERTY. Brass, proof. 13.

1108 Oval medalet. Bust to left. Rev. MARTYR TO LIB ERTY. Bronze and brass, gilt. Loop; perforn. 14x16. 2 pcs

1109 Mint medalets. Bust to right. Rev. Bust of Grant (varieties, "Broken column," "The crisis demands his reelection," "Inaug. second term." *Silver*; proof. 12. 6 pcs

3 1110 Similar lot; one with square and compases on rev.
        Bronze and w. m. ; very fine. 12.   6 pcs

3 1111 Bust to right. ABRAHAM LINCOLN 1864. Rev.
        Heads of Washington, Franklin, Grant, Indian
        head (2), broken column, arms in wreath (2),
        eagle, etc. Cop., brass and w. m., proof ; all
        rare, one pierced. 12.   11 pcs

2 J- 1112 Same obv. Rev. Bust of McClellan to left. *Silver ;*
        proof. 12.

3 0 1113 Same obv., the rev. also the same. Struck on a
        cent. of 1855. Bright red.

J- 1114 Two other impressions like last, on copper plan-
        chets ; one very much damaged. Proof.   2 pcs

J-J- 1115 Another reproduction of the "Salvator patriae"
        medal, an exact facsimile, but size 10. Bronze
        and w. m., proof. 10.   2 pcs

4 J- 1116 Head to left. ABM LINCOLN PRESIDENT, 1864. Rev.
        AMERICA and 13 stars in wreath. Rare copper-
        head ; *silver,* very fine.

J-0 1117 But to left. 1864. Rev. Sedgwick & Co.'s card.
        Rare copperhead ; silver, very fine.

1 ½ 1118 Copperheads, each with head of Lincoln. Rev. O.
        K., square and compasses, etc. A rare lot. Copper
        and brass. All different and uncir.   13 pcs

1   1119 Miscellaneous. Wide-awakes, etc. Copper and
        brass. Av. size 12.   11 pcs

1 0 1120 Impressions in rubber of scarce Lincoln medals.
        Fine ; pierced. 17.   4 pcs

2 0 1121 Perpetual calendar, metallic shells, portraits on
        metallic shells, mourning badge, etc. All very fine
        and rare.   8 pcs

1   1122 Melanotypes, etc., in metallic shells. Large and
        small; a fine and rare lot.   17 pcs

2 J- 1123 Bust to left over axe in rail. Rev. "50" in oval,
        oblong square, pierced at corners, 8x13 ; also pin-
        shaped hatchet, "Honest Abe." Brass ; fine and
        rare.   2 pcs

ANDREW JOHNSON.

1 J-0 1124 Bust to right by *Barber.* 1867. Rev. WITH COUR-
        AGE AND FIDELITY, etc., in wreath of oak and
        laurel. Bronze ; perfect. 48.

8 0 1125 Naked bust to right by *Paquet.* 1865. Rev. Draped
        female with American flag, grasping the hand of
        an Indian, before the bust of Washington on
        pedestal. Bronze ; perfect. 40.

1426 Bust to left. Rev. PUBLIC RECEPTION AND BAN-
QUET, etc.; New York Aug. 29, 1866. *Silver*;
nearly proof. 5 struck in this metal. 20.

1427 The same. Bronze; perfect. 20.

1428 The same. Copper; proof. 20.

1429 Duplicates. Cop. and w. m.; proof. 20.   2 pcs

1430 Same obv. Rev. "Pro patria," "The people must
be trusted," "Dickeson's safe." Three very rare
if not unique combinations. Cop. (spotted) and
w. m.; proof. 20.   3 pcs

1431 Bust to right. Rev. Hands joined; THE PEOPLE
MUST BE TRUSTED, etc. Brass; proof. 20.

1432 Eagle displayed. 1865. *Bricham's* series. Bronze;
proof. 19.

1433 Bust to right. Rev. 17 PRESIDENT. Varieties.
W. m.; proof. 11 and 12.   2 pcs

GEO. B. McCLELLAN.

1434 Military bust to left. Rev. THE UNION AND THE
CONSTITUTION TO BE PRESERVED, etc. Tin, silvered; fine. 36.

1435 Military bust to left. Rev. Names of battles, a
small bust of Washington below. Tin, partly gilt;
very fine. 32.

1436 Bust to left. Rev. AMORE PATRIÆ. BELLEGHEM.
I. C. Carpenter, Co. A. 23 *Regt. P. V.* engraved.
Barely fair but interesting rebellion medal. 28.

1437 Laureated bust in toga to left. No inscription;
rev. blank. Unique artist's proof by Lovett. Tin.
26.

1438 Miscellaneous, including dupl. of 1435 & '37. W.
m., fine or proof. 2 pierced. 19 to 32.   9 pcs

1439 Military bust to left in wreath of laurel by *Smith*.
Rev. "We can ask no higher honor," etc., "The
fall of Sumter will be avenged." Eagle crushing
an eagle. Bronze; perfect, rare. 21.   3 pcs

1440 Military bust facing. Rev. Bombardment of Fort
Sumter. *Silver*; proof. 21.

1441 Naked bust to left. Rev. NEC QUEMERE NEC SPER-
NERE HONOREM. Bronze; perfect. 21.

1442 Military bust to left by *Key*. Rev. THE CONSTITU-
TION AS IT IS, etc. Brass; proof. 20.

⌐ 1143 Military bust to right. 1864. Rev. Shield and trophy of flags. German silver and copper ; proof. 20.   2 pcs

⌐ 1144 Bust to left in wreath. Rev. Bust as in last no., also same as last. German silver, copper and brass ; proof. 20.   3 pcs

/ 6 1145 Military bust to left. Rev. Eagle over a trophy of arms and flags. UNITED STATES ARMY, etc. Copper; proof. 19.

8 0 1146 Bust three-quarter face to right. GENERAL G(UN) B(OAT) MC CLELLAN, etc. Rev. I COULDN'T BE PRESIDE NT IN 1865, etc. Satirical medal. *Silver;* proof. 20.

9 1147 The same. Copper and brass ; proof, very scarce.   2 pcs

9 1148 Duplicates of last no. Same condition.   2 pcs

9 1149 Bust to left (several varieties). Rev. Names of soldiers with letter of company, number of regiment, etc, two blank. *Silver* (1), brass (5), fine ; w. m. (2) poor ; all but one pierced. Rare. 12 and 18.   9 pcs

⌐ 1150 Military bust to left. Rev. "Democratic candidate," a monitor, Key (varieties) and Warner's cards. Copper, brass, and w. m. proof. 17.   7 pcs

6 0 1151 Military bust to left over branches of oak and olive crossed. Rev. Shield inscribed with names of battles. Copper proof ; a very pretty medal, rare. 17.

⌐ 1152 Military bust to left by *Key.* Rev. Same as in No. 1150, excepting "Warner's" card. Bronze, copper, and w. m., proof. 18.   4 pcs

/ 5⁻ 1153 Military bust to left by *Key.* Rev. INAUGURATED GOVERNOR, etc., 1878. Brass, proof. 16.

5 1154 Same as last. W. m. pierced, with pins. 16.   3 pcs

2 ½ 1155 Miscellaneous, one duplicate. All very fine ; 5 pierced. Bronze, cop., brass, and w. m. 12 to 22.   15 pcs

5 1156 Copperheads, or war tokens with bust or name of McClellan. All different and uncir. or proof. German silver (2), copper (11) and brass (9). A rare lot.   22 pcs

1157 Chaplin's McClellan medal. Bust nearly facing
"The great American Hesitator. Theodor peri
theles epis." *Leather*; fine and rare, but an in-
famous aspersion on the character of gallant little
Mac. 48.

1158 Trial piece of obverse copperhead. "Spades are
trumps," a shell; metallic pins, melanotypes, etc.
All fine and scarce. 12 pcs

ULYSSES S. GRANT.

1159 Bust to left. Joint resolution of Congress, Dec.
1863; for Vicksburg, Chattanooga and the Mississippi River. A *perfect* electrotype. 64.

1160 Bust nearly facing. Rev. PATIENT OF TOIL, etc.,
in five lines. Bronze proof; a *very beautiful* and
extremely rare medal by *Bovy*. 38.

1161 Duplicate, in gilt metallic rim, ornamented with
stars on leaves of oak, an eagle and loop above.

1162 Bust to left by *Bovy* Rev. Same as last. Bronze;
perfect. 38.

1163 Short bust to right over branch of olive and Indian
pipe, ornamental border of U. S. shields and wreath
LET US HAVE PEACE, etc. Rev. A globe surmounted by a Bible, over a trophy of agricultural
implements. ON EARTH PEACE, etc. 1871. Bronze;
perfect. 40.

1164 Bust to right by *Key*. Rev. INAUGURATED, etc.,
1869, in wreath of oak and laurel. Bronze; perfect. 32.

1165 Naked bust to right by *Barber* Rev. LIBERTY
THE TRUE FOUNDATION, etc., on tablet. Mint
series. Bronze; perfect. 28.

1166 Short bust to right by *Barber*. THE OCEANS UNITED
BY RAILWAY, 1869. Rev. Mountain scenery, the
Pacific ocean in the distance. Mint series.
Bronze; perfect. 28.

1167 Bust to right. LIEU. GEN. U. S. GRANT and 13
stars, surrounded by wreath of laurel. Rev.
Blank shield surrounded by trophy of flags.
Copper proof. 26.

1168 The same. Shield on rev. stamped with name,
company, regiment, etc., of volunteers in U. S.
service. W. m., proof; pierced. 26. 3 pcs

ʃ- 1169 Busts jugata of Grant and Colfax by *Sigel*, to right. Rev. FOR PRESIDENT, etc.. 1869–1873. W m. proof. 24.

ʃ 0 1170 Bust to left. Rev. THE WILL OF THE PEOPLE, etc. Thick pl., w. m. proof. 20.

ʹ 0 1171 Bust to left. REPUBLICAN CANDIDATE, etc. Rev, I INTEND TO FIGHT IT OUT, etc. Cop. and brass. proof. 20. 2 pcs

/ 2 1172 Same obv. Rev. "Pro patria," " Dickeson's coin safe." Same as last. One pierced ; brass and w. m., proof. 20. 4 pcs

6 1173 Bust to right. ,LIEU GEN. U. S. GRANT and 13 stars on border. Rev. "Capture of Richmond," "Reception of Volunteers, N. Y. 1865," "Grant and Colfax invincibles, 1868," ornamental star. One pierced. Bronze, silvered, brass and w. m., proof. 20. 4 pcs

ʃ- 1174 Bust to right in wreath of oak and olive. LIEU. GEN. U. S. GRANT. Rev. "Grant invincibles," and "the peoples choice," 1868. Brass and w. m., proof. 20. 2 pcs

3 1175 Bust to right, a circle of 31 stars near border. Rev. "The peoples choice," " Republican candidate, 1872," " Grant and Colfax, 1868," bust of Colfax. Cop., br. and w. m. (pierced). Proof. 20. 4 pcs

/ʃ- 1176 Bust to left. 1864. Rev. U. S. on oval shield in trophy of arms and flags, an eagle above. German silver ; very fine. 19.

ʹ 7 1177 Eagle displayed. 1869. *Brichaut's* series. Bronze, proof. 19.

ʃ- 1178 Bust to left by *Jacobus*, 1868. Rev. SOLDIER STATESMAN AND PATRIOTS, etc. Cop. and brass, proof. 2 pcs

3 1179 Same obv. Rev. "The hope of the nation," " First in the hearts of his soldiers." W. m., proof, 20. 2 pcs

4 1180 Bust in civilian dress to right, without inscription. Rev. RECEPTION AT PHILADELPHIA, etc., 1879. Bronze and w. m., proof, the latter pierced. 18. 2 pcs

3 1181 Bust nearly facing. 1868. Rev. I PROPOSE TO FIGHT IT OUT, etc. Cop. and brass, proof. 17. 2 pcs

3 1182 Same obv. Rev. Bust of Colfax and same as last (one thick planchet). Bronze and w. m. Fine and proof. 3 pcs

1183 Bust to left by *Key*, 4 stars widely spaced below.
Rev. "Republican candidate." "Protection to
American industry," "The Constitution and the
Union," "In honor of the 15th amendment."
"Surrender of Lee," bust of Wilson, and Key's
card. A rare lot. Bronze and w. m. proof. 18.

7 pcs

1184 "Key's" card and "Surrender of Lee." A rare if
not unique combination. Brass proof. 20.

1185 Bust to left by Key, 4 stars closely spaced below.
Rev. SURRENDER OF GEN LEE and "In honor of
the 15th amendment." Thick pl., bronze proof.
18.

2 pcs

1186 Same obv. Rev. "Republican candidate," "Protection to American industry," "28 battles," and
varieties of Key's card. Brass and w. m. proof.
18

5 pcs

1187 Large bust to left by *Key*. Rev. SURRENDER OF
GEN LEE, etc., also C. K. Warner's card. Nickel
and w. m., silvered. Proof. 18.

2 pcs

1188 Busts jugata to left of Grant and Colfax. Rev.
LET US HAVE PEACE, in wreath; another with
similar inscription. Brass proof. 18.

2 pcs

1189 Busts of Grant and Colfax facing each other, and
another. Rev Blank. Artist's trial piece in lead.

2 pcs

1190 Large bust to left. IT OUT ON, above. Trial piece
in lead. 23x18.

1191 Miscellaneous. Campaign and political medals,
pierced, with metallic pins, etc. W. m. proof. 18.

5 pcs

1192 Bust to right. GENERAL U. S. GRANT. Rev. Naked
bust of Washington to right by *Lovett*. Copper;
very fine. 18.

1193 Same obv. Rev. "Republican candidate, 1872,"
"The people's choice, 1868," and bust of Washington as in last no. One pierced, brass and w. m.
proof. 18.

4 pcs

1194 Bust to right by *Key*. Rev. PATIENT OF TOILS, etc.
1872. Thick pl., copper proof. 16.

1195 Bust to right by *Bolen*. Rev OUR NEXT PRESIDENT,
etc. Brass proof. 46.

1196 Miscellaneous. All with bust and different, includes "Unconditional surrender," etc. Brass
and w. m. 3 pierced. Fine to proof. 14 to 16.

7 pcs

25- 1197 "Bolen die sinker" stamped on incuse impression of U. S. ½ dime (?) surrounded by a solid rim inscribed v. s. GRANT, 1869. Tin ; unique. 16.

12 1198 Bust to right. MAJ. GEN. U. S. GRANT. Rev. Eagle over VICTORY. The Vicksburg medalet. Brass proof ; rare. 15.

16 1199 Bust to right. PRES 1869 TO '77 on label, in exergue. Rev. "Born at Point Pleasant" etc. ; "Civis Londiniensis, 1877." etc. ; "Civis Edinburgensis, 1877," etc.; bust of Washington to left, McPherson on horseback. Copper proof. 13.   5 pcs

3 1200 The same. Brass proof. 13.   5 pcs

15 1201 Same obv. Rev. "Born at Point Pleasant," "Civis Londiniensis," "Civis Edinburgensis" as before. *Silver* proof. 13.   3 pcs

10- 1202 Duplicates of last no. *Silver* proof.   3 pcs

20 1203 Same obverse, struck on bright red cent of 1850.

10 1204 Duplicate of last number. Same condition.

10 1205 Bust to right. 1868. Rev. "Society army of the Tennessee, Washington 1876" "Pater patriæ," McPherson on horseback and Parmelee Webster & Co's card. Copper proof. 13.   4 pcs

8 1206 The same. Brass proof. 13.   4 pcs

2 1207 Bust to left. 1868. Rev. Eagle and flags. Bronze pr. 13.

4 1208 Bust to left (varieties). Rev. All different. *Silver* (3), bronze (2), copper (1), brass (1) and w. m. (2). Proof. 12.   9 pcs

3 1209 Bust to left. Copperhead reverses. Cop. and brass proof. Rare.   4 pcs

4 1210 SCHUYLER COLFAX. Bust to left and facing. Copper and w. m. proof. 20 and 17.   2 pcs

40 1211 Leather Medal. Busts jugata to left. THE NATICK COBBLER, THE GALENA TANNER, 1872, etc. Fine and rare. 24.

6 1212 Metallic shells, campaign badges, etc. ; round, shield shaped, with and without ornamental pins, nearly all silvered ; also brass shell similar to $20 gold piece. All with bust and a fine lot. 20 pcs

7 1213 Melanotypes with metallic mountings ; sleeve buttons, portrait of Grant, etc. A fine lot. 32 pcs

3 1214 Hard rubber medals. Head and legend in high
relief and different colors, etc. 9 pierced for
ribbons; a beautiful lot. Average size 20.
17 pcs

HORATIO SEYMOUR.

5 1215 Miscellaneous; includes "No North, no South,"
etc.; bronze, copper and white metal. All different; one pierced, proof. 12 to 24. 12 pcs
4 1216 Metallic shells with bust, silvered or gilt. All
very fine. 8 pcs
3 1217 Melanotypes mounted in metallic and ornamental
shells, with and without pins, etc.; also a few rubber cards. All round, and a very fine and varied
lot. 40 pcs
3 1218 A similar lot, few if any dupl. of last. 46 pcs
2 1219 Melanotypes; ornamental metallic shells; square,
star and shield shaped, etc. 45 pcs

HORACE GREELEY.

5 1220 Head to left in ornamental tressure. Rev. THE
HONEST OLD FARMER, etc. Brass, proof. 20.
2 1221 Same obv. Rev. CANDIDATE FOR PRESIDENT, etc.
1872. Copper and brass proof. 20. 2 pcs
5 1222 Bust to left. Rev. "Liberal republican candidate," etc., "Democratic candidate," head of
Gratz Brown. Cop., brass and w. m., proof.
18. 6 pcs
4 1223 Bust to right. Rev. EDITOR AND FOUNDER, etc.
Cop. and brass, proof. 16. 2 pcs
4 1224 Same obv. Rev. FOR PRESIDENT, etc. Bronze
and w. m. (pierced with metallic pins). Fine. 16.
4 pcs
5 1225 Bust to right. Rev. AMNESTY, 1872, etc. Cop.,
brass and silvered; pierced, good. 14. 4 pcs
5 1226 Metallic pins, melanotypes with metallic frames,
campaign badges, etc., includes about ten different Greeley hats. A fine and varied lot. 46 pcs

RUTHERFORD B. HAYES.

4 1227 Bust to left by *Morgan.* Rev. INAUGURATED
MARCH 5 1877, etc. Bronze proof. 48.

3 1228 Head nearly facing. CENTENNIAL, etc. Rev.
Bust of Wheeler. Varieties of obverse and rev.
Copper, brass and silvered ; two pierced. Good
to fine. 20.   5 pcs

2 0 1229 Eagle displayed. 1877. *Brichaut's* series. Bronze,
proof. 20.

3 1230 Bust to left. Rev. PRESIDENT R. B. HAYES, etc.
1876. Nickel, copper and w. m. (pierced); proof.
16.   3 pcs

6 1231 Miscellaneous. Bronze, cop., and w. m., proof.
One pierced. 14 to 16.   7 pcs

6 1232 Shield-shaped badge with detached pin. Busts of
Hayes & Wheeler to right, etc. 1876. *Silver*
plated ; very fine. 18x20.

6 1233 Campaign pins, melanotypes mounted in metallic
shells, etc. All fine.   21 pcs

4 1234 Boys in blue, oval glazed pin : celluloid medals.
5 pcs

SAMUEL J. TILDEN.

√-0 1235 Bust nearly facing ; double semi-circle of 39 stars.
Rev. CANDIDATE FOR PRESIDENT OF OF (sic) THE
UNITED STATES, etc. Copper proof ; rare. 20.

2 3 1236 Same obv. Rev. Same, error in "of," corrected.
Cop. and w. m. proof. 20.   2 pcs

2 2 1237 Bust nearly facing. CENTENNIAL 1876. Rev.
Bust of Hendricks. Nickel plated ; fine, pierced,
edge reeded. 20.

/3 0 1238 Bust nearly facing. SHAMMY TILDEN. DEMOCRATIC
PARTY DIED OF TILDENOPATHY, etc. 1876. Rev.
"I DONT CARE ABOUT YOUR PIECE OF CAKE," etc.
1877. *Silver;* proof. 20.

3 8 1239 The same. *Silver,* copper, brass and w. m. proof.
4 pcs

0 0 1240 Same obv. Rev. Catafalque. GONE TO THE OLD
WORLD, etc. Brass proof. 20.

0 2 1241 The same. Cop., brass and w. m. proof. 20. 3 pcs

/2 0 1242 Similar bust in a slightly depressed circle. O MY
OFFENCE IS RANK AND SMELLS TO HEAVEN, etc.
1876-1878. Rev. THE GREAT FRAUD, etc. *Silver*
proof. 20.

4 8 1243 The same. Cop., br. and w. m. proof. 20. 3 pcs

4 5 1244 Bust to right. TILDEN'S "CONVENTION" BITTERS,
etc. Rev. DRAKE'S PLANTATION BITTERS, etc.
Silver, gilt and w. m. proof. 18.   3 pcs

5 2   1245   Duplicate set.   3 pcs

3 0   1246   Bust facing. THE AGGRESSIVE LEADER. etc. Rev.
Bust of Hendricks. Copper and gilt. proof.
14.   2 pcs

O   1247   Miscellaneous ; also campaign badges. Mounted
melanotypes. Metallic shells, etc. All fine   10 pcs

2   1248   Celluloid campaign charms and badges; a variety
of colors, etc. 14.   13 pcs

JAMES A. GARFIELD.

1249   Bust nearly facing. Rev. All-seeing eye over the
inscription GOD REIGNS AND THE GOVERNMENT AT
WASHINGTON STILL LIVES ; BORN, etc. Bronze
proof. 24.

1250   The same. W. m., proof. 24.

3 0   1251   Bust to right in heavy wreath of laurel. Rev.
INAUGURATED PRESIDENT U. S., MARCH 4 1881.
Bronze proof. 24.

8   1252   Similar obv., a star above. Rev. SOUVENIR. BORN
NOV 19 1831, ASSASSINATED JULY 2 1881, etc.
Bronze proof. 24.

6 0   1253   Bust to left. FOR PRESIDENT. etc. 1880. Rev.
Eagle on shield. W. m. Fine. 20.

1254   Bust to left. THE NATION'S CHOICE FOR PRESIDENT,
etc. Rev. Canal boat, etc. FROM THE TOW PATH
TO THE WHITE HOUSE. Cop., gilt, proof. 17.

1255   Same obv. Rev. "July 2d 1881" in wreath.
DANGER THAT FOUND HIM FAITHFUL CROWNS HIM
GREAT. Silver, proof. 17.

1256   The same. Silver, gilt and bronze proof.   3 pcs

8 0   1257   Same obv. Rev. Bust of W. S. Hancock ; THE
PEOPLE'S CHOICE FOR PRESIDENT 1880. Silver ;
proof. 17.

1258   The same. Silver, and copper proof.   3 pcs

1259   Bust to right. Rev. REPUBLICAN CANDIDATE, etc.
1880. Br. pr. 16.

1260   Bust to left. Rev. CANAL BOY, etc. Gilt proof.
16.

1261   Busts jugate of Garfield and Arthur to left. Rev.
Shield; UNION, etc. Silver ; pierced, uncir. 16.

1262   Bust to left. Rev. REPUBLICAN CANDIDATE, etc.
1880. Silver, nickel, cop., brass and w. m.
proof. 12.   5 pcs

26 1263 Same obv. Rev. Bust of Hancock. *Silver*, nickel, cop., br. and w. m. proof. 12.   5 pcs
20 1264 Bust to right. Rev. SOUVENIR. W. m. pr.   12.
11 1265 Duplicates of preceding lots. 4 pierced ; gilt and w. m. proof.   6 pcs
10 1266 Melanotypes, all handsomely mounted on metallic shells, in a great variety of designs and several metals. A beautiful and rare lot.   40 pcs
19 1267 Solid enameled campaign badges (3), gilt oak leaf with portrait, metallic star, scarf pin, and sleeve buttons, busts of Garfield and Arthur. All fine and rare.   9 pcs
75 1268 Solid metallic pig, said to have been extremely popular among our democratic friends before the election. Length, 1 in., also metallic profile of Garfield.   2 pcs
30 1269 Star-shaped easel, bust of Garfield. Length 6 in.
40 1270 Large gilt bust on chocolate-colored frame of plastic materials ; one of Garfield, the other of Arthur. Both perfect and handsome parlor ornaments. 5 in.x5 in.   2 pcs

WINFIELD S. HANCOCK.

18 1271 Miscellaneous. All different. Cop., gilt and w. m., one pierced; proof. 16 to 20.   7 pcs
14 1272 Bust to left. Rev. DEMOCRATIC CANDIDATE, etc. 1880. *Silver*, nickel, cop., br. and w. m. proof. 12.   5 pcs
19 1273 Metallic campaign badge, handsome enamel on gilt ground, sleeve buttons, scarf pin with portrait, trefoils, oak leaf, etc. A fine and rare lot.   11 pcs
10 1274 Melanotypes, all handsomely mounted on metallic shells, in a great variety of designs and several metals. A fine and rare lot.   37 pcs
65 1275 Metallic pig, and little man as in 1268, but a different photo.   2 pcs
25 1276 Portraits of Hancock and English, gilt on square frames. Same material, size and style as 1270.   2 pcs
42 1277 Clover leaf-shaped easel, bust of Hancock. Length, 6 in.

1278 Bust to left. Award Medal of the Franklin Insti-
tute of the State of Pennsylvania; not named.
Bronze; perfect. 34.

1279 Similar medal. 1824. Named on rev. *Silver*; very
fine. 32.

1280 Same obv. as last. Rev. Different inscriptions,
not named. Bronze; perfect 32.   2 pcs

1281 Franklin Institute, Syracuse, N. Y. Award medal,
not named. W. m., silvered, fine. 32.

1282 Bust to left by *Morin* in wreath of leaves of laurel.
Rev. Broad wreath of oak and laurel. W m.,
fine; very rare. 32.

1283 Bust to left by *Dupré*. MDCCVI. Rev ERIPUIT
COELO, etc. in wreath. Bronze; perfect. 29.

1284 Same obv. Rev. Angel standing, same inscription.
Bronze; perfect. 29.

1285 Busts jugata of Franklin and Montyon. Rev. LES
SOUSCRIPTEURS, etc. Bronze; perfect. 26.

1286 Franklin Mechanics' Literary Association, Rochester. Award medal, not named. Bronze; very
good. 26.

1287 Bust to left. Rev. Masonic emblems; LES MAC
FRANC.'. A FRANKLIN M.'. DE LA L ⊤ DES 9
SOEURS O.'. DE PARIS 5778, 5829. Bronze; fine, and
a very rare medal. 26.

1288 Bust to right; LIGHTNING AVERTED, etc. Rev.
Beaver gnawing the trunk of an oak tree. 1776.
Bronze; perfect. 26.

1289 Bust to left. Series numismatica. Bronze. Perfect. 26.

1290 Duplicates. Bronze; perfect.   2 pcs

1291 Youth studying; the bust of Franklin on pedestal
to right. GOD GIVETH ALL THINGS TO INDUSTRY.
etc. Rev. Beehive. Scarce medal by *Davis, Birmingham*. Tin, pierced, fine. 28.

1292 Bust in fur cap to left. Award medal of the Franklin Inst., Pa. Not named; bronze, perfect. 34.

1293 Bust to left. BEN° FRANKLIN L. L. D. Bronze; perfect, scarce. 23.

1294 Bust to left by *Mitchell*. THE GIFT OF FRANKLIN
MDCCXC. Rev. AWARDED TO on scroll. Named.
Silver; fine. 22.   2 pcs

1295 Bust to left by *Wright & Bale.* Rev. REWARD OF MERIT, etc. Named. *Silver;* pierced, fine. 20. 3 pcs

1296 Pens crossed over book. THE GIFT OF FRANKLIN. Rev. ADJUDGED BY THE SCHOOL COMMITTEE, etc. Named. *Silver;* pierced, fine. 22.

1297 Bust to left. Rev. "TIME IS MONEY" and Masonic temple, Boston. Cop. fine. 19. 2 pcs

1298 Bust in fur cap to left. Rev. Blank. Brass; fine and rare. 18.

1299 Same obv. with addition of *Wright & Bale* under bust. Rev. Wright & Bale's card in 7 lines. Brass; thick and thin pl.; fine and rare. 18. 2 pcs

1300 Miscellaneous. Includes R. Lovett's card, "Good for one glass of soda," "Penny saved," etc. Each with bust of Franklin. *Silver*, copper, brass and w. m., proof. 12 to 17. 9 pcs

1301 Electros and shells. 3 pcs

1302 Profile bust of Franklin to right in fur cap. Oval bronze cast medallion of the period, in solid brass rim. Fine and very rare. $2\frac{1}{4}$x$2\frac{3}{4}$ in.

1303 Bust to right. Oval bronze shell; very fine. $2\frac{1}{2}$x$3\frac{3}{4}$ in.

MEDALS OF LAFAYETTE.

1304 Military bust to right by *Caunois.* Rev. APPELÉ PAR LE VOEU UNANIME, etc., in 7 lines. Bronze, perfect. 32.

1305 Large head to left by *Gatteau.* 1789–1830. Rev. A LAFAYETTE L'ARRONDISSEMENT DE MEAUX JUILLET 1830 in wreath of oak. Bronze; perfect, rare. 32.

1306 Large head laureate to right by *Oleszczynski.* Rev. Poland mourning at a funeral altar. OBIIT 20 MAII 1834. Bronze, perfect, and a rare and beautiful medal. 32.

1307 Military bust to left. LE G. LAFAYETTE COMEND^{T} G^{L} DE L'ARMÉE PARISIENNE, etc. In exergue DÉPUTÉ D'AUVERGUE EN 1793. Rev. Blank Tin, bronzed, dotted border. 30.

1308 Bust to right by *Caunois*. Rev. THE DEFENDER, etc., in wreath of oak. Bronze, perfect. 30.

1309 Similar bust. Rev. LAFAYETTE BORN SEPT 6 1757, etc., in 10 lines. Tin, pierced. Fine. 30.

1310 Similar bust. *J. Bale* under the shoulder. Rev. Blank. Bronze, perfect. 30.

1311 Similar bust. Rev. VIVE LA CHARTE ET LA LIBERTE 29 JUILLET 1830 in wreath. Varieties. Lead. Good and rare. 28 and 30. 2 pcs

1312 Large military bust to right. Rev. DEFENSEUR DE LA LIBERTE EN AMERI, etc., in wreath. Tin or lead; said to be unique. See 3287 Holland sale. Fine. 26.

1313 Military bust to left. Dedicated by the artist, Duvivier, to the National Guard. Rev. French inscr. in 12 lines. Bronze; perfect. 26.

1314 Bust to left. GLOIRE AUX DEFENSEURS DE LA PATRIE (sic), etc. Rev. VIVE LOUIS PHILIPPE, etc. Lead; fine. 24.

1315 Military bust to left, by *Dumarest*. Series of patriotic Frenchmen. Bronze, gilt. Fine. 22.

1316 The same. Bronze, fine. 22.

1317 Bust to right. Rev. Head of Washington. *J. F. W. des*. N. Y. Medal Club series No. 1. Copper, proof. 20.

1318 Same obv. Rev. STATUE IN N. Y. UNVEILED SEPT 6 1876 CENTENNIAL. Brass proof. 20.

1319 Same obv. *N. Y. M. C. Series No. 2*, below. Rev. Ground floor of Masonic Temple. Silver, proof. 20.

1320 The same. Silver, bronze and copper. Fine and proof. 20. 3 pcs

1321 Small bust to right, *H. and B.* below. THE HERO OF TWO SUCCESSFUL REVOLUTIONS. Rev. Bust to left. PHILIPPE), etc. Copper; fine. 20.

1322 Bust to right. Rev. Inscription (French) in 10 lines. Bronze; fine, pierced. 20.

1323 Large draped bust to left. LAFAYETTE above. Rev. *Engraved* "To John Allan, from his friend, James Wellstood, alias Edie Ochiltree, pilgrim to the land of Burns." Silver; fine. 24.

1324 Silver medal of the Veterans of the 55th Regiment Lafayette Guard, struck to commemorate the unveiling of Lafayette's statue in New York, 1876. Guard and ribbon. Fine and very rare. 20.

/2 1325 Bust to right. 1757–1834. Rev. THE UNTIRING ADVOCATE, etc. Brass proof. 18.

27 1326 Same obv. Rev. Masonic emblems. Copper proof. 18.

7 1327 Military bust to left. 1757–1834. Rev. Names of different battalions, regiments and legions, under Lafayette, in 1830. All different. Bronze; fine. 8 pcs

8 1328 Head to left. Different inscriptions on rev. Bronze, fine. 13. 2 pcs

/0 1329 Bust to right. Rev. THE DEFENDER, etc. Brass, fine. 14.

/0 1330 Miscellaneous. Dupl. 1318 and 1321, also electro of rare medal with eagle and pyramids on rev., etc. One pierced; fine 5 pcs

26 1331 Oval medalet. Bust on each side. IN PEACE FRIENDS, IN WAR ENEMIES. Tin proof. 11x14.

60 1332 Head to right on either side, one gilt. GENERAL LAFAYETTE. *Silver ;* oval, loop, fine. 8x10.

3/ 1333 Head to left on either side ; gilt, on silver planchet. Loop, fine and rare. 9.

25⁻ 1334 Head to right. GENERAL LAFAYETTE. 1824. Rev. Blank. *Silver ;* fine and rare. 9.

/2 1335 Bust to right. French medalets ; all different. *Silver ;* German silver, and bronze. Fine. 6 to 9. 3 pcs

75⁻ 1336 Naked bust to left. General Lafayette. Bronze shell (?) encased in square lackered frame, a short historical sketch pasted on the back. An interesting memento of his visit to the United States. Perfect and very rare. 4x4½ in.

40 1337 Cupid on dolphin. Rev. LAFAYETTE CADETS, engraved Bronze, cast, loop. 34.

50 1338 Bust of Lafayette impressed on piece of heavy wood, stained black, suitable for paper weight. Fine. 40.

30 1339 Military bust to right. White on red ground, inscription in eight lines on back ; under glass on each side. Perfect. 26.

1340 Five dollars, gold. Mormon coinage. 1860. HOLI-
NESS TO THE LORD, etc. Very good ; rare.

1341 California gold. 1853. One dollar, octag. Uncirculated.

1342 1853, half dol. round, and 1872 ¼ dol.. head of
Washington, octagonal. 2 pcs

1343 Half dime. 1800. Sharp and ~~uncirculated~~. Rare

1344 Quarter dollars. Counterstamped with names of
firms, etc. Good. 3 pcs

1345 1818. Pattern cent. Electrotype (?) Very fine. 12.

1346 1809. Pattern dime. Liberty seated. Rev. 8d.
mic. cop. Reeded edge ; nearly proof.

1347 1800. Pike's Peak gold. $20 and $5. 1834. $5.
1849, Cal. $24 and 1861 $2.50. Copper and brass.
6 pcs

1348 James I. Tin plantation piece. King on horseback.
Rev VAL 24 PART REAL HISPAN. Pewter : fine. 17.

1349 Duplicates. Good and fine. 2 pcs

1350 Satirical token on Law's Mississippi scheme. Mercurius prostrate. Rev. VISIBILIS. INVISIBILIS.
Tin : very good and scarce. 16.

1351 Colonial jeton. Bust of Louis XV. Rev. Indian
advancing from a grove. COL FRANC DE L'AM.
1751. Copper : very fair and scarce. 18.

1352 Another jeton. 1755. A galley on reverse. Very
good. 18. 2 pcs

1353 New York. 1787. Cent. Rev Liberty seated to
left. Good.

1354 Massachusetts. 1787. Half cent. Olive color :
sharp and uncirculated.

1355 Rhode Island. 1778. Satirical medal. without
ornament under ship. Brass : very fine. 26.

1356 The same. Pewter ; uncirculated.

1357 North Carolina brass token. Fine. 16.

1358 Castorland token. 1796. Thin pl. : bronze, nearly
proof and original. 20.

1360 Ship. Colonies and Commerce. British and American flags ; one with W & B. N Y, the other with
Cash & Co, stamped in exergue. 16. 4 pcs

2 o 1360 Miscellaneous. Includes R. I. token, Louisiana
R. F. and electro of the *New Yorke in America*
token. 6 pcs

/. o-o 1361 BOLEN'S COPIES. Liber natus, etc. Rev. Neo
Eboracus 1787. *Silver;* fine and rare. 18.

/. o-o 1362 Liber natus. Rev. Excelsior. *Silver;* uncirculated. 17.

3 o 1363 George Clinton Cents. Bust. Rev. Eagle, arms
of New York, and blank. Copper ; uncirculated.
3 pcs

3 o 1364 Duplicates ; also "Non dependens status," Bra-
shier's doubloon and Hog Island shilling. Copper
and brass ; uncirculated. 7 pcs

3. 5 o 1365 Square copper planchet with four impressions on
each side from Bolen's dies of Colonial coins.
Unique. 2¾x2¾ in.

7 1366 Continental seals. Varieties. Copper proof. 24.
3 pcs

4 1367 The same. W. m. proof. 24. 3 pcs

2 1368 Brass Buttons. Washington, New Hampshire,
Jackson, etc. Fair to fine. 6 pcs

ASSAY MEDALS.

/. / o 1369 1869. ANNUAL ASSAY in wreath, LET US HAVE
PEACE on scroll above. Rev. Liberty seated.
Copper ; proof. Rare. 21.

/. 5 -o 1370 1869. Same obv. Rev. Liberty seated ; 13 stars
on border. Aluminum proof. Rare. 21.

/. 2 o 1371 1869. Same obv. Rev. Peace with torch setting
fire to implements of war. MINT OF THE UNITED
STATES, PHILAD. Slightly spotted : aluminum.
Rare. 21.

/. / o 1372 1870. ANNUAL ASSAY in wreath. Bronze ; perfect. 21.

o o 1373 1873. ANNUAL ASSAY. Tomb inscribed ECKFELDT.
Silver; proof. Rare. 21.

/. o o 1374 1874. Same design. *Silver;* proof. Rare. 21.

ADMIRAL VERNON MEDALS.

5 -5 1375 One, two, and three figures on obverse. Rev. View
of bombardment and capture of Porto Bello,
1739, and Carthagena, 1741. No duplicates ;
brass and copper (2). 4 pierced near edge. Average condition fine, and contains a number of rare
varieties. 24. 22 pcs

1376 Duplicates. 2 copper, balance brass. Average
fine. 24. 8 pcs

1377 Bust of Vernon. TOOK PORTOBELLO, etc. Brass:
one poor, one fine. 17. 2 pcs

AUG. B. SAGE'S TOKENS.

1378 Historical tokens. No. 1 to 14, inclusive. Copper
and bronzed. A rare and interesting set. In nearly
proof condition. 19. 14 pcs

1379 Duplicates. Same condition. 12 pcs

1380 The Old Jersey. Rev. Faneuil Hall. *Silver*:
proof. 19.

1381 A. B. Sage's Numismatic Gallery. Nos. 1, 2, and
5. Copper proof. 19. 3 pcs

1382 Aug. B. Sage's Numismatic Gallery. Nos. 3, 5, 6,
7, 8 and 9. Copper proof. 19. 6 pcs

1383 Miscellaneous. A. B. Sage & Co's card, etc. Copper and w. m. (1) proof. 19. 6 pcs

FEUCHTWANGER CURRENCY.

1384 Obverse, FEUCHTWANGER AMERICAN SILVER COMPO-
SITION 2 CORTLANDT ST NEW YORK in 7 lines.
Rev. HOUSE AND HOUSEHOLD FURNITURE, INSTRU-
MENTS, BEER PUMPS, PILLARS, GRATES, SPOONS,
FORKS, AND DINING SETS in 6 lines. Composition
metal ; fine and of extreme rarity. 16½.

1385 Obverse, DR L. FEUCHTWANGER AMERICAN SILVER
COMPOSITION 877 BROAD WAY NEW YORK. Rev.
Same as last. Composition metal ; fine and
extremely rare. 16½.

1386 Duplicate of last number. Barely fair: pierced.

1387 Eagle on a rock, 1837. Rev. THREE CENTS in
wreath of laurel. FEUCHTWANGER'S COMPOSITION.
Reeded edge ; very fine and rare. 15½.

1388 Arms of New York, 1837. Rev. THREE CENTS,
four stars and two roses in wreath of laurel,
FEUCHTWANGER'S COMPOSITION. Reeded edge :
very fine. 15½.

1389 Eagle grasping a snake, 1864. Rev. 3 THREE CENTS
in wreath of oak. FEUCHTWANGER'S COMPOSITION.
Reeded edge : very fine. 15½.

1390 Feuchtwanger cents. 1837. Fine to unciir. 4 pcs

JACKSONIAN TOKENS, STORE CARDS, ETC.

3. 2 5⁻ 1391 Bust to right. ANDREW JACKSON. Rev. THE UNION MUST AND SHALL BE PRESERVED in wreath, and THE BANK MUST PERISH near border. Engrailed edge. Copper ; fine and *very rare.* 17.

2. 2 0 1392 Ship sailing to left. FOR THE CONSTITUTION HURRA. Rev. *Les trois jours* APRIL 8 9 and 10 1834. Brass ; fine ; rare. 16.

1. 2 0 1393 Ship sailing to right. FELLOW CITIZENS SAVE YOUR CONSTITUTION. Rev. Liberty cap in diverging rays. THE GLORIOUS WHIG VICTORY 1834. Copper ; fine, but pierced. 17.

7½ 1394 Hard times tokens. Includes "a plain system," "balky and b. b. donkey," "Loco-foco," etc. Average strictly fine. 32 pcs

1. 2 5⁻ 1395 Jackson in money chest I TAKE THE RESPONSIBILITY. Rev. Donkey inscribed L.L.D. *Brass ;* fine.

1. ᴄ⁻0 1396 Small bust of Jackson. MY SUBSTITUTE, etc. Rev. Running hog. PERISH CREDIT, etc. *Brass ;* very good.

8 1397 Early Store cards, size of the Hard times tokens, many combined with them. Fair to very fine. 39 pcs

1. 3 5⁻ 1398 Ship. AGRICULTURE AND COMMERCE. Rev. J. GIBBS, MANUFACTURER OF MEDALS AND TOKENS, ETC., BELLEVILLE, N. J. Copper ; very fair, rare. 17.

⁴⁻0 1399 Barnum's Museum. Copper ; uncirculated. 24.

1 6 1400 Brewster, J. & L., Buchan, Boutwell, Browning Brothers. Copper and brass ; fair to uncirculated. 17 and 18. 7 pcs

1 1 1401 Bolen, J. A. Miscellaneous. Includes his card combined with "Confederatio 1785," and other rarities. Copper (9), brass (2) and w. m. All very fine. 16 to 18. 12 pcs

1 9 1402 Cleaves, Doremus, Suydam & Nixon, Doremus & Nixon, Day, Newell & Day, Durkee & Co. (Feuchtwanger composition). Copper and brass ; fair to very fine, 2 pierced. 11 to 17. 10 pcs

1 0 1403 "Ebling's Columbian Garden," and "S. M. W. Gouverneur," stamped on Spanish ¼ (2) and ⅛ dol. Fair. 3 pcs

1404 Green & Wetmore, Gowans & Co., Hallock & Bates,
Hallock, Dolson & Bates, Hardie, Hewett, Dr. J.
C., Henning, Houghton, Merrell & Co. Copper,
brass and silvered. 14 to 20. 9 pcs

1405 Hotels. German silver, copper and brass. Good
and fine. 12 to 20. 18 pcs

1406 Jennings, Wheeler & Co., Judson, Loewe, Leviek,
Law, Leverett & Thomas. Copper, brass and w.
m. Fine. 11 to 18. 6 pcs

1407 Key, F. C. & Sons. Includes their card combined
with "Thomas Wildey," "David M. Lyle,"
"Continental currency," etc. 18 and 24. Copper,
brass and w. m. proof. 10 pcs

1408 F. C. Key, also Woodgate & Co. Rev. E. Hill,
etc. *Silver*, pr. 18. 2 pcs

1409 Jury, Soulsby, Vaux Hall, Baltimore. (Feuchtwanger composition metal.) Good and fine; rare.
10. 2 pcs

1410 Lovett, Geo. H., R., and J. D. *Silver* (1), composition, copper and brass. All very fine. 9 to 20.
20 pcs

1411 Miscellaneous. Includes many scarce cards,
frequently catalogued singly. Copper and brass.
Nearly all uncirculated. 17 to 21. 50 pcs

1412 Another lot. Same metals and condition. 50 pcs

1413 Another lot. Same metals and condition. 14 to
20. 50 pcs

1414 Another lot. German silver, copper and brass.
Good to uncirculated. 11 to 18. 94 pcs

1415 Copper and brass, pierced or poor, and w. m. Good
to uncirculated. 10 to 21. 44 pcs

1416 "New Congress Hall, 1860," "R. Lovett." *Silver*. Fine. 12 and 16. 3 pcs

1417 Mott, New York, 1789. Copper; fine. 17. 2 pcs

1418 Mullen, Mott, Wm. H., Maverick Coach, N. Y. and
Harlaem. Nickel, copper and brass. Round and
octagonal. Fine. 12 to 20. 7 pcs

1419 Nicholson's. State of Missouri. Half dime.
Nickel; very good and rare. 10.

1420 Omnibus, Paid, Prescott's, 11 Wall St., N. Y.,
Patterson Brothers. Nickel and copper. 11 to
18. Fine. 6 pcs

/2 1421 Peale's Museum. Parthenon, New York, 1825
and Philadelphia. Varieties. Copper; fine and
scarce. 20 and 22.	3 pcs

√0 1422 Prentice, F. "First product by mill process in the
Lah-Ranagat Mining district, Nevada, 1867." *Silver*; fine. 20.

√- 1423 Randel, J. Jr., C. & D. Canal. 1825 in wreath.
Rev. Blank. Copper; fine and rare. 14.

4 1424 Rickeys, Robinson, S. McD. & Co. 25 cents,
Squire & Merritt, Smithsonian, Thomson, Tredwell, Kissam & Co., Thomas. Copper and brass.
16 to 24. Fine.	12 pcs

8 0 1425 Risley & McCollum's Hippodrome. Brass; fine.
20.

30 1426 Talbot, Allum & Lee. New York, 1794. From
different dies. Very good. 18.	3 pcs

2 0 1427 The same, muled with different English halfpenny
tokens. Fine. 18.	2 pcs

/ 1428 Van Nostrand & Dwight, Wilbur, Webb, Wolfe,
100th St. Copper and brass (2). Fine. 16.	9 pcs

9√- 1429 Wilson, T. B. "Half dime" in wreath. Rev.
BREAD. W. m., uncirculated. 10.

3 1430 Centennial store cards. "Libertas Americana"
(4), "Carpenter's Hall" (3), "Coat of Arms of
Maryland" (4), "Capital at Washington" (2),
"Double head" (3), "Public Buildings, Phila."
(4), "Liberty Bell," varieties (9), "Independence
Hall" (53), "Continental soldier" (51). Rev.
Various business advertisements. Bronze, and a
few copper and brass. No duplicates in the same
metal. Proof. 14.	134 pcs

/ 1431 Similar lot. W. m. proof.	62 pcs

2 1432 Liberty bell. Rev. Various business advertisements. No duplicates in the same metal. Bronze
(8) and brass. Proof. 16.	10 pcs

2 1433 Stiner's Centennial token. Varieties. Brass proof.
24.	2 pcs

2 0 1434 1 and 5 c. encased postage stamps. Various cards
on back. Fine and scarce.	12 pcs

√- 1435 Brass shells, in imitation of $20 gold, silver dollars,
etc.; includes several very rare varieties. All
fine.	39 pcs

// 1436 Rubber cards, etc. Round, square, oval. Includes several rare Centennial; etc. All perfect.
55 pcs

1437 Copperheads or War tokens. A very fine lot, large and small. 390 pcs

1438 Henry C. Montz. Orpheus Hall. Rev A TOKEN OF THE WAR FOR THE UNION, 1863. Struck over an English Colonial shilling. Fine; rare.

1439 The same, copper; another with "Millions for defence, not one cent for tribute" on rev. Fine. 2 pcs

1440 Silver (4) and German silver, three with head of Lincoln. Fine. 7 pcs

1441 Sutlers' checks. 5 cents to one dollar. Used during the rebellion in Western armies. Names of sutlers, regiments, etc. Copper (2), tin (1), the balance brass. All different, fine and rare. 10 to 16. 63 pcs

1442 Spielmarks, etc. Brass; fine. 10 to 24. 13 pcs

1443 Calendars, coats of arms of New York, Pennsylva. and Ohio. Brass (12) and w. m. 14 to 26. 14 pcs

ARMY AND NAVY MEDALS.

REVOLUTIONARY PERIOD.

1444 Battle scene. Rev. GERMANTOWN OCT 4 1777 in wreath. Tin; a rare medal. 28.

1445 Horatio Gates. For surrender of Burgoyne at Saratoga. Bronze; perfect. 34.

1446 The same. Tin; cast.

1447 De Fleury. For storming of Stony Point. 1779. A warrior with glaive and captured flag on the ruins of a fort. VIRTUTIS ET AUDACIAE MONUM ET PRAEMIUM, etc. Rev. View of the fort, etc. Bronze; perfect, and an excessively rare medal by du Vivier. 28.

1448 Fine electrotype of last number.

1449 Antony Wayne. For Stony Point. Indian princess presenting a crown to Wayne. Rev. View of the storming of fort. Two copper shells, soldered like an electro. Very fine; rare. 34.

1450 Obverse of the extremely rare medal give to Capt. John Stewart for Stony Point. Lead; fine. 26.

1451 The same. Obverse and rev. Lead; cast. 28.

/. *OO* 1452 Henry Lee. For Paulus Hook. 1779. Bronze: very fine. 28.

U⁻O 1453 The same obv. Rev. Blank. Bronze; perfect.

/. / *O* 1454 John Paul Jones. For victories off coast of Scotland. 1779. Fine original by *Dupré*. Bronze; nearly proof. 36.

/ *ᴄ⁻O* 1455 The same. Without *Dupré*. Bronze; perfect. 36.

/. / *O* 1456 Daniel Morgan. For battle of Cowpens, 1781. Beautiful bronze medal by *Dupré*. 35.

U ᴜ̃ 1457 John Egar Howard. For battle of Cowpens. Fine bronze medal by *Duvivier*. 28.

/ *c* 1458 Nathaniel Green. For battle at Eutaw Springs. 1781. Perfect tin cast of this very rare medal. 35.

ᴜ⁻ᴜ̃ 1459 Silvered electrotype copy of the medal granted the captors of Major André by Congress. Oval; perfect. 26x36.

ʂ ᴜ̃ 1460 Thomas Truxton. Naval victory over French frigate La Vengeance, 1800. Without inscription on rim. Bronze proof. 36.

/. *ʂ O* 1461 Edward Preble. Bombardment of Tripoli, 1804. Bronze; perfect. 40.

WAR OF 1812.

ʂ O 1462 Colonel Geo. Croghan. For defense of fort on Sandusky bay. 1813. Bronze proof; by *Furst*. 40.

ʔO 1463 Governor Isaac Shelby For battle of the Thames. 1813. Bronze; perfect. 40.

ʂ ᴜ̃ 1464 General Peter B. Porter. For Chippewa, Niagara, and Erie. 1814. Bronze; perfect. 40.

ʂ ᴜ̃ 1465 General Eleazer W. Ripley. Same battles; bronze, perfect. 40.

ʂ ᴜ̃ 1466 General Jacob Brown. Same battles; bronze, perfect. 40.

ʔ O 1467 General James Miller. Same battles. Rev. View of engagement; bronze; perfect. 40.

ʂ ᴜ̃ 1468 The same. Rev. A trophy. Bronze; perfect. 40.

ʂ ᴜ̃ 1469 General Alexander Macomb. For battle of Plattsburgh, 1814. Bronze; perfect. 40.

ʂ ᴜ̃ 1470 General Edmund P. Gaines. For battle of Erie. 1814. Bronze; perfect. 40.

ʂ ᴜ̃ 1471 Captain Isaac Hull. For capture of frigate Guerriere. 1812. Bronze; perfect. 40.

1472 Captain Jacob Jones. For capture of Frolic. 1812. Bronze; perfect. 40.

1473 Commodore S. Decatur. For capture of Macedonia. 1812. Bronze; perfect. 40.

1474 Captain William Bainbridge. For capture of frigate Java. 1812. Bronze; nearly proof. 40.

1475 Captain James Lawrence. For capture of brig Peacock. 1813. Bronze; perfect. 40.

1476 Lieut. Edward R. McCall. For capture of sloop Boxer. 1813. Bronze; perfect. 40.

1477 Lieut. W. Burrows. Capture of Boxer, in which action he was killed. Bronze; perfect. 40.

1478 Captain Oliver H. Perry. Defeat of British fleet on Lake Erie, 1813. Bronze; perfect. 40.

1479 The same. Smaller medal, with view of action on rev.; presented him by the government of Pennsylvania. Bronze; perfect. 37.

1480 Same obv. as last. Rev. Inscription and wreath. Bronze; perfect. 37.

1481 Captain Jesse D. Elliot. Defeat of British fleet on Lake Erie. 1813. Bronze; perfect. 40.

1482 View of the engagement on Lake Erie. Rev. TO - BY RESOLUTION OF THE KENTUCKY LEGISLATURE, etc. 1860. Bronze; perfect. 26.

1483 The same. Brass proof. 26.

1484 Captain Louis Warrington. For capture of brig Epervier. 1814. Bronze; perfect. 40.

1485 The same. For capture of sloop Reindeer. 1814. Bronze; perfect. 40.

1486 Thomas MacDonough. For victory over British fleet on Lake Champlain, 1814. Bronze; perfect. 40.

1487 Captain Robert Henley. For victory on Lake Champlain, 1814. Bronze; perfect. 40.

1488 Lieut. Stephen Cassin. For the same victory. Bronze; perfect. 40.

1489 Captain Charles Stewart. For capture of English men-of-war Levant and Cyane, 1815. Bronze; perfect. 40.

1490 Captain James Biddle. For capture of British ship Penguin. 1815. Bronze; gilt; perfect. 40.

1491 Medalet. Bust of Commodore S. Decatur. Rev. Bust of Captain J. Lawrence. W m.; fine. 24.

MEXICAN WAR.

1492 Lieut. Colonel Bliss. Bust to right. Rev. Arms
of the State of New York. Presented for gallant
services in Mexico by the State of New York.
1849. Fine and rare bronze medal by *Wright.* 44.

1493 Arms of the City of New York. Rev. Victory
landing in Vera Cruz. Names of battles, etc.
Presented by the City of New York to the N. Y.
Regt. of Volunteers in Mexico. Bronze; perfect
and rare. 32.

1494 Shield. Wreath enclosing a castle, a nopal plant
and the date 1848. MEXICO above. Ship and
cannon in angles; 29 stairs in curving lines below,
the whole surrounded by border with names of
battles. *John S. Lynch,* 11*th Inf.,* engraved on
rev. Copper ; perfect and rare. 34x36.

1495 Smaller shield, similar to last, engraved on rev. as
before. *Silver;* perfect and rare. 20x22.

MEDALS AND TOKENS OF THE REBELLION.

1496 Hartford Wide-awakes. 1860. ~~Silver~~, copper and
Brass. Uncir. or proof. 17.   3 pcs

1497 Farmer in star-spangled garb. I AM READY.
1861. Varieties. *Silver* and brass. Uncir. 19.
                                                 3 pcs

1498 View of bombardment of Fort Sumter April 12
and 13 1861. Rev. TO MAJOR ROBERT ANDERSON
FROM THE CITIZENS OF NEW YORK CITY, etc., in
wreath. W. m., silvered; fine. 44.

1499 Eagle to right. MASSACHUSETTS. 1866. Rev.
LEXINGTON APRIL 19, 1775, BALTIMORE APRIL 19
1861. Copper, brass and w. m., proof. 17. 3 pcs

1500 Encased melanotypes of Anderson, Ellsworth and
Brownell the Avenger ; one with calendar on
back. Fine. 16 to 26.   4 pcs

1501 Merrimac and Monitor. 1862. Copper proof. 20.

1502 California Union medal. 1861 W. m., pierced.
20.

1503 National Union League. Varieties. Copper, brass
and w. m., the latter pierced with guard and
ribbon. Fine or proof. 16 to 22.   4 pcs

1504 Death to traitors. Medal of the Iron Brigade, N.
Y. Vols. W. m., pierced. 24.

1505 Medals of several designs, with engraved names or
blank space on rev. for the names of Volunteers,
companies, regiments, etc.; 8 pierced. Copper,
brass and white metal, good to proof. A scarce
lot. 17 to 20. 46 pcs

1506 Columbia seated. HONOR IS THE REWARD OF LOY-
ALTY. Rev. WAR OF 1861, etc.; all different, 3
pierced. Copper (1) and w. m.; fine or proof.
20. 4 pcs

1507 General Naglee on horseback to right, charging
rebel redoubt. FAIR OAKS above. 1862. Rev. TO
GENERAL H. NAGLEE, etc. Bronze proof. Rare.
37.

1508 Naked bust of Mead to right by *Paquet*. Rev.
Meade receiving a laurel wreath from seated
female. Beautiful and rare bronze medal in perfect
condition, presented to General George G. Meade,
the victor at Gettysburg, by the Union League of
Philadelphia. 50.

1509 Bust to right of General G. K. Warren. Rev. 5th
corps badge. Bronze : fine and rare. 24

1510 Same obv. Rev. Trophy and names of battles,
" Return of State flags," etc. " Pennsylvania
volunteers," and Key's card. Brass (1), and w. m.
24. 4 pcs

1511 Trophy, State Flags, Pa. Vols., and Key's card,
reverses of last two. combined together, making 4
varieties. All very fine. Copper (1), brass (2)
and w. m. silvered. 24. 4 pcs

1512 Bust of General Ambrose E. Burnside facing. Rev.
Names of battles. W. m., proof. 25

1513 Bust of Custer. 3 Cav. Div. Rev. Inscription.
W. m. proof : loop. 23.

1514 Bust of General Jesse L. Reno to left. Rev.
" Awarded to ——." and Fame writing on a rock.
Bronze and w. m. proof. Rare. 29.

1515 Head of General N. P. Banks to right. Rev. Blank.
Cop.; very fine. 21.

1516 Bust of General Philip Kearney, surnamed " the
one armed devil." Rev. Trophy of arms. UNITED
STATES ARMY, etc. Copper proof and rare. 30

1517 Bust of Gen. J. W. Geary. Rev. Same. Cop.,
very fine. 20.

1518 Bust of General Wright in centre of 6th Corps
badge. Rev. Trefoil. W. m., good and rare. 20.

0 1519 Bust of General W. T. Sherman. Rev. Corps
badges, trophy, etc. All different obverses; a fine
and scarce lot. Copper, brass and w. m. 20. 5 pcs

2 ʊ⁻ 1520 Bust of Gen. Joseph Hooker. Rev. Same as rev.
of 1516. Copper; very fine. 19.

2 ʊ⁻ 1521 Bust of General H. G. Berry. Rev. KILLED AT
CHANCELORVILLE, VA MAY 1863. Nickel proof.
18.

ʊ⁻ 1522 Bust of General A. A. Humphreys. Rev. Trefoil.
W. m. fine, pierced. 20.

ʃ 1523 Bust of Gen. John F. Hartranft. Rev. THE HERO
OF FORT STEADMAN AND 24 BATTLES. Brass; proof.
17.

1 2 ½ 1524 Bust of Gen. James A. Beaver. Rev. Corps badge
etc. Bronze and w. m. proof. 16.   2 pcs

ʃ⁻ 1525 Bust of Grant. Rev. McPherson, Society of Army
of the Tennessee, etc. All different. Copper and
brass proof. 12.   4 pcs

ʊ⁻ 1526 Sanitary Fair of Wapakoneta, O. Eagle on trophy
and inscription. Brass; silvered. Fine and rare. 14.

/ 1527 Miscellaneous. A few duplicates of last nos. Cop.
(4), brass (3) and w. m. Good to proof ; 4 pierced
12 to 26.   19 pcs

8 0 1528 Colored volunteers charging a redoubt. Rev. CAM-
PAIGN OF RICHMOND 1864, etc. Bronze : perfect
and rare. 25.

ʊ⁻0 1529 Names of officers killed during the Rebellion in
wreath of oak and laurel. Rev. TO OUR FALLEN
BRAVE 1861–1865. Issued on the occasion of the
semi-centennial celebration of the Washington
Grays. Bronze ; perfect. 32.

3. 7 0 1530 Bust to left under a double wreath, TO GEORGE F.
ROBINSON, etc. Medal awarded by Congress for his
heroic conduct in saving the life of Wm. H Seward, April 14, 1865. Rev. Scene of the assault.
A beautiful and rare medal by *Paquet.* Bronze ;
perfect. 48.

ʊ⁻ʊ⁻ 1531 Silver badge. Hooker's old division, etc. Diamond shape ; pin gone. 20x26.

ʊ⁻ʊ⁻ 1532 Silver badge. 38 Regiment; Excelsior Brigade.
Guidon shaped pin. Length 1½in.

ʊ⁻ʊ⁻ 1533 Signal Corps. Shield shaped, with pin : signal flag,
red centre. *Silver*; fine. 22x26.

1534 Ornamental shield-shaped medal of honor presented by the City of Brooklyn to returned veterans. Guard and pin attached. *Silver*; in perfect condition and rare. 20x28.

1535 The same. Bronze ; pin gone.

1536 Veteran Corps medal. 1861-1865. Solid ornamental pin with ribbon attached. Bronze ; perfect ; oval. 22x27.

1537 Star-shaped badge. Columbia in centre crushing Treason with shield. Eagle-shaped pin above. Copper ; perfect. 34.

1538 Shield-shaped badges. Busts of Kearney and Hooker. Nickel plated ; one pin gone. 17x19.
2 pcs

1539 Metallic pins. Flag and shield shaped, etc. Fine.
7 pcs

1540 Bust of Lincoln. Rev. SURRENDER OF GENERAL LEE, etc. W. m Fine. 17. 2 pcs

1541 Connecticut battle flags returned. 1879. Fine. W. m. 19.

1542 Arms of New York. Rev. Inscription. N. Y. State medal to returned veterans. Bronzed proof. 23.

1543 Eagle surrounded by a circle of 24 corps badges. Rev. Soldier and sailor before Columbia in cluster of stars, 1861-65. VETERAN GRAND ARMY OF THE REPUBLIC, etc. Bronze proof. 32.

1544 Volunteer soldier before encampment. Rev. Eagle. 16TH NATIONAL ENCAMPMENT G. A. R. BALTIMORE 1882. Bronze proof. 24.

1545 The same. W. m. proof. 24.

1546 Arms of Baltimore. Rev. Similar to Rev. of No. 1543. Bronze proof. 24.

1547 Jefferson Davis hanging to gallows. 1861. DEATH TO TRAITORS, etc. Brass ; fine and scarce. 16.

1548 "No submission to the North." Rev. The wealth of the South, etc. Several varieties. Copper 11 and brass, 1 pierced. Good to uncir. 14. 5 pcs

1549 Bust of T. J. Jackson, Stonewall, by *Cuqué*. Rev. Names of battles. Tin ; uncir. 32.

1550 Full military figure of Stonewall Jackson on pedestal, by *Kohler*. JACKSON HOPE MEDAL. THE GIFT OF ENGLISH GENTLEMEN. Rev. DISTINGUISHED GRADUATE VIRGINIA MILITARY INSTITUTE, etc. Tin ; very fine and rare. 42.

3. 0—0 1551 Similar to last. Tin ; very fine and rare. 28.

? 0 1552 Gallery of American traitors. Rev. J. B. FLOYD,
JOHN BELL, JEFF DAVIS, etc. *Silver;* very fine,
scarce. 20.

6 0 1553 Confederate half-dollar. Arms. Rev Inscription.
W. m., fine. 19.

/5⁻ 1554 Metallic portrait of Wade Hampton. Nickel plated,
fastened on wooden frame. Perfect. 4¾x4¾ in.

MISCELLANEOUS.

5⁻5⁻ 1555 Declaration of Independence. Rev. Names of
Signers. *Electrotype;* perfect. 56.

7 0 1556 Same obv. Rev. DISCOVERY OF NORTH AMERICA,
etc. in 18 lines. *Electrotype;* perfect. 56.

/5· 1557 Electrotype copy of the obverse of this medal.
Fine. 56.

9 5⁻ 1558 Placque. View of the signing of the Declaration
of Independence, as in last obv., surrounded by a
copy of the document with signatures of signers.
Copper ; perfect. 8x7¼ in.

/ 2 0 1559 Medal awarded by Congress to Commander Dun-
can N. Ingraham for gallant and judicious conduct
at Smyrna on the 2d July, 1853 Bronze ; very
perfect *electrotype.* 64.

4 0 1560 Life-saving medal. Heraldic eagle and scene of
wreck. Bronze ; perfect. 42.

/ C—0 1561 Bust of Commodore M. C. Perry by *Mitchell.*
Rev. PRESENTED BY MERCHANTS OF BOSTON, etc.
1854. Bronze ; perfect. 40.

/. 6 0 1562 View of rescue of crew from disabled steamer and
inscription medal. presented by the State of Virginia to the widow of Captain William Lewis
Herndon, U. S. Navy, as a testimonial of respect
for her virtuous son, etc. 1858. Bronze, perfect;
a rare medal. 36.

/ 5⁻0 1563 Rescue of the crew of U. S. brig Somers in the har-
bor of Vera Cruz by foreign war ships. 1846. PRO
VITA (sic) AMERICANA. Suppressed design ;
bronze, perfect, rare. 36.

5 0 1564 Medal of the Life Saving Benevolent Association
of New York. Not named on rev. Bronze ;
perfect. 32.

1565 Medal of the Humane Society of Massachusetts. Shield surmounted by house of refuge. Rev. Name of recipient, engraved. 1873. *Silver;* very fine. 30.

1566 Same obv. Rev. Names of the officers of the Society, etc. 1854. Bronze; perfect. 36.

1567 Humane Society medal. 1850. Bust and inscription; name in blank. W. m.: proof. 25.

1568 Bust to left. JOHN HORN. Granted by Congress for heroic exploits, etc. 1874. Bronze; perfect. 30.

1569 View of two ships amidst Arctic scenery. Rev. PRESENTED BY THE BRITISH RESIDENTS OF NEW YORK TO *William Lincoln,* etc., for American Arctic expedition sent by Henry Grinnell. 1851. Original; *silver;* pierced with loop, fine. 24.

1569a Monument. U. S. MILITARY ACADEMY, WEST POINT. Rev. FROM THE CORPS OF CADETS TO J. H. B. LATROBE ESQ 1825; an eagle with motto on ribbon above. *Silver;* thick pl., very fine and rare. 16.

1570 Company F. 5th Regiment Jefferson Guard. August 11 1859, etc. Rev. Wreath. Copper; corroded on border, but fine and rare. 26.

1571 Regimental badge of the 7th Regt. Inf. N. G. State of New York. Bust of Col. Clark and view of the new armory. 1879. Bronze; fine and rare. 17x18.

EARLY AMERICAN AND PEACE MEDALS.

1572 Bust in armor and high ruffled collar of Peter Heinius, nearly facing. PET; PETRI. HEINIVS. FOED; BELG; ORD; ARCHITALASS. Rev. View of a naval engagement. HEINIAD NVT SENSIT SPOLIATA MATANCA 1628. *Silver;* very fine. 38.

This beautiful and excessively rare medal, never before offered in an American sale, was granted by the States of Netherlands to Peter Heinius, admiral of the Dutch squadron, who captured the whole laden silver fleet on its way from Mexico to Spain off Matanza, Cuba.

1573 Victory crowning a trophy. In exergue. INCENSA GALLOE CLASSE HISPAN OPES AMERIC INTERCEPT. Rev. View of ships attacking the port of Vigo. *Silver;* fine. 26.

Commemorates the capture of Spanish silver fleet by the Dutch and English fleets off Vigo, 1702. One of the earliest medals with direct reference to America.

$9\,0$ 1574 Britannia riding in chariot drawn by a lion ; Justice and Liberty at her side ; names of victories over the French on border, among them (Fort) DUQUESNE, etc. Rev. Shield with inverted fleur-de-lis and names of battles 1759. Brass ; very fine and scarce. 27.

$1.\,0\!\cdot\!0$ 1575 Bust of Louis XIV. to right by *Mauger*. Rev. Indian princess with French shield seated. For St. Christopher 1666. Bronze ; restrike, perfect. 26.

$1.\,0\,5^-$ 1576 Similar bust by *Dollin*. Rev. Indian chief gazing at a fallen warrior before prow of a ship. For victory over the Dutch at Martinique. 1674. Bronze ; restrike, perfect. 26.

$1.\,0\!\cdot\!0$ 1577 Same obv. Rev. Female reclining against the shield of France. For maritime tranquility. 1674. Restrike ; bronze; perfect. 26.

$1.\,1\,0$ 1578 Same obv. Rev. Neptune with trident and French flag, riding over the seas. For recapture of Cayenne 1676. Restrike ; bronze, perfect. 26.

$1.\,1\,0$ 1579 Same obv. Rev. Victory over a galley. For Tabago, 1677. Bronze restrike ; perfect. 26.

$1.\,1\,0$ 1580 Same obv. Rev. Explosion of fort. For capture of Tabago, 1677. Bronze restrike ; perfect. 26

$1.\,1\,0$ 1581 Similar bust by *Mauger*. Rev. Female at the foot of a palm tree pouring out coins from an urn. For capture of Spanish treasury at New Carthage 1697. Bronze ; original, fine. 26.

$\mathcal{C}\,\mathcal{J}\!\cdot\!0$ 1582 Bust of Louis XV. to right. Rev. Plan of the Island of Guadaloupe, 1721. Bronze restrike ; perfect. 26.

$1.\,1\,0$ 1583 Female with palm branches kneeling before Britannia. GVADALOVPE SVRRENDERS May 1 1759. Rev. Britannia with trident and standard on pedestal. MOORE BARRINGTON in the field. Plain edge ; copper, extremely fine. 25.

$5\,0$ 1584 Bust of George II. to left. Rev. Indian and white trader at council fire, smoking the pipe of peace, a sun above. LET US LOOK TO THE MOST HIGH, etc. 1757 Bronze ; perfect, the die cracked on obverse. 28.

$5\,\mathcal{J}$ 1585 The same. Die cracked on both sides. Bronze ; perfect.

40 1586 Coat of Arms. THE GIFT OF THE CORPORATION OF
THE CITY OF PHILADELPHIA. Rev. KITTANING
DESTROYED 1756. Like the two last a restrike;
bronze, perfect. 28.

30 1587 Head of Liberty with small liberty cap to left.
LIBERTAS AMERICANA 4 JUIL. 1776. Rev. Gallia
protecting America from the attacks of the British
lion, the dates of surrender at Saratoga and Yorktown in exergue. Very fine bronze medal by
Dupré. Very scarce. 30.

20 1588 Peace medal. Indian holding a cherub who crowns
a monument at the foot of which are the arms of
England, France, etc. EUROPAE ALMAM NE TAE-
DET PACEM 1762. Rev. Mercurius seated near
the Batavian lion, bales of merchandise, ships in
the distance and a liberty cap on staff. A very
fine and rare *silver* medal by *Holtzhey.* 28.

40 1589 Victory to right on prow of ship. Rev. Wreath
within which, EXIMIAE VIRTVTES PRAEMIVM.
Granted to officers of the Dutch fleet who fought
against England at the battle of Doggersbank
August 5, 1781, oval; loop gone. *Silver;* fine, a
rare medal. 18x22.

10 1590 Batavia and Batavian lion to right over implements
of war. INJVRIIS COACTA. Rev. Names in 7 wreaths
of officers killed at Doggersbank. August 5, 1781.
Silver; very fine and rare. 28.

50 1591 Fame supporting the crowned shields of Holland
and the United States (13 stars). EXCISTISSIMO
FOEDERE JVNCTAE DIE VII. OCTOB MDCCLXXXII.
Rev. Mercuries crowning a monument, etc. *Silver;*
very fine and rare medal by *Holtzhey.* 38.

20 1592 The same medal, reduced to size 22. *Silver;* fine
and rare.

40 1593 A warrior with American flag presenting a branch
of olive to seated Batavia. EN DEXTRA FIDESQVE
DIES 7 OCTOBER 1782. Rev. (Dutch) ALL YE FREE
MADE AMERICANS, etc. *Silver;* very fine and
rare. 20.

9 1594 Female with staff surmounted by liberty cap and
fasces. NEDERLAND VERKLAART AMERIKA VRIJ,
etc. Rev. Trophy of flags over bales of merchandise. 1782. Copper; fine, probably a restrike,
and the only one of the Dutch Peace medals restruck at the present time. 21.

1595 Louis XVI. seated, pointing to American shield (thirteen bars) suspended on a column surmounted by a liberty cap, a female figure before him. LIBER-TAS AMERICANA MDCCLXXXIII. Rev. Female with four linked shields. COMMUNI CONSENSU. Tin ; original, fine. 28.

1596 The OPE VVLCANI 1783, Peace medal. Tin ; original, very fine. 28.

1597 Female with branch of olive and cornucopia on section of globe. ON EARTH PEACE GOOD WILL TO MEN. Rev. Inscription in wreath. Ghent Peace medal, 1814. Tin ; fine. 28.

1598 Staff with liberty cap inscribed FREE ; near border CITY OF CHARLESTOWN and *No.* 33 engraved in the field. Old bronze cast, pierced above ; barely fair. Oval. 22x26.

MEDALS OF DISTINGUISHED AMERICANS.

1599 Military bust to right. GEN. ALEX. HAMILTON SEC. TREAS. UNIT. STA. Rev. TO PUBLIC CREDIT. Bronze; perfect. A beautiful and rare medal. 30.

1600 Bust to left by *Gobrecht.* TO CHARLES CARROLL OF CARROLLTON. Rev. THE SURVIVING SIGNER OF THE DECLARATION OF INDEPENDENCE AFTER THE 50TH ANNIVERSARY. Near border, UPON ENTERING HIS 90TH YEAR SEP. XX MDCCCXXVI. *Silver ;* nearly proof. Rare and beautiful. 32.

1601 Bust nearly facing. GEORGE WHITEFIELD. Rev. AN ISRAELITE INDEED, etc., DIED 30 SEPT 1770. Bronze ; fair, scarce. 24.

1602 Similar bust. THE REV. GEORGE WHITEFIELD A. M. Rev. Mortuary inscription in 8 lines on tablet. Bronze, very fine. 23.

1603 Bust to right by *Furst,* DE WITT CLINTON MAYOR. Rev. View of City Hall, New York. FOUNDED MAY 26 1803, etc. W. m. ; fair, rare. 21.

1604 Bust to right. WILLIAM PENN B. 1644 D. 1718. Rev. Penn grasping the hand of Indian chief. BY DEEDS OF PEACE. In exergue, PENSYLVANIA SETLED 1681. Bronze ; fine and rare. 25.

1605 The same. *Series numismatica.* Electro. 26.

1606 Bust in wreath of Penn to left. IN PEACE FRIENDS. Rev. Bust of Lafayette. IN WAR ENEMIES. Tin ; uncir. Oval 11x14.

8 ✓ 1607 Bust to left by *Smith*. MAJOR GENERAL BARON
STEUBEN. Rev. Within two branches of palm.
BORN NOV 15 1730, etc., DIED NOV 28 1794 AT STEU-
BENVILLE N. Y. Bronze; perfect. 24.

3 0 1608 Bust of Joseph Priestley, divine, to left. Rev. Long
inscription ending with DIED IN NORTHUMBERLAND
TOWN IN PENNSYLVANIA FEB 6 1804. Tin proof.
32.

7 2 5 1609 Full figure in the costume of a burgher of the 17th
century on pedestal inscribed 1642. TRISTRAM
COFFIN THE FIRST OF THE RACE THAT SETTLED IN
AMERICA. Rev. Four hands joined. DO HONOUR
TO HIS NAME. BE UNITED. Bronze; fine and rare.
34.

3 0 1610 Steamboat to right, flying the American flag. Rev.
SACRED TO THE MEMORY OF ROBERT FULTON ONE OF
THE MOST ILLUSTRIOUS BENEFACTORS OF MANKIND.
Tin, silvered; very fine and rare. 32.

4 6 1611 The same design as last, from different dies. W. m.,
fine, pierced. 32.

5 0 1612 Bust of Fulton nearly facing. Rev. STEAM NAVIGA-
TION ESTABLISHED, etc. 1807. Brass; nearly proof.
22.

3 0 1613 Daniel Webster. Bust to right by *Wright*. Rev.
Column surmounted by a globe; I STILL LIVE on
base. LIBERTY AND UNION, NOW AND FOREVER,
ONE AND INSEPARABLE. Bronze; perfect. 48.

6 0 1614 Duplicate of last no. Bronze; perfect. 48.

0 1615 Bust of Webster to right. Rev. DEFENDER, etc.
Lead; cast. 25.

5 1616 Bust to right by *Merriam*. Rev. I STILL LIVE in
wreath, and Jos. H. Merriam's card. Cop. and
brass. Very fine. 19. 3 pcs

5 1617 Bust in Roman toga to right. DANIEL WEBSTER.
Different reverses. W. m., proof. 18. 7 pcs

2 0 1618 Bust to right by *Bolen*. Rev. THE ABLE DEFENDER,
etc. Brass; fine. 16.

3 0 1619 Naked bust to left by *Hennig*. Rev. Heavy
wreath of oak and laurel, within which WASHING-
TON IRVING BORN APRIL 3 1783 DIED NOVEMBER
28 1859. Bronze; perfect. 43.

6 0 1620 Bust of Fenimore Cooper to left by *R. Lovett*. Rev.
Inscription in wreath. Bronze; fine. 32.

20 1621 Bust facing. THOMAS BRAINERD L.L.D., DIED AUGUST 22 1866. Rev. View of the Third Presbyterian Church, Phila., built 1768, etc. Bronze; perfect. 24.

10 1622 Bust to left. HON THOMAS SWANN MAYOR OF THE CITY OF BALTO 1856. Rev. United States shield surrounded by 20 stars. Tin; fine and very scarce. 27.

7 1623 Head to left by *Knox & Lang.* JOHN DAVIS; heavy wreath of oak and laurel on broad border. Rev. REP TO CONGRESS FROM DEC 1825 TO JAN 1834, etc., in 13 lines. Tin proof. 24.

7 1624 Bust to left. DAVIS MEDAL. Rev. Blank. Copper; fine. 21.

90 1625 Bust nearly facing; JOHN T. HOFFMAN. Rev. GOVERNOR OF THE STATE OF NEW YORK 1869—1871. *Silver;* very fine. 21.

75- 1626 Head to left by *Barber.* W. H. FURNESS D.D, Rev. Within heavy wreath of laurel, 1825–1875 IN HONOR OF A PASTORATE OF 50 YEARS OVER THE FIRST UNITARIAN SOCIETY PHILADELPHIA. Bronze; perfect. 40.

3 25- 1627 Head to right by *Ellis.* A GRATEFUL COUNTRY TO HER GENEROUS SON, CORNELIUS VANDERBILT. Rev. Columbia with sword and shield, a steamer in the distance, etc. Struck by order of Congress in acknowledgment of his gift of the steamer Vanderbilt to the U. S. at the beginning of the rebellion, 1861. Bronze; perfect. 48.

580 1628 Cyrus W. Field. Perfect electrotype copy of the larger medal granted him by Congress, 1867. Equal in appearance to an original. 64.

U5- 1629 The same. Perfect electrotype copy of the medal presented him by the Chamber of Commerce, N. Y. 42.

U5- 1630 The same. Draped bust to right by Lovett. Rev. PRESENTED BY A FEW OF HIS FRIENDS, etc. Bronze; perfect. 32.

29 1631 Duplicate of last no. Bronze; fine. 32.

125- 1632 Smaller medal presented to Cyrus W. Field by the Chamber of Commerce, New York. Steamers sailing from each other. Rev. Male and female figures stretching a wire over the ocean, etc. Published by *Tiffany & Co.;* bronze, perfect. 37.

85 1633 Bust of Field to left. Rev. Arms. FROM THE STATE OF WISCONSIN, etc. Bronze; perfect. 41.

75 1634 Bust in high relief to left by *Landry*. L. AGASSIZ 1807-1873. Rev. In heavy wreath of olive, VIRO INGENIO, LABORE, SCIENTIA PRÆSTANTISSIMO. The Swiss medal; a masterpiece of metallic art. Bronze proof. 57.

9·0 1635 The same. Bust to right. Smaller mortuary medal by *Barber*. Bronze; perfect. 28.

7·0 1636 Elisha Kent Kane, Arctic Explorer. Head to right over tablet with view of Arctic regions. Rev. Ground-floor of Masonic temple, etc. 1859. Bronze; perfect. 42.

1·2 1637 Bust to right. DR. E. K. KANE. Rev. BORN IN PHILA. PA FEB 3 1822, etc., in 8 lines; also one with F. C. Key's card. Bronze, brass and w. m.; very fine. 24.   3 pcs

1·0 1638 Arms of the United States surmounted by an eagle on globe, a female figure on each side. Rev. View of the discovery of the open Polar Sea. Fine electrotype. 50.

4·5 1639 Similar obv. Rev. Two figures in Arctic costumes on iceberg, the open sea in the distance. Fine bronze medal, published by *Tiffany & Co.* 38.

7·0 1640 Arctic scene; hunters slaying a walrus, a sledge drawn by dogs in the distance. Rev. Blank. Oval; type metal, cast. 34x44.

8·8 1641 Naked bust to left by *Barber*. DAV. RITTENHOUSE 1ST DIRECT U. S. MINT 1792-1795. Rev. Inscription. Medal series. U. S. Mint. Bronze; perfect. 28.

2·5 1642 Naked bust to left by *Wright*. ROBERT M PATTERSON DIRECTOR OF THE U S MINT 1835-51. Rev. A PARTING TOKEN, etc. 1851. Bronze; perfect. 40.

8·0 1643 Bust to right by *Furst*. ADAM ECKFELDT CHIEF COINER U. S. MINT 1814—1839. Rev. A FAREWELL TRIBUTE, etc. Bronze; perfect. 32.

7·0 1644 Bust facing by *Paquet*. PRESENTED TO JAMES ROSS SNOWDEN, DIRECTOR OF THE MINT, ETC 1861. Rev. View of the U. S. Mint, Phila., 1856, etc. Bronze; perfect. 50.

7·0 1645 Bust to left by *Barber*. HON JAMES POLLOCK L.L.D. Rev. Inscription in 9 lines. Bronze; perfect. 28.

SS 1646 Bust to left by *Key.* JOSEPH J. MICKLEY 1867.
Rev. PRESIDENT OF THE NUMISMATIC AND ANTI-
QUARIAN SOCIETY OF PHILADELPHIA. Yellow
bronze; perfect. 32.

1.10 1647 Bust to right by Miss *Lea Ahlborn.* JOSEPH J.
MICKLEY PRAES SOCIET NUMISM, etc. Rev. Heavy
wreath of oak, within which STAT SINE MORTE
DECUS. Bronze proof. 32.

1.10 1648 Bust to left. ELI K PRICE PRESIDENT 1879. Rev.
Arms of the Numismatic and Antiquarian Society
of Philadelphia and inscription. Bronze; perfect.
26.

1.55 1649 Bust to right. JOHN PINTARD. Rev. View of the
building of the New York Historical Society,
1857. Bronze proof medal by *Smith & Hartmann.*
40.

2.25 1650 Bust to left by *Smith & Hartmann.* EDWIN FOR-
REST. Rev. Heavy wreath of olive entwined
with the names of his principal characters, within
which, BORN IN THE CITY OF PHILADELPHIA PA
MARCH 9 1806, etc. Bronze; perfect. 48.

1.0 1651 Head of Forrest to left. Rev. ROSE BY HIS OWN
EFFORTS, etc. Copper proof. 20.

5 1652 Bust to right. EDWIN FORREST, the rev. all different. W. m., very fine or proof. 18.   7 pcs

1.0 1653 Bust to left. WILLIAM J. MULLEN PRISON AGENT,
etc. Rev. Inscription in 17 lines. Copper, nearly
proof. 23.

1.20 1654 The Thiers medal. Presented to A. Thiers, French
statesman, by Frenchmen in Philadelphia, for
distinguished services to the French Republic,
1873. Arms of Philadelphia and inscription.
Bronze; perfect and rare. 40.

3 1655 Bust to right. ELIAS HOWE JR. Brass shell. 33.

4.0 1656 Bust to right of John Pintard. Rev. Born in the
city of New York 1759, etc. W. m. proof. 40.

4.0 1657 Bust to right of Will Page 1848. Rev. A pallet,
etc. Bronze; perfect. 30.

MEDALS OF EDUCATIONAL INSTITUTIONS, SOCIETIES, ETC.

UU 1658 Bust of Edward Everett to left. Rev. PENNSYLVA-
NIA INSTITUTE 1856. Bronze; proof. 28.

50 1659 Bust to right by *Paquet.* SUYDAM, 1870. Rev.
NATIONAL ACADEMY OF DESIGN, NEW YORK. Bronze;
fine. 40.

660 Bust to right by *Wright*. WASHINGTON ALLSTON. Rev AMERICAN ART-UNION 1847. Bronze; perfect. 40.

661 The same medal, the rev. from different dies. Bronze; perfect. 40.

662 Bust to right by *Wright*. From the same society. 1848. Bronze; perfect. 40.

663 Bust to left by *Wright*. Rev. Same design as last. 1849.

664 Head to left by *Müller*. ASHER B. DURAND 1863. Rev. ARTISTS' FUND SOCIETY, NEW YORK. Bronze; perfect. 32.

665 Bust to left by *Furst*. BENJAMIN COUNT RUMFORD, DIED 1814. The Rumford medal for discoveries in light or heat, etc. Bronze; nearly proof. Rare. 40.

666 Female bust to left by *Key*. THE NEW YORK FREE ACADEMY WAS FOUNDED 1847, etc., in 13 lines. Bronze; perfect. 38.

667 Bust of Peter Cooper. To graduate of full course in the Cooper Union, New York. Bronze; perfect. 32.

668 College of the City of New York. Kelly prize medal, founded 1868. *Silver* proof. 24.

669 The same. Claflin prize medal; different reverses. Bronze; perfect. 22.   2 pcs

670 Free Academy, New York. Prize medal; bronze; fine. 22.

670a Another. 1853. Bronze; perfect. 32.

671 College of St. Francis Xavier, New York. Prize medal; brass; fine. 24.

672 Union College, Schenectady, N. Y. Blatchford oratorical prize medal. *Silver*; very fine. 24.

673 Other medals of this college, one with name engraved on rev. Bronze and w. m. ; fine. 17.   2 pcs

674 Hamilton College, N. Y. Prize medals, with busts. Bronze; fine. 26.   2 pcs

675 Public Schools of Buffalo, N. Y. Bust of Jesse Ketchum. 1782-1867. Bronze; perfect. 22 and 30.   2 pcs

676 Randolph Macon College, Virginia. Bust of Bishop Joshua Soule, founder. Rev View of the college building. Yellow bronze; fine. 28 and 32. 2 pcs

�4 0 1677 Fulton Institute, Lancaster, Pa. Bust to right.
Award medal; bronze, perfect. 32.

6 0 1678 Pittsburgh Female College. Thomas McKee prize
medal, for superior excellence in music. Bronze;
perfect. 26.

4 5 ̄ 1679 Peabody medal. Bronze; perfect. 28.

2 5 ̄ 1680 Lowell Schools. James C. Carney medal. Bronze;
perfect. 24.

1. 1 0 1681 Hungerford Collegiate Institute. 1864. Award
medal. *Silver* proof. 32.

2 5 ̄ 1682 Worcester High School Bullock medal. Bronze;
perfect. 26.

2 5 ̄ 1683 Girls High School of Boston Mass. Award medal;
bust of Mrs. H. M. Dodd. Bronze; perfect. 21.

1 1 1684 Miscellaneous. Sands medal, Mechanics Society
School, Sisters of Bethany, Topeka, Kan., Union
School, Cooperstown, N. Y. *Silver* (pierced),
bronze and w. m. Fine. 16 to 26   6 pcs

7 5 ̄ 1685 Presbyterian College, Montreal. Christina prize
medal, founded 1874. Bronze; perfect. 28.

1. 0 5 ̄ 1686 Haverford College. Bust to right. CHARTERED
1833 SEAL OF THE CORPORATION MDCCCXXIII.
Isaac F. Wood's series "B" No. 2. Rev. View
of the college buildings, 1876. *Silver* proof. 26.

2 2 1687 The same. Bronze and w. m. Perfect. 26. 2 pcs

1 8 1688 View of College, as in rev. of last. Rev. A
chapel; ALUMNI ASSOCIATION, etc. W. m. proof.
26.

7 5 ̄ 1689 View of College; 1869. Rev. Lamp over a Bible;
FOUNDED BY THE SOCIETY OF FRIENDS 1833. ME-
MORIAL OF CLASS OF 1862, etc. *Silver:* proof. 26.

2 0 1690 The same. Bronze; thick planchet, perfect. 26.

1 7 1691 The same. Bronze and w. m. Perfect.   2 pcs

3 3 1692 The same. *Silver*, bronze and w. m. Perfect.
3 pcs

1 0 1693 A chapel, as in No. 1688. Rev. FOR UNDER-
GRADUATE ORATION. Bronze and w. m.   2 pcs

1 2 1694 Bust to left of David M. Lyle, Phila. Fire Dept.
Rev. Inscription and Key's card. Bronze; perfect. 24.   2 pcs

1 1 1695 Grand Parade Phila. Fire Dept., 1865; w. m., proof.
32; Fireman's medal, 1860; brass, proof. 19.
2 pcs

1696 Medal struck from first copper produced in Colorado, 1866. View of the mining works and inscription. Copper ; uncirculated. 40.

1697 Challenge cup for sloops. Award medal, 1874. Sloop sailing to right. Published by *Tiffany & Co.* ; bronze, perfect. 36.

1698 Bust laureate to left. Rev. United Bowmen of Philadelphia around a wreath. Name and date 1840 engraved on edge. *Silver*; perfect and rare. 24.

1699 International Regatta. Philadelphia, 1876. Oarsman in skiff, etc. Bronze ; fine and rare Centennial medal. 22.

1699*a* German shooting festival. Philadelphia, 1876. A target surmounted by eagle, etc. Bronze ; fine. 28.

1700 Medal of the New Haven Numismatic Society, founded 1862. Fac-similies of 8 Colonial coins around a Washington cent, and inscription on rev. Tin ; fine and rare. 28.

1701 Pittsburgh Numismatic Society, 1878. W. m. Fine. 22.

1702 New England Historical Genealogical Society, 1873. *Isaac F. Wood's memorial series.* Thick pl. *Silver* proof. 20.

1703 The same. *Silver*, cop. and brass proof. 20.

3 pcs

1704 Duplicates. Copper and brass, proof. 4 pcs

1705 Delta Psi Fraternity, 1860. Nickel ; proof. 15.

1706 Savannah Benevolent Association, 1876. The good Samaritan on the way-side and cross. Bronze ; perfect and rare. 24.

1707 Marksman's medal of the German-American shooting festival, 1868. Arms of New York and eagle with target, etc. *Silver* ; very fine, rare. 24.

1708 Plattdeutsches Volksfest, New York. 1875. Bust facing of two bier fiends, the champion bier drinkers at the festival ; an oak tree on rev. W m., bronzed, with loop. Uncir. ; rare. 22.

1709 New York 1865-1875. Miscellaneous medals struck to commemorate German carnival, shooting and gymnastic festival, including a dupl. of last no. W. m. 5 with loop or pierced. A fine and rare lot. 18 to 32.

8 pcs

7 1710 Swiss National festival. New York, 1872 & '73.
German silver and brass ; loop. 17.   4 pcs

/8 1711 Irish Republic. Centennial of the birthday of
Daniel O'Connell, 1875. His bust. Rev. A harp
and sprigs of shamrock. Brass ; proof. 20.

6 1712 Medalets struck in honor of the grand Fenian
parades in New York, 1874 and 1875, each with
harp. W. m., proof ; rare. 19 and 20.   2 pcs

/2 1713 Ship to left. F. B. Rev. Hands joined ; IRELAND,
AMERICA, 1866, etc. Brass, pierced, uncir. 18.

6 1714 Head of Liberty to left, 13 stars around it, LIBERTY
below. Rev. Harp, PARNELL LAND LEAGUE. 1881.
Copper ; proof. 12.

o'2 1714a Flying eagle grasping a harp to left, holds a
label inscribed AMERICAN MANUFACTURES AND
IRELANDS INDEPENDENCE SOLIDARITY. Rev. WE
PURPOSE 'FORE HIGH HEAVEN, etc., 39 stars.
Brass proof. Pierced, and large green and gold
ribbon, with pin, attached. 24.

/2 1715 Bust of Louis Kossuth to right. THE WASHINGTON
OF HUNGARY. Rev. NOW IN THE NAME OF
ETERNAL TRUTH, etc. in 12 lines. Brass ; uncir.
17.

6 1716 Same obv. Rev. Eagle. UNITED STATES OF
AMERICA. Brass ; fine. 17.

/7 1717 Same obv. Rev. Small bust of Bolivar. Copper,
proof, rare. 17.

7 1718 Bust of Kossuth to left. NOTHING IS IMPOSSIBLE,
etc. Rev. Eagle. UNITED STATES, etc. Brass,
fine. 17.

3./0 1719 Bust of Kossuth to left. THE WASHINGTON OF
HUNGARY 1852. Rev. Steamer to right, DRY
GOODS AND UPHOLSTERY, etc. Copper ; uncir.
and rare. 17.

4/ 1720 Same obv. Rev. A hat. FRANCISCO & CO. HAT-
TERS. Copper ; uncir. and rare. 17.

AGRICULTURAL SOCIETIES, FAIRS, ETC.

50 1721 Adams Co., Ill. Agri. & Mech. Bronze ; fine.
32.

20 1722 Boston Peace jubilee, 1872. Bust of Gilmore.
Rev. View of the Coliseum. Shells, joined with
a broad edge and silvered. Loop. Proof. 24.

1723 Badge in shape like a Maltese cross, struck for the
same occasion. W. m., silvered ; perfect. 33.

1724 Edrom Agric. Society. Bronze ; perfect. 32.

1725 Erie Co. Agri. Society. W. m. ; proof. 28.

1726 Hudson River Agric. and Driving Park Assoc.
Poughkeepsie, N. Y. W m., proof. 28.

1727 Farmers' and Mechanics' Club, Hicksville, L. I.,
1877. Bronze, perfect. 28.

1728 Fine Art Exp. Galesburg, Ill., 1873. Brass, pr.
29.

1729 International Indus. Exhibition, Buffalo, N. Y.
Bronze ; perfect. 38.

1730 Mechanics' Fair, Louisville, Ky., with H. Miller &
Co.'s card (die sinkers). Copper ; perfect. 21.

1731 Massachusetts Hortic. Soc. 1845. Bust of Samuel
Appleton. Bronze ; perfect. 26.

1732 Mass. Charitable Mech. Assoc. Br. perfect. 24.

1733 Nashville, Tenn. Agr. & Mech. Assoc. Br.; perfect. 24.

1734 New York, 1853. Exhibition medal. Bronze ;
perfect. 36.

1735 N Y. State Agr. Soc. Bronze ; perfect. 33.

1736 The same. Smaller award medal. Copper and
brass, proof. 20.   2 pcs

1737 N. Y. State Poultry Soc. 1869. Name engraved on
rev.; silver, perfect. 28.

1738 New York, 1853. Exposition of all nations, with
view of Crystal Palace. W. m., proof. 46.

1739 The same. Crystal Palace, varieties. W. m.
proof. 39.   2 pcs

1740 The same. Crystal Pal., and Columbia seated. Yellow bronze ; fine. 28.

1741 Crystal Palace. Rev. Latting observatory. Tin ;
fine. 34.

1742 Crystal Palace. Rev. Flags of all nations. Tin ;
good. 35.

1743 Erie Canal, 1825. Tin ; very fine. 50.

1744 Smaller Erie canal medal. In box (damaged) made
from wood brought from Erie in first Canal Boat,
" the Seneca Chief," etc. Tin ; fine. 28.

1745 Croton Aqueduct, N Y., 1842. Bronze ; fine. 32.

1746 Miscellaneous. No duplicates. Nickel, copper,
brass and w. m. ; very fine or proof. 18 to 32.
                                                     7 pcs

3 0 1747 Ohio State Board of Agric. W. m., proof. 32.

v ~0 1748 Pennsylva. Hortic. Society. Bronze ; perfect. 32.

3 0 1749 Pennsylva. State Agr. Fair. Phila. 1880. Copper gilt ; proof. 16.

v ~ 1750 Bazaar of Nations. Phila. 1875. Y. M. C. A., w. m., fine, pierced. 24.

9 0 1751 Portsmouth, Va. Building flying the Confederate flag, a trophy of arms in exergue. Rev. Wreath around which, PRESENTED BY THE COUNCIL OF THE TOWN OF PORTSMOUTH, VIRGINIA. Bronze, proof medal by *Mitchel.* Rare. 40.

3 1752 Ridgeway and Shelby, N. Y. Union Agricultural Society. 1858. Varieties. W. m. proof. 28.
2 pcs

3 1753 Rome, Georgia, 1857. National Exposition. W. m.; proof. 20.

/ 6 1754 St. Lawrence Co. Agr. Soc. Member's badge. Bronze ; perfect. 19.

/ 0 1755 Syracuse Mechan. Assoc. W. m., silvered. Very fine. 29.

/ 4 0 1756 Utica Mechanics' Assoc. 1852. Name of recipient engraved on rev. *Silver ;* fine. 36.

4 0 1757 Yonkers Horticultural Soc. Bronze ; perfect. 26.

/ 6 1758 Brooklyn Bridge. 1883. W. m., pierced ; proof. 22.

/ 6 1759 Hotel Brighton. Rev. Manhattan Hotel, Coney Island. W m., proof. 25.

RELIGIOUS AND TEMPERANCE TOKENS AND MEDALS.

v ~6 0 1760 Church penny or token, issued by the Presbyterian Church at Albany, N. Y. D. CHURCH PENNY. Rev Blank. Struck over a copper coin. Fine ; very rare. 16.

v ~v ~ 1761 Church token. Open bible over crossed branches. COMMUNICANT'S TOKEN. Rev. THIRD REFORMED PRESBY CONGR' N. Y W m.; very fine. Oval ; 14x18.

v ~0 1762 Copper token. DONT SPEND ME FOR LIQUOR. Rev. I AM PLEDGED FOR TEMPERANCE. Battered ; good, very rare. 16.

/ 0 1763 Bust of Robert Raikes to left by *Thomas, N. Y* Rev. SUNDAY SCHOOL OF ST THOMAS'S CHURCH NEW YORK INSTITUTED A. D. 1827. W. m., good, pierced, 22.

/ ⊃ 1764 St. Matthew's Church, New York. 50th jubilee, New York, 1867. Luther nailing his thesis at cathedral door, and inscription (German). *Silver*; very fine. 25.

/ 0 1765 American Lutheran Zion Church, New York, 1857. Christ rising from the grave, and inscription (German). W. m. loop; fine. 22.

⟁⁻ 1766 Bust of Wesley. Rev. CENTRAL M. E. CHURCH BROOKLYN E. D. ORGANIZED MARCH 1858. Brass; shells, fine. 24.

⟁⁻ 1767 Temperance medals. THE OLD OAKEN BUCKET, etc. W. m., all different; good to choice, 3 pierced. 20 to 28. 7 pcs

⟁⁻ 1768 American Juvenile Temperance Society, N. Y. Organized 1856. Varieties; bronze, fine. 20. 2 pcs

⟁ 1769 Meriden Excelsior Truth Division. Temperance pledge medal. Copper and brass pierced. Fair. 24. 2 pcs

⟊ 1770 Herkimer and Montgomery Temperance Society. Clover leaf surrounded by 13 stars, etc. W. m., good. 23.

⟁⁻ 1771 Moses striking the rock. GOD GAVE THEM WATER. Rev. Blank. Rare medal by *Thomas*. W. m. proof. 22.

⟁ 1772 Sabbath School Jubilee, July 4, 1842. Blank reverse. *Silver*; very fine. 21.

⟁ 1773 Hands joined. ST VINCENT KINGSTOWN 1840. Rev. FRIENDLY CHURCH OF ENGLAND SOCIETY. *Silver*; pierced, fine. 20.

⟁⁻ 1774 Temperance medals. Order of Rechabites, Bible and Scenes, etc. All different and very fine or proof, 10 pierced. W. m. 24 to 38. 18 pcs

⟁⁻ 1775 Nova Scotia. TEMPERANCE SOCIETY; TOKEN OF MEMBERSHIP, etc. Tin; pierced. Poor; rare. 24.

⟁⁻ 1776 Epiphany Temperance Guild, 1877. Star-shaped member's badge; also mint piece of the same on pentagonal planchet. W. m. proof. 32. 2 pcs

⟁ 1777 Miscellaneous. Religious and temperance medals of American Societies. Ten pierced, one or two dupl. Copper, brass and w. m.; average condition, fine. 15 to 26. 21 pcs

3 S 1778 Bust of Father Mathew to right. Rev. Rev. Father
Mathew addressing a group of converts. Fine
bronze medal by *Wyon.* 36.

/ S 1779 Bust of Father Mathew by *Jacobus.* Rev. Temperance pledge. W. m., proof. 26.

/ S 1780 Bust of Father Mathew by *Kieserling, Chicago.*
Rev. T. A. & BENEV SOC ST LOUIS MO. W. m.,
pierced. 26.

/ S 1781 Temperance medals with busts of Mathew and
Burke. Yellow bronze; proof. 21.   2 pcs

7 0 1782 Roman Catholic temperance medal. Shield supported by male and female figures. Rev. Large
cross and inscription. *Silver;* pierced, very fine.
28.

7 0 1783 Temperance Association of the 3d Regt. Irish
Brigade, N. Y. Vols. 1861. Cross on altar and
inscriptions. *Silver;* pierced, fine and rare. 22.

S 1784 Roman Catholic temperance medals. American,
Canadian, and Irish. One each copper and brass,
balance white metal. Many pierced, average condition fine, and average size 25.   21 pcs

2 1785 Bust of Pius IX. Rev. Golden jubilee, etc. Issued
in New York. Three varieties. W. m. proof,
one. pierced. 21.   5 pcs

/ S Z) 1786 Bust of Gregory XIII. Rev. VGONOTTORVM STRAGES
1572. Bronze; perfect. 19.

2 1787 Roman Catholic amulets, charms, etc.; one, size 16,
silver, balance copper and brass, and smaller. All
fine.   9 pcs

MASONIC MEDALS.

7 0 1788 Bust of Kane to right over square tablet, with view
of Arctic scenery. Rev. Ground floor of Masonic
temple MDCCCLIX Bronze; fine. 32. Marvin
291.

G S 1789 The same. Yellow bronze or brass; proof. Not
mentioned by Marvin as struck in this metal.

G 0 1790 Pittsburgh No. 1. W. m., proof. 27. Marvin
297.

O S 1791 Armory, Seventh Regiment. CORNER STONE LAID
Oct. 13, 1877, etc. Bronze proof. 25. Marvin
711.

1792 New Masonic Temple, Phila. DEDICATED SEP-
TEMBER 28 A. D., 1873, etc. Bronze proof. 24. Marvin 284.

1793 The Old Round House, Le Roy, N. Y. Rev.
Square and compasses OLIVE BRANCH □ NO. 39.
etc. Copper proof. 22. Marvin 288.

1794 Similar. Copper proof impression from the second
or altered dies. See Marvin's notes. No. 288.

1795 Obverse as in two last numbers. Rev. DEDICATED
TO THE SCHOLARS, etc. Copper proof. 22. 2 pcs

1796 Masonic Temple. Boston. W. m. silvered; fine.
19. Marvin 24.

1797 Arms supported by a lion and an eagle. HOLLAND-
SCHE LOGE STAAT VAN NIEW YORK 5787, etc.
Rev. Inscription. *Silver* proof. 20. Marvin 302.

1798 The same. Copper, br. and w. m. proof.   3 pcs

1799 The same. Bronze, cop. and brass ; proof.   3 pcs

1800 Same obv. Rev. Old Masonic Hall, New York.
Copper, proof. 20. Marvin 700.

1801 Same obv Rev. New Masonic Hall, New York.
Copper proof. 20. Marvin 303.

1802 Same obv. Rev. Ground floor of Masonic Temple.
Copper proof. 20. Marvin 710.

1803 Old Masonic Hall, New York. Rev. New Masonic Temple, New York. *Silver* ; nearly proof.
20. Not in Marvin.

1804 The same. Copper and brass proof. 20.   2 pcs

1805 Old Masonic Hall, as before. Rev. Ground floor of
Masonic Temple. Copper and brass ; proof. 20.
2 pcs. Marvin 304.

1806 Duplicates of last no. Proof.   2 pcs

1807 Same obv. Rev. Altar on ground floor. YOUTH,
MANHOOD, OLD AGE. Copper proof. 20. Marvin
36.

1808 New Masonic Temple. Rev. Ground floor of Masonic Temple. Copper proof. 20. Marvin 37.

1809 Duplicates of Nos. 1800, '02, '04 and '08. Copper
and brass proof.   4 pcs

1810 Egyptian Obelisk, New York, 1880. Bronze ; proof.
21. Marvin 712.

1811 Mount Vernon Chapter, No. 228, N. Y. Bronze
proof. 20. Marvin 704.

3 0 1812 Bust of Lafayette. Rev. Ground floor of Masonic temple. Copper, proof. 20. Marvin 280.

2 0 1813 Masonic temple. Rev. DEDICATED JUNE 24 1874, SPRINGFIELD, MASS. W. m. proof. 17. Marvin 287.

2 5 1814 Head of Washington to right. Rev. LAKE CITY LODGE NO. 27, LAKE CITY, FLA. Copper proof. 17. Marvin obv. 270, combined with obv. 290; not mentioned by him.

2 5 1815 Same obv. Rev. Plumb, level and square, same as rev. of Marvin 290 ; a combination not mentioned by him. Copper proof. 17.

2 5 1816 The same as in two last nos. W. m. proof. 17.
2 pcs

5 5 1817 Mark Lodge. Rev. EXCELSIOR NO. 216. Copper ; fine, 15. Marvin 306.

5 5 1818 Duplicate. Same condition.

7 0 1819 Square and compasses. Rev. HOPKINS LODGE NO. 180 BLACK JACK GROVE TEXAS. *Silver ;* proof. 13. Marvin 30.

2 0 1820 The same. Cop. and brass proof. 2 pcs

2 0 1821 Duplicates of last No. Same condition 2 pcs

3 5 1822 Head of Washington to right. Rev. Square and compasses on Bible. *Silver* (pierced) and gilt, proof. 12. 2 pcs

2 0 1823 Masonic temple New York. Shield-shaped badge, struck on the occasion of the dedication of the New Masonic temple, New York, 1875. Bronze ; perfect. 25x36. Marvin. 38.

1 5 1824 Another, with metallic pin. Silvered ; perfect.

5 0 1825 Seal of Lamoka Lodge No. 465, Tyrone, N. Y. Perfect impression in lead. 26.

5 0 1826 Seal of Weston N. Y. Lodge No. 463. Perfect impression in lead. 28.

2.6 0 1827 Silver planchet in the shape of Keystone, engraved *Columbian Chapter D. C.* Perfect. 19x22.

2.1 0 1828 Shield-shaped silver badge; engraved Masonic implements, etc. John Sullivan 5795 *I. R. A. L. No.* 2. Perfect ; rare old Masonic medal. 28x42.

3.3 0 1829 Engraved silver badge with triple loop. All-seeing eye, surrounded by symbolic letters. Rev *Elisha Hiacock of Washington State of Connecticut Init in Franklin Chap June* 13 1797. Fine. 29.

CENTENNIAL MEDALS.

Many other Centennial Medals will be found among the Washington Medallic series.

1830 Eagle on American shield, surrounded by trophy of flags, anchor, 13 stars above, etc. NATIONAL JUBILEE 1826. Rev. DECLARATION OF INDEPENDENCE SIGNED JULY 4 1776, etc. Tin, silvered, pierced ; fine and rare. 25.

1831 Centennial celebration of the founding of St. Matthew's Church, Walker St., N. Y., October 1852. View of the church and inscription in German. W. m.; fine and rare. 27.

1832 Centenary Anniversary of the birth of Schiller ; New York 1859. Bust to right and inscription in German. Bronze ; perfect. 26.

1833 Another. Large bust to right. W. m., silvered ; proof. 25.

1834 Bust of John Wesley to left by *Key.* 1866. Rev. View of the old Wesley Chapel and Parsonage, John St., New York, as it appeared in 1768. Yellow bronze ; proof. 32.

1835 Wesley as a boy, kneeling before his mother, *rev.* SUSANNA WESLEY, TEACHING HER SON JOHN, etc. Rev. Similar to last rev. W. m. proof. 26.

1836 Same obv. Rev. Dickinson College, 1866. Copper and bronze proof. 26. 2 pcs

1837 Bust of Wesley to right. Rev. SUNDAY SCHOOL CENTENARY CHAIR, INDIANA UNIVERSITY. Copper proof. 19.

1838 Similar medal of Albion College, Albion, Mich. Copper proof. 19.

1839 Centenary medal of Ashbury, 1866. Copper, silvered and pierced; another w. m. proof. 18 and 20. 2 pcs

1840 Fiftieth Anniversary of Odd Fellows, Phil. 1869. Emblematic figures and inscription. Bronze ; fine. 32.

1841 Pilgrim Jubilee. 1620—1870. Landing of pilgrims and holy bible. Bronze ; gilt. Proof. 29.

1842 Semi-Centennial of All Saints Church, New York. May 1874. Bronze, proof. 25.

1843 Duplicate. Same condition. 25.

1844 Bust of Rev. William Otterbein. Rev. A church ; SABBATH SCHOOL CENTENARY, etc. 1774—1874. W. m. proof. 26.

6 ✓ 1845 Liberty cap and hornet's nest on shrub over two joined hands 1775—1875. Rev. MECKLENBURG DECLARATION OF INDEPENDENCE 20 MAY 1775. *Silver;* proof. 19.

2 ✓ 1846 The same. Copper proof. 19.

4 0 1847 Charleston Centennial Antique Association 1875. Old militia man with gun and flask. Rev. Inscription in 15 lines. Tin ; silvered, pierced. 39.

3 2 1848 Lexington Centennial 1875. Militia man on shield and inscription. Bronze ; perfect. 24.

/✓ 1849 The same. Brass : pierced. Fine. 24.

2 2 1850 Bust of Gen. Joseph Warren. Rev. BUNKER HILL BATTLE GROUND 1875. W. m., good. 22.

2 / 1851 Seventh Regt. N. G. N. Y. Vols. to Bunker Hill, 1875. Copper proof. 20.

2 / 1852 Bunker Hill Centennial Anniversary 1875. Scene of the death of Warren and Monument. Brass, pierced. Proof. 17.   2 pcs

/. 4 ✓ 1853 American eagle displayed, a shield on his breast, an olive branch in his right talon and thirteen arrows in his left, 13 stars in radiant sun above. THE UNITED STATES OF AMERICA. Rev. Mercurius presenting cornucopia to Indian princess seated, etc., TO PEACE AND COMMERCE IN JUL MDCCLXXVI. Reproduction by *Barber* of *Dupré's* design. Bronze ; perfect. 42.

7✓ 1854 Columbia seated to left ; near border four small medallions representing the four parts of the world, and chain of 38 stars. Rev. INTERNATIONAL EXHIBITION PHILADELPHIA MDCCCLXXVI, etc. Rejected design of the Centennial Commission award medal. Very perfect electro. 48.

✓✓ 1855 Large and small medals commemorative of the hundredth anniversary of American Independence. Columbia with glave pointing to a constellation of 13 stars above. 1776. Rev. Columbia crowning kneeling figures, etc. 1876. Copper gilt (2), bronze and w. m. proof. 36 and 24. In velvet-lined morocco case.   4 pcs

5✓ 1856 The same. Large commemorative medal. Bronze ; perfect. 36.

/ 8 1857 The same. W. m., nearly proof. 36.   2 pcs

2 8 1858 Independence Hall 1776. Rev. Memorial Hall 1876. TO COMMEMORATE THE CENTENNIAL ANNIVERSARY, etc. Copper gilt, proof. 36.

3 o 1859 The same. Bronze; perfect. 36.

2 3 1860 Main building and art gallery. FAIRMOUNT PARK PHILADELPHIA 1876. Copper gilt; proof. 32.

4 0 1861 The same. Bronze proof. 32.

1 5 1862 Three Exposition buildings, superposed. 1876. Rev. Declaration of Independence. 1776. W. m. proof. 32. 2 pcs

3 0 1863 Full figure of John Witherspoon, SIGNER OF THE DECLARATION OF INDEPENDENCE, etc. Rev. Bible inscribed PROCLAIM LIBERTY, etc. W. m. silvered, proof. 32.

J 5 1864 Knights of Pythias. AUG 22 1876. Fine Centennial medal. W. m. gilt. 32.

5 0 1865 The same. W. m. proof. 32.

3 0 1866 Liberty Lodge 272 I. O. O. F. SEPT 20 1876. Centennial medal. W. m. proof. 32.

1 0 1867 Greek head of Liberty to left, by *Voyral*, a circle of pellets on border. Rev. American and French flags crossed 1776-1876 UNITED STATES OF AMERICA INDEPENDENCE. Bronze proof and the most artistic of all Centennial medals. 32.

2 ½ 1868 Busts of Victoria, McMahon, Pius IX, and William of Germany. Rev. SEE HOW WE PROSPER. Fine Centennial medals by *Laubenheimer*. Bronze; perfect. 28. 4 pcs

1 0 1869 Exposition building, Philadelphia. 1876 in shield below. Rev. Horticultural Hall. Copper proof. 26.

1 5 1870 Same obv. Rev. Art Gallery. Copper; perfect. 26.

1 0 1871 Same obv. Rev. ILLUSTRATING, etc., in 6 lines. Copper; proof. 26.

2 1872 Horticultural Hall and Art Gallery. Copper; proof. 26.

3 1873 Horticultural Hall and inscription as in 1871. Cop. pr. 26.

5 1874 Art Gallery and inscription as before. Cop. pr. 26.

4 1875 Set of Centennial buildings, the same as in preceding 6 nos. Yellow bronze, proof. 26. 6 pcs

3 1876 Grand entrance, Exposition building, Phila. 1876. Rev. Dimensions of building, etc. W. m. gilt, proof. 26.

2 1877 The same. W. m. proof. 26. 2 pcs

7 1878 Same obv. Rev. U. S. MEDALLION ADVERTISING CO., etc. W. m. 26.

/ o 1879 Head of Washington to right, panels of infantry and cavalry on border. Rev. Declaration of Independence. Thick pl., good. 26.

/ 2 1880 John Hancock's signature. Rev. Same as last, but *Demarest* in exergue. W. m. pr. 26. 2 pcs

6 1881 H. G. Sampson's card. Rev. Same as rev. of 1879. W. m. proof. 26.

7 1882 Declaration of Independence, as in 1879. Rev. IN COMMEMORATION, etc W. m. gilt. 26.

2 s- 1883 Head of Washington to right. Rev. Unfinished Washington monument, stone uncut. Wood's satirical medal. Bronze; thick pl., good. 25.

/ 2 1884 Bust of Lincoln to right. Rev. OUR NATION'S FREEDOM, etc. W. m. proof. 25.

/. 2 s- 1885 Soldiers saluting a bell. Rev. Mining scene. Struck from Nevada *silver* ore at International Exhibition 1876. Nearly proof. 24.

J - 1886 Large cracked bell. PROCLAIM LIBERTY, etc. 1776–1876. Rev. Independence Hall, 1776. Copper and brass proof. 24. 2 pcs

/ 3 1887 Same obv. Rev. CENTENNIAL MEMORIAL OF SILOAM M. E. CHURCH, PHILADELPHIA, etc. Copper and brass proof. 24. 2 pcs

/ / 1888 Same obv. Rev. CENTENNIAL MEMORIAL OF THE CUMBERLAND ST. M. E. CHURCH, PHILADELPHIA, etc. Brass proof. 24.

/ 2 1889 Same obv. Rev. UNION AVENUE BAPTIST SUNDAY SCHOOL, etc. Copper proof. 24.

/ 2 1890 Small bell. PROCLAIM LIBERTY, etc. Rev. Independence Hall, 1776. Bronze and brass proof. 24. 2 pcs

/ 0 1891 Independence Hall. 1776–1876. Rev. CENTENNIAL CELEBRATION CHOSEN FRIENDS LODGE NO 100. I. O. O. F. Brass; very fine. 24.

/ 3 1892 Columbia seated to left. FREE AND UNITED STATES. 1876. Rev. BIRTHPLACE, etc. 1776. Copper and brass; very fine. 24. 2 pcs

~ 1893 Same obv. Rev. AMERICAN COLONIES 1776. Brass; very fine. 24.

8 s- 1894 Same obv. Rev. Ornamental border, the field blank. *Silver;* very fine and rare. 24.

1895 Centennial fountain. Fairmount Park. 1876. Copper and brass. Very fine. 24. 2 pcs

1896 Continental Currency. 1776. Rev. Chain. Copy: copper proof. 24.

1897 The same. Cop. and w. m. proof. 24. 2 pcs

1898 Head of Liberty with Grecian helmet to left. Rev. HOMMAGE DE F. F. F. MAC., D'ERBOIS, etc. 5776–5876. Bronze proof. 23. Marvin 86

1899 Square and compasses. Rev. Same as last. Bronze and brass proof. 23. Marvin 85. 2 pcs

1900 Bust of Lafayette. Rev. STATUE IN NEW YORK UNVEILED, SEPT. 6, 1876. Copper proof. 20.

1901 Trophy of arms. Rev. Chain of 13 links inscribed with names of States. CENTENNIAL LEGION 1776–1876. Copper, proof obv. 20.

1902 The same. Pierced, with metallic pin. Bronze: very fine. 2 pcs

1903 Centennial Exposition of Chicago. 1876. Rev. EAT GUNTHER'S CANDY, etc. W. m. Uncirc. and very rare. 19.

1904 Memorial Hall. Rev. Eagle. *Schwerdtle f.* Loop: w. m. proof. 18. 2 pcs

1905 Liberty with American flag. 27 stars near border. Rev. 4TH JULY CELEBRATION 1776–1876. Loop: w. m. proof. 18.

1906 P. H. crowned and inscriptions. 1876. The Brazilian medal for Philadelphia Exposition. Copper, uncirc. 17.

1907 Miscellaneous. Includes "Stockton Hotel" and other rare Centennial medalets. W. m. proof: a few pierced. 11 to 17. 18 pcs

1908 Hawk-like eagle. CENTENNIAL 1776–1876. Rev. INTERNATIONAL EXHIBITION. A British medalet. Loop: copper, silvered, uncirc. 16. 2 pcs

1909 Seated female, spinning. Rev. Monogram and inscription. The Lowell, Mass. centennial medalet. *Silver:* proof. 15.

1910 Pine tree. MASSACHUSETTS. Rev. SAIL ON O UNION STRONG AND GREAT. 1776–1876. *Silver,* pierced: very fine and rare. Oval. 12×16.

1911 Centennial ball. Rev. "Greenpoint Sunday School," "Sommernachtsfest," and American flag. Bronze: proof. 16. 3 pcs

7 1912 Independence Hall. 1776. Memorial medalet struck within the international exhibition 1876. Copper gilt, proof. 15.

ʋ 1913 Duplicates. One pierced. Fine. 2 pcs

ʋ 1914 Head of Liberty to left, 13 stars near border. Rev. Eagle, 1876. CENTENNIAL. Brass, pierced, very rude impressions, but as fine as known. 14.

ʋ 1915 Eagle, as in last No. Rev. Incuse. Same metal, etc.

2 0 1916 Lafayette Restaurant checks. 50, 10 and 5 cents. Brass; scarce. 3 pcs

16 1917 Duplicate set. Equally fine. 3 pcs

19 1918 10 and 5 cents tokens. 1876. P. L. & CO. in monogram. Nickel; fine and scarce. 2 pcs

ʋ 1919 Bell and Independence Hall (4), Art Gallery, Carpenter's Hall, etc. Cop. (3), brass (3) and w. m., 3 pierced. Fine. 14. 7 pcs

ʋ 1920 Large and small bell. Rev. Independence Hall, (3 var.), head of Washington, and Children's Centennial party. Pottsville. Bronze, cop. and brass proof. 11. 20 pcs

/2 1921 Large and small bells. Rev. Indep. Hall. *Silver;* nearly proof, 1 pierced. 12. 2 pcs

16 1922 Lord's prayer in 15 lines. Rev. "Struck in the main building on first steam coin press," etc. 1876 and 1877. Varieties, 2 pierced. *Silver;* very fine. 9 and 11. 4 pcs

6 1923 Duplicates of the 1877 medalet. Brass ; one pierced, fine. 12. 2 pcs

ʋ 1924 Bell. 1776-1876. Rev. A CENTURY OF LIBERTY I. The smallest Centennial medalet. German silver, copper and brass, one pierced. Uncirc. 8. 4 pcs

ʋ 1925 Bell and Independence Hall, glass surface (2) ; bell with pin, etc. W. m. ; all very fine. 14 to 24. 4 pcs

6 1926 Memorial Hall, International Exhibition, Phila., 1876. Incuse impression on smooth steel planchet. Rev. Blank. Pierced. 27

6 1927 Bell-shaped badge with guard and pin of Philadelphia Commandery No. 2. CENTENNIAL 1876. *Silvered;* perfect. 32x32

/2 1928 Shield-shaped badge of Mary Commandery No. 36. Masonic Knights Templar, struck to commemorate 100th anniversary of Independence, 1876. W m., perfect. 22x29.

1929 Cross-shaped badge with metallic pin of Hugh de Payens Lodge No. 1, Jersey City, N. J. Struck for Knights Templar Reunion at Philadelphia, June 1, 1876. Silvered; perfect. 8¼x3¼.

1930 Centennial guard. Detective badge. Perfect. 20.

1931 Calendars. Independence Hall, Liberty bell. Metallic discs on green and black rubber frames. Perfect. 30. 2 pcs

1932 Views of Philadelphia, New York and San Francisco, in metallic boxes, impressed with bell and head of Liberty. 1876. Perfect. 39. 3 pcs

1933 Centennial rubber and celluloid medals. 24. 3 pcs

1934 Odoriferous amulet, SOUVENIR D'AMERIQUE. 1776-1876. 23.

1935 View in high relief of the declaration of Independence, from Trumbull's painting at the Capitol, 46 correct likenesses of signers. Rev. Copy of the declaration of Independence and names of signers on two tablets. Copper shells, bronzed. Perfect and rare. Diameter 6½ in.

1936 Views of Centennial Exposition buildings, heads of Goshorn and Hawley. Wooden medals; all perfect. 38 to 48. 7 pcs

1937 Views of Centennial Exposition buildings, etc. Rev. "Three millions of Colonists," etc. Compressed wood, square 2¼x4 inches. 5 pcs

1938 Liberty seated. Rev. Exhibition Philadelphia 1876. Red, black and bronzed terra cotta. Perfect. 42. 4 pcs

1939 "Two minute man," rubber; "Women's pavilion," porcelain, etc. Perfect, average 36. 3 pcs

1940 Liberty bells of 1776, in miniature. Various sizes and metals; one with stereoscopic views of Centennial building, etc., the balance with clappers. 11 pcs

1941 Pins, charms, waist belt, etc.; bell-shaped, etc. 7 pcs

1942 Centennial pins and badges. Various designs and metals, one Masonic, several with ribbons. Metallic shells; all very fine. 35 pcs

1943 Metallic watch charms, etc. Bells, buildings, monograms. 5 pcs

1944 Centennial toy watches. Perfect. 2 pcs

J⁻ 1945 Ladies' scarf pins. Views of buildings in metallic colors, with crystal covers. Red, green, blue, gold, etc. All perfect. 22. 5 pcs

J⁻ 1946 Oval ladies' breast pins, gilt setting. Views of Centennial buildings painted on imitation ivory under glass covers. Very fine. 24 to 52. 3 pcs

J⁻ 1947 Rubber ladies' pins : oval, cross and anchor shaped, etc., one with metallic setting. All perfect. 9 pcs

J J⁻ 1948 Tortoise-shell sleeve buttons. Lion grasping eagle, 1776 ; eagle grasping lion, 1876. Perfect pair.

J 0 1949 Nickel-plated tobacco box. Eagle over shield, etc. 1876 on top. Perfect.

2 J⁻ 1950 Solid metallic sleeve buttons. Centennial buildings ; pretty designs, French enamel. A pair.

J⁻ 1951 Sleeve and shirt buttons, etc. Metallic shells. 19 pcs

J⁻ 1952 Miniature weights 1776-1876, etc. 2 pcs

4 J⁻ 1953 Bust of Genl. John Stark. Rev. Three shields. Centennial of the battle of Bennington. 1877. Bronze ; perfect. 25.

4 J⁻ 1954 Surrender of Burgoyne. Rev. Saratoga monument. Bronzed copper, proof. 22.

4 J⁻ 1955 Bust of Genl. Anthony Wayne. Rev. Storming of fort. Centennial of the Storming of Stony Point, 1879. Bronze; perfect. 22.

/ 0 1956 The same. Bronze and w. m. proof. 22. 2 pcs

2 J⁻ 1957 Monument and inscription. Centennial of the battle of Newtown. N Y. 1879. W. m. proof. 25.

2 J⁻ 1958 Centennial celebration of the capture of Major André, Tarrytown, N. Y. 1880. Monument and facsimile of medal granted by Congress to captors. Copper gilt. perfect. 22.

J 0 1959 Bust of Major André. Rev. Old Dutch Church, Tappan, where his trial was held. Bronze ; perfect. 22.

C 0 1960 Bust facing of George Calvert, the first Lord of Baltimore. Rev. Monument. 1730-1880, etc. copper, proof. 20.

4 0 1961 Busts jugata of Washington and Rochambeau. CENTENNIAL, YORKTOWN, VA. 1881. Rev. The surrender. W. m. proof. 32.

2 J⁻ 1962 Busts of Washington, de Grasse, and Lafayette. Rev. Monument at Yorktown. 1781-1881. W. m. proof. 20.

2 1963 Bust nearly facing of Washington. Rev. sortye-
ste, etc. Yorktown Centennial. W. m. proof,
pierced. 20.

5 1964 Baltimore Festival. ORIOLE. 1881 and 1882.
Bronze and w. m. proof. 16 to 22.   3 pcs.

3 1965 Bust of William Penn to left. Rev. BI-CENTEN-
NIAL OF PENNSYLVANIA. 1882. Bronze proof.
22.

0 1966 Same obv. Rev. Penn's house, 1682; City Hall,
1882. W. m. proof. 22.

5 1967 Same obv. Rev. UPLAND 1682, CHESTER 1882, in
wreath. Bronze proof. 22.

6 1968 Duplicate of 3 last Nos. 3 pierced, with pins. W.
m. pr. 5 pcs.

3 1969 Full figure of Penn. Rev. PENN'S HOUSE, 1682-
1882. W. m. proof. 20.

0 1970 Penn's treaty. Rev. BI-CENTENNIAL, TREATY CEL-
EBRATION 1882. W. m. proof. 19.

0 1971 Bust nearly facing of Penn. Rev. Arms. Copper gilt medalet distributed by employes of U. S.
mint during the celebration 1882. 46.

5 1972 Similar bust. Rev. The Lord's prayer in 14 lines.
Silver proof. 9.

0 1973 The same. Copper, gilt. 2 pcs.

7 1974 Phillipse Manor, Yonkers, N. Y. Bi-centennial
celebration of the erection of the manor, Yonkers,
1882. Copper proof. 20.

5 1975 Figure seated to left. GEN. JAMES OGLETHORPE.
Rev. SESQUI CENTENNIAL OF THE SETTLEMENT OF
GEORGIA, 1733-1883. Bronze proof. 22.

6 1976 The same. W. m. proof. 22.

MISCELLANEOUS MEDALS, ETC.

5 1977 Set of presidential series, residence on reverse.
Complete from Washington to Lincoln. W. m.
~~proof~~. 22. 16 pcs.

6 1978 Busts jugata to left. ROBERT AND LOUISA GILMOR
of Baltimore. In exergue, MARRIED FIFTY YEARS
THE 25TH SEPTEMBER, 1841. Rev. A cupid, TO
CONJUGAL HAPPINESS. Fine and rare bronze
medal by *Faulkner*. 25.

*5 ⅌-*1979 Bust on each side said to be portraits of Governor Clinton and wife; beaded border and ornamental loop. Hollow shells soldered and silvered; fine. Oval. 16x20.

⅌ 1980 Bust of Jefferson to right by *Bolen.* Rev. EQUAL AND EXACT JUSTICE, etc. Cop. and w. m. proof. 16. 2 pcs.

⅌ 1981 Bust of Jackson, rev. battle of New Orleans; French and American shields surmounted by a liberty cap; Our flag trampled upon (2); Beware of foreign influence; War-fund committee of Brooklyn, etc. One brass, balance w. m.; nearly all rare, but average only fair, 4 pierced. 22 to 27. 9 pcs.

2 0 1982 Battle of Bunker Hill. Rev. SUCCESS TO THE FAIR. 1840. Bronze; fine. 27.

2 7 1983 Bust to left of Jenny Lind. Rev. FIRST CONCERT IN AMERICA AT CASTLE GARDEN N. Y., SEP. 11, 1850, etc. W. m., nearly proof. Rare. 26.

4 0 1984 Bust nearly facing of John Brown. SLAVERY THE SUM OL ALL VILLANIES. Rev. John Brown's body hanging to a gibbet. GIVE ME LIBERTY OR GIVE ME DEATH, etc. Copper proof; scarce. 20.

1 4 1985 Military bust to left of Anthony Wayne. Rev. Names of battles. Copper and brass proof. 22.

2 1 1986 Bust to right of Major André. Rev. Old Dutch Church, Tappan, where he was tried. Copper; perfect. 22. 2 pcs

1 6 1987 Balloon. GREAT AIR SHIP CITY OF NEW YORK. Rev. Inscription. Copper; proof. 22.

5-0 1988 Hog hanging. 1837-1857. NEVER KEEP A PAPER DOLLAR, etc. Satirical on the financial panics of '37 and '57. Copper; very fine. 22.

1 ⅌ 1989 Old Middle Dutch Church, Nassau St. Rev. A RIDING SCHOOL, etc. Brass; nearly proof. 22.

1 ⅌ 1990 Odd Fellow's Hall, New York. CORNER STONE LAID JUNE 4TH, 1847. Rev. Odd Fellow's emblems. W. m.; fine, pierced. 24.

*3 5-*1991 Bust to left. DEDICATED TO CHARLES A. DANA, EDITOR OF THE NEW YORK "SCUM," etc. 1876. Rev. THE CHINESE STINK-POT OF AMERICAN JOURNALISM. etc. Copper and brass; proof. Rare satirical medal. 20. 2 pcs

3 2 1992 Duplicates of last number. 2 pcs

1993 Bust of Tilden to right. Tilden's "Convention" Bitters, etc. Rev. DRAKE'S "PLANTATION" BIT- TERS S. T. 1860-X. Copper gilt ; proof. 17.

1994 Great Eastern. 1859. Copper (3) and w. m. Three varieties ; fine to proof. 19. 4 pcs

1995 Constitution and Guerriere. 1812. Cop. and br.; pr. 20. 3 pcs

1996 Penn's treaty. 2 varieties. Cop., br. and w. m. pr. 20. 3 pcs

1997 Atlantic telegraph. Varieties. Copper and w. m. pr. 20. 2 pcs

1998 Miscellaneous medalets, each with bust. Lincoln, Grant, Geary, Buckalew, Clymer, Hartranft, Fisk, Heenan, Sayers. Copper and brass, two pierced. Uncirculated. 14 to 21. 9 pcs

1999 Miscellaneous. W. m.; fine, 2 pierced. 14 to 19. 10 pcs

2000 U. S. Armory. Springfield, Mass. Copper, proof. 17. 2 pcs

2001 Steamer Hancock. "329." FOR SALT RIVER DIRECT; etc. Rev. THE GREAT REPUBLICAN VICTORY OF 1880. Copper; proof. 18.

2002 Anchor on shield. HOPE. 1844. Rev. BOSTON LIGHT DRAGOONS, hound, rabbit. Yellow bronze ; proof. 18. 3 pcs

2003 Tom Thumb. Varieties. W. m. proof. 24. 3 pcs

2004 Liberty and Commerce, 1794, rev. "John Howard"; Liberty and Security, 1795, rev. Hope; etc. Cop- per ; poor to good, 2 pierced. 18. 6 pcs

2005 1838. Loco-foco cent. Very fine ; scarce.

2006 Jackson, Harrison, Clay, Seward, Verplank, Kos- suth, etc. Brass tokens : several very scarce ; average fine ; 18 pierced. 12 to 18. 31 pcs

2007 Brass jetons, spiel-marks, etc. Average fine, 2 pierced. Cop., brass and w. m. 12 to 34. 17 pcs

2008 Stephen Girard. Rev. BORN AT BORDEAUX, etc. Brass ; proof. 20.

2009 Firemen's medals. Three varieties. Brass ; pr. 19. 4 pcs

2010 Eagle and 16 stars. Rev. PERRY. Brass ; fine. 14.

2011 George Washington. Bust, shell ; Washington token, 1833(2); Sumner medalet ; Columbia token. Copper ; fine. 12. 5 pcs

2012 Female watering a plantation. 1736, etc. The Cistern medal. *Silver ;* good. 25.

2013 Engraved U. S. quarter-dollar, pierced.

2014 Pocket detector of U. S. counterfeit silver coins. Nickel plated ; fine. 24.

2015 Bust of Simmebujen Nokami. Rev. "Chief of Japanese Embassy, Washington, D. C., U. S. A. 1860"; *engraved* on copper planchet. Fine. 22.

2016 Encased melanotypes, sleeve buttons with photo. of Beach, pins, badges, etc. 17 pcs

2017 Collection of silk badges, worn on public banquets, celebrations, funerals, etc. Henry Clay, Scott, Grant, Hayes, Tilden, Garfield, Hancock, Centennial, etc., several with metallic pins. A fine and scarce lot ; large and small. 25 pcs

2018 U. S. flags (miniature), Centennial paper and linen badges, colored lithographs of presidents, etc. 26 pcs

2019 Indian wampum. String of 91 beads ; several shades of color and varieties of shape. Rare.

FOREIGN MEDALS, TOKENS, ETC.

ENGLAND.

2020 Bust of Aelfred. Rev. BRITISH EMPIRE, UNITED STATES ANGLO-SAXONS EVERYWHERE. 1849. W. m. Fine. 22.

2021 Edward VI. Fine portrait bust. Rev. Monument and mortuary inscription. Bronze, cast ; fine, small hole near edge. 25.

2022 Busts jugata of James III., pretender and Clementina. Rev. PROVIDENTIA OBSTETRIX. Bronze ; very fine. 26.

2023 Bust of Anne to left. Rev. View of engagement. One of the Vigo medals. Bronze, cast ; good. 27.

2024 George IV. Coronation medal, 1821. Bronze, perfect. 22.

2025 William IV. Coronation medal, 1831. Bronze, fine. 28.

2026 Victoria. Bust to left by *Wyon.* For visit to the corporation of London, 1837. Bronze ; fine. 34.

2027 The same. Bust to right. Award medal of the Society of Florists, *named. Silver;* fine. 24.

2028 Busts jugata of Victoria and Albert by *Helfricht*
Rev. The royal pair in chariot drawn by cupids,
etc. Bronze ; fine marriage medal, nearly proof.
28.

2029 Bust facing of Alfred, Prince of Wales. Rev.
Victoria bridge, Montreal. Bronze : perfect. 27.

2030 Another medal, struck on the same occasion. W.
m. proof. 32.

2031 The same. Bust. VISITED THE UNITED STATES
OCT. 1860. Bronze, cop. and brass, proof. 20.
3 pcs

2032 London Exposition medals. 1851. One with bust
of Prince Albert, bronze ; balance w. m. All different ; fine to proof. 24 to 32. 4 pcs

2033 William Pitt. Bust to left. Rev. THE MAN WHO
HAVING SAVED THE PARENT PLEADED WITH SUC-
CESS FOR HER CHILDREN. With and without
name under the shoulder. Bronze ; fine. 26.
2 pcs

2034 The same. Bust to left. Rev. WITH FORTITUDE,
etc. Tin ; one bronzed. Fair only. 33. 2 pcs

2035 Bust to left. Rev. Mortuary inscription, ending
with DIED JAN. 23, 1806. Bronze ; very fine. 34.

2036 Another mortuary medal. Bust. Rev. Britannia
weeping at the foot of a monument. Tin ; nearly
proof. 32.

2037 The same. Draped bust to left. Rev. HE SAVED
HIS COUNTRY in heavy wreath. Silvered. Fine.
32.

2038 The same. Similar bust. Rev. Pitt on a rock ;
English ship in the distance. Bronze ; fine. 32.

2039 Similar obverse, the rev. emblematic of England's
tranquility in the midst of foreign wars, etc. W.
m. proof, in solid metallic frame. 32.

The three last medals were issued by the Pitt club, 1813.

2040 Carolus Grey, Gwyllim Lloyd Wardle, Daniel de
Lisle Brock, etc. Tin and bronze cast. Good
and fine. 28 to 38. 4 pcs

2041 Bust of Rev. William Knibb, Jamaica. Rev.
King's Chapel, Jamaica. Copper ; fair. 28.

2042 Rural Deanery of Middlesex, Jamaica. A TOKEN
OF ESTEEM. Copper ; pierced, good. 26.

2043 A vase. THE THOMASON METALLIC VASE, 24 FEET
IN CIRCUMFERENCE, etc. Fine bronze medal. 43.

2 0 2044 Bust to left; rev. a balloon. VINCENT CUNARDI, first aerial traveler in England. 1781. Copper : good. 22.

2 5- 2045 Ancient Order of Druids. Bust of Druid facing. Rev. Initiation scene. Bronze ; pierced, cast. 32.

J 0 2046 Stonehenge on Salisbury Plain. 1843. Rev. Old Sarum deserted 1217. W. m. Fine. 32.

6 2047 Chronological medals of the rulers of England, to George IV. Varieties : pierced. W. m. 24 and 30.
                                                   2 pcs

2 / 2048 Another to Victoria. W. m. proof. 28.

/ 4 2049 Chinese Junk. "Arrived at England 27 Mar. 1848." W. m. Fine. 17 and 28.   2 pcs

5-0 2050 Ship sinking in a gale. ROYAL GEORGE ADMIRAAL KEMPENFELT 1783. Rev. View of Gibraltar. GEBLOOUFERDE GIBARALTAR 1783. Dutch satirical token; copper gilt. Fine. 21.

/ 0 2051 Bust nearly facing. THOS HARDY SECRETARY TO THE LONDON CORRESPONDING SOCIETY NOV 1794 NOT GUILTY. Rev. Names of Jurors. Penny size; copper, fine.

/5- 2052 Mrs. Newsham the white negress. Curiosity house penny token, 1795. Uncirculated.

/ 2 2053 Bust of Sir George Chetwind. Grendon halfpenny. Very fine.

2. 75- 2054 Bust of Wellington. Rev. Names of battles. *Silver ;* fine. 18.

2 6 2055 Bust of Col. Percie Kirk. Rev. Britannia seated. BRITONS OWN HAPPY ISLE 1686. Halfpenny size ; uncirculated.

3 5- 2056 Satan leading Napoleon to Elba, inscription on rev. Brass ; fine. 16.

/ 0 2057 Miscellaneous. Includes Portsmouth and Chichester halfpenny, silver shell inscribed "Waterloo," Earl of Elgin Jamaica, Vigo medalet, etc., various metals. 1 pierced. 10 to 19   10 pcs

ANTI-SLAVERY MEDALS.

6 5- 2058 Negro in chains. AM I NOT A MAN AND A BROTHER. Rev WHATSOEVER YE WOULD, etc. Brass ; very good. Rare. 20.

/ 3 2059 Similar. From different dies. W. m. Fine. 20.
                                                 2 pcs

2060 Colonist and negro grasping hands. WE ARE ALL
BRETHREN. SLAVE TRADE ABOLISHED BY GREAT
BRITAIN 1807. Rev. Arabic inscription. Copper
proof. 22.

2061 Duplicates. Fine; scarce. 2 pcs

2062 Others. Fair and fine. 2 pcs

2063 Negro with uplifted hands. ENGLAND I REVERE,
GOD I ADORE, NOW I AM FREE. 1834. Rev. COLO-
NIAL SLAVERY ABOLISHED, etc. Very fine and
rare bronze medal. 32.

2064 Negro with broken shackles. JUBILEE 1834. Rev.
IN COMMEMORATION OF THE EXTINCTION OF COLO-
NIAL SLAVERY, etc. Red bronze ; extremely fine,
rare. 27.

2065 Duplicate. Bronze; fine. 27.

2066 Same as last and other emancipation medals of
1834, including "a voice from Great Britain to
America." All different. W. m. proof. 5 pierced.
20 to 28. 6 pcs

2067 Negroes kneeling at the foot of Justice. AM I NOT
A WOMAN AND A SISTER. Rev. Names of English
abolitionists entwined in heavy wreath of flowers.
TO THE FRIENDS OF JUSTICE MERCY AND FREEDOM.
Bronze ; very fine and rare. 26.

2068 Bust of Revd. William Knibb, Jamaica. Rev.
Monument erected to his memory by emancipated
Africans. 1838. W. m. proof ; pierced. 26.

2069 Bust of Joseph Sturge. Rev. Emancipated negroes
under a palm tree. 1838, etc. W. m. proof;
pierced. 26.

2070 Duplicates of two preceding nos. and two other
emancipation medals of 1838. One poor, balance
fine ; w. m., pierced. 24 and 26. 4 pcs

2071 Bust of Thomas Clarkson. Rev. Negro in chains.
FOREIGN ANTI-SLAVERY SOCIETY. Struck in commemoration of the general anti-slavery convention,
held in London, 1840. Bronze ; very fine. 32.

2072 Bust facing ; similar to last. W. m., fine. 28.

2073 Female figures on pedestal. AMERICAN ANTI-
SLAVERY SOCIETY INSTITUTE DEC. 1833. THERE
ARE MORE THAN 2,500,000 SLAVES IN THE UNITED
STATES. Rev. Inscription. W. m.; very fine and
rare medal by *Bridgens, New York.* 25.

2 2074 Baptist mission jubilee. 1842. W. m. proof. 28.
2 pcs

ſ-ſ- 2075 Head to right of F. A. Isambert, a French jurist.
Rev. In wreath of palm and oak, A LEUR DÉFEN-
SEUR, LES NÈGRES ET LES MULATRES RECONNAIS-
SANTS 1838. Bronze ; fine and rare. 32.

7 ſ- 2076 Jubilee medal of the London Missionary Society.
1844. Indian, Chinaman, Negro, etc., gathered
around an angelic figure. Rev. Tablet with inscription. Bronze ; very fine. 28.

ſ-ʊ 2077 Liberia medal. Ship sailing toward the African
coast. THE LOVE OF LIBERTY BROUGHT US HERE.
Rev. LIBERIA FOUNDED MARCH 1821, DECLARED
INDEPENDENT 1847, and names of the chief officers.
Tin ; very fine. Rare. 26.

2 ſ- 2078 Bust to right of Isaac T. Hopper. Rev. Colonist
raising a negro from the ground. TO SEEK AND
TO SAVE THAT WHICH WAS LOST. W. m. Very
fine. 34.

FRANCE.

/./0 2079 Louis XII. Bust to right. Rev. A hedge-hog,
crowned. Bronze, mint restrike ; very fine. 36.

90 2080 Henry IV. Bust laureate to right. Rev. A trophy.
VICTORIA YVRIACA. Bronze, mint restrike ; very
fine. 31.

/.0ſ- 2081 Louis XIII. Draped bust to right. Rev. Youth-
ful figure driving a quadriga, the 12 signs of the
zodiac on broad border. Fine ; bronze, mint restrike. 44.

80 2082 Louis XIV. Bust to right. Rev. Laudatory inscription in wreath. Bronze ; very fine mint restrike. 46.

/.ʊ0 2083 Louis XV. Bust in armor to right. Rev. Inscription commemorative of the Indies Company of
France. Bronze, mint restrike. Very fine. 37.

/.ʊʊ 2084 The same. Bust to right. Rev. View of Louis-
burg ; LUDOVICOBURGUM FUNDATUM ET MUNITUM
MDCCXX. Bronze, silvered ; mint restrike. 26.

4/ſ- 2085 Accolated busts of Louis XVI., Marie Antoinette,
and Elizabeth. Rev. The several dates of their de-
capitation in wreath of palm. Bronze ; original,
very fine. 25.

2086 Bust of Louis XVII. Rev. A broken flower. circi
DIT ET FLOS VIII Junii MDCCXCV., the date of
his death, in exergue. Bronze; original, very fine.
26.

2087 Bust to left of Louis, 2d son of Louis XVI. Rev.
Angel writing on tablet. Very fine *silver* medalet
by *Loos*. 18.

2088 Napoleon I. Bust laureate to right. Rev. Infan-
tile bust of his son with title NAPOLÉON II. EMP DES
FRANÇAIS XX JUIN MDCCCXV. Original : *silver*.
fine. 25.

2089 Naked figure. BONUS EVENTUS. Rev. Frigate
sailing. Bronze; original, fine. 20.

2090 The same. Bust laureate to right. Rev. Napoleon
in coronation robes, carried by two figures. *Gold* ;
very fine. 9.

2091 The same. Medalets with bust (5), and 2 of Napoleon III. *Silver*; very fine. 8 to 11.   7 pcs

2092 Similar. Bronze (9) and brass. All very fine. 8
to 14.   12 pcs

2093 Military decoration with bust of Napoleon I. Rev.
CAMPAGNES DE 1792 À 1815, etc. Bronze; loop.
very fine. 12x16.

2094 Fine bust of Marie Louise by *Andrieu*; blank reverse. Tin, very fine. 42.

2095 Busts jugata of Henry IV. and Louis XVIII. Rev.
Restoration of the statue of Henry IV. Bronze ;
good. 20.

2096 Henry V. Bust to left. Rev. Crown over two
crossed sceptres. Probably a pattern for a 5 franc
piece. Struck in copper ; uncirculated. 24.

2097 Medalets commemorative of the destruction of the
Bastile, the erection of the Vendôme and July
columns, birth of princes, etc. Bronze ; fine to
uncir. 16 and 17.   12 pcs

2098 Louis Philippe. Capture of Constantine. 1837.
Bronze restrike ; very fine. 32.

2099 The same. Enlargement of the Palace of the
House of Peers. 1836. Bronze restrike ; very fine.
42.

2100 The same. Construction of the buildings of the
Normal School. 1841. Bronze restrike ; very
fine. 42.

2101 The same. Portraits of the royal family in ovals,
obv. and rev. Bronze ; original, very fine. 47.

2 5- 2102 Napoleon III. 1853. Marriage medal. Busts jugata, etc. Bronze restrike ; fine. 32.

5-5- 2103 Busts jugata of Napoleon III. and Eugenie. Rev.
Industrial palace, 1855. Bronze restrike ; very
fine. 42.

2 3 2104 The same. 1859. Exposition at Rouen. Bronze
restrike ; nearly proof. 26.

8 0 2105 The same. Military medal for Italian campaign,
1859. *Silver;* loop. Very fine. 19.

1. 5-0 2106 The same. Other military medals granted for valor
and discipline. Eagle above and loop. *Silver ;*
fine and rare. 16x27.

8 0 2107 Napoleon (IV). Bust to left by *Merley.* Rev. 16
MARS 1874. Bronze ; original, very fine. 28.

1 3 2108 Bust of Louis, Cardinal of Guise. Blank rev.
Bronze ; fine. 24.

7 0 2109 Bust of Andrew Hercules de Fleury, cardinal. etc.
Rev. Females gathered around a column surmounted by French shield. MDCCXXXI. Bronze;
original; die cracked on rev. Fine. 42.

6 0 2110 Bust of the Count de Chambord. Fine bronze
medal, struck on the occasion of the visit paid
him by French legitimists. 1872. 23.

1 8 2111 Naval victory at Navarin 1827. Brass ; fine. 22.

5 0 2112 Railway from Paris to St. Germain. 1835. Early
style of locomotive. etc. Copper gilt ; fine. 28.

1 8 2113 Crimean medal. 1854. French and English inscriptions. W. m. ; fine. 28.

4 5- 2114 Bust of Blanchard, aeronaut. Rev. A balloon and
parachute. Ascent at Warsaw 1788. Bronze ;
very fine. 18.

4 2 2115 Paris. 1753. *Silver* jeton. Arms of Louis Basile
de Bernage, etc. Fine. 20.

6 0 2116 Bust of Liberty, crowned with stars. LIBERTE
EGALITE FRATERNITÉ. *F. B. Smith, N. Y.,* under
the bust. Cross-shaped decoration. probably
issued by French residents in New York on the
establishment of the Republic. *Silver* ; very fine.
21.

2 5- 2117 Brass jeton issued at the International Congress of
Americanists, at Nancy, 1875. Brass, loop, uncirculated ; rare. 15.

2118 Louis XIV, XV, XVI, Napoleon I. (gros consuli),
Henry V. Napoleon III, etc. Copper and brass
jetons and medalets, several with loops; a fine
lot. 26 pcs

SWITZERLAND, ITALY, GERMANY, ETC

2119 View of Geneva and Lake Leman. Rev. Liberty
with staff and cap resting on the Bible, cherubs
plying useful arts about her. Fine Reformation
medal by *Dassier*. Bronze; original.

2120 General Dufour. Commander Swiss Federal Army,
1847. Fine bronze medal by *Bovy*. Proof. 24.

2121 The same. Old head to left. Fine bronze medal
by *Bovy* on the completion of the military map
of Switzerland. 1866. Proof. 38.

2122 Bust of Hans Herzog, General of the Swiss army
during the late Prusso-French war. Rev. Helvetia with shield and glaive guarding the Alpine
passes. Extremely fine bronze medal by *Richard*.
32.

2123 Federal shooting festival, Bale. 1844. Five francs,
struck in *bronze*. Proof.

2124 Octagonal bronze medal. Opening of the Roanne
Canal. Arms of Geneva, etc. Very fine. 20.

2125 Sardinia. Victor Emanuel. 1815. Peace medal.
Bronze; very good. 26.

2126 Victor Emanuel II. War medal for Italian independence. *Silver*, loop; fine. 20.

2127 Head in high relief to left. Rev. Fool's head formed
entirely of phallus. Old Italian bronze medal,
cast; fine and rare. 25.

2128 Bust of Emperor Frederic Barbarossa to left.
FED. AE NOB IMP. Rev. Empress on donkey's
back, holding its tail in indecent posture; kneeling burgher behind. ECCO LA FICO. Old Italian
bronze medal, cast. Very fine and rare. 32.

2129 Male figure reclining; three ladies around him.
Rev. Blank. Old Italian bronze, cast and pierced
above. The subject may possibly have been in-
spired by Boccaccio's "La jardinier du Convent."
Fine. 34.

2130 Poland. Thadeus Kosciuszko. *Series Numismatica*. Bronze; very fine. 25.

2131 Duplicate. Equally fine. 25.

$ʃ ʃ - 2132 Prussia. Crowned bust facing of William, title
" German Emperor." Rev. Germania with glave
and wreath. 1870–1871. Beautiful bronze medal
for victories over Napoleon III. 35.

6 0 2133 Military bust of Prince Bismarck, Chancelor of the
German Empire. Rev. Germania seated with
glave and branch of laurel. POSCIMUR 1870–1871.
Bronze proof medal by *Bovy*. 28.

ʊʊ- 2134 The same. Bust facing by *Bovy*. 1870. Rev.
Arms. Bronze proof. 38.

6 2135 Miscellaneous. Dr. (theologiae) George Michael
Wiltman, etc. Bronze, pierced (1) and w. m. 21
to 28.   3 pcs

/. 3 0 2136 Satirical. The Queen of Hungary putting on the
breeches. Rev. The Queen naked. etc. 1742.
Copper ; fine. 25.

ʊ 0 2137 Lovers' medal. Doves over two hearts. Rev.
Hands grasping a flaming heart, over a globe
broken asunder. German inscriptions. Bronze,
cast ; fine. 29.

/. 8 0 2138 Male and female heads with one body. Rev. Hands
joined, etc. Latin inscriptions. *Silver*, fine. 28.

/. ʊ-0 2139 Cuckold riding a cock. Rev. Chest. German inscriptions. *Silver* ; very good. 20.

8 ʃ- 2140 Doves cooing. Rev. Cock treading a hen. German inscription. Brass ; very good. 15.

/. / 0 2141 Cupid on a box. WEN DU NICHT TREU WILT SEIN.
. . . . Rev. The usual German emblem of
love. *Silver* ; fine. 14.

/ 8 2142 Doves cooing. Rev. As before. Copper, silvered ;
fine. 10.

.2 2143 Bronze spielmarks or jetons. Atalanta picking
up the apple and Moneta. Fine. 18.   2 pcs

ʊ- 0 2144 Bark in a storm. EMD. ASSECUR. COMP. 1772. Rev.
Female seated. BENE MERENTI. Early medal of
Insurance Co. *Silver ;* fine. 27.

ʃ-0 2145 A hand pointing to a fruit on plant, which the
Batavian lion is about to grasp. 1672. A JEHOVAH
HOC FACTVM EST, etc. Rev. Arms. Old Dutch
medal ; yellow bronze, cast. Fine. 25.

SPAIN, WEST INDIES, ETC.

ʊ-/0 2146 Busts jugata of Velasco and Gonzales. Rev. Explosion of powder magazine in fortress. IN MORRO
VIT GLOR JVNCT, 1763. Bronze ; fine. 30.

2147 Barbadoes. Medal commemorative of the hurricane, August 11, 1831. English inscription on each side, giving details of the awful calamity and of the help received, etc. *Silver ;* very fine and rare. 25.

2148 Mexico. Hemispheres with broken chains ; triple rings inscribed INDEPENDENCIA, UNION, RELIGION. Rev. Wreath. SECUNDA EPOCA. Copper ; fine. 31.

2149 Bust to right of Augustine, Emperor of Mexico. Rev. Inscription in 5 lines. 1823. Copper ; uncirculated. 25.

2150 Maximilian. War medal. Bust to right. Rev. AL MERITO MILITAR. Bronze ; loop. Fine. 20.

2151 Cornucopia and Mercury staff crossed before bouquet of Colonial products. BANCO DE BAHIA. Rev. Blank. Copper ; thick planchet ; fine and rare. 22.

2152 Agricultural trophy surmounted by the arms of Jamaica. THE CLARENDON CONSOLIDATED MINING COMPANY OF JAMAICA. Rev. Blank. Copper ; very fine. 35.

2153 Havana. 1858. Inauguration of the Havana-Matanzas railway. Building and inscription. W. m. proof. 24.

2154 Neptune driving a quadriga of sea-horses, a crowned shield in front. Rev. Inscription. Fine bronze medal struck on the opening of water-works at Havana, 1858. Rare, oval. 37x39.

2155 Statue on pedestal and inscription. Erection of the statue of Christopher Columbus at Havana, 1862. *Silver.* Fine and rare. Oval. 22x26.

2156 Three shields crowned. Rev. Shield surmounted by crest and inscription. Struck in honor of the arrival at Havana of Francisco Lersundi y Ormaechea, captain-general. 1867. Bronze ; very fine. 26.

2157 Bust of Amadeus. Rev. Rising sun between pillars and shields. War medal granted to Cuban volunteers, 1871. *Silver ;* oval, projecting border of oak and laurel branches, loop. Very fine and rare. 26x27.

2158 Havana Transportation Co. 1881. Steamer. Rev. Locomotive. *Silver* and copper proof. 12. 2 pcs.

2 ✓‾2159 Bust of Isabella II. Rev. Paschal lamb on rock. Award medal of the Royal Academy at Porto Rico. Oval ; fine, impression but damaged on border. *Silver.* 13x17.

/ 6 2160 The same. Copper ; uncirculated.

✓ 0 2161 Crowned shield. Rev. Books, globe, etc. Award Medal of the Faculty of Philosophy in the Royal University at Havana. *Silver* (?) ; fine and rare. 23.

✓ 0 2162 Award medal of the Royal College of Jesuits at Havana. Copper, fine and rare. 26.

2 7 2163 Crowned arms and Justice with scales. Bronze medal of Louis Susini é hijo, Havana. Fine. 36.

8 0 2164 c. r. s. & ca. Cigarette manufactury, Havana. Copper ; oval, very fine. 18x25.

/ ✓‾ 2165 Matanzas. Premium medal for application to studies. Copper ; uncir. 18.

✓‾J 2166 Santiago de Cuba. Inauguration of Gas Works, 1857. Inscription on either side. *Silver ;* nearly proof. 25.

/ / 2167 Birth medalets. 1862 and '78. Copper proof. Loops. 10 and 16.   2 pcs

2. 6 0 2168 Haiti. Military bust to left. alexander petion, died 1818. Brass shell ; fine, rare. 40.

6 0 2269 Military bust to right. j. p. boyer president d'haiti. Elected 1818. Copper shell ; fine, rare. 44.

/ 0 2170 Brazil. Military bust to left. petrus II. imperat. brasiliarum ; different reverses. 1841. W. m., one pierced ; fine. 26.   2 pcs

/. ✓ 0 2171 Sandwich Islands. Bust facing ; his majesty kamehameha IV. Rev. Bee-hive ; john thomas waterhouse importer, etc. W m. silvered. 22.

CATHEDRALS, CHURCHES, EDIFICES, ETC.

8 ✓‾2172 Bust of Pius IX. Rev. Interview of St. Paul's church. Massive electro. 52.

6. 0 2173 Bust of Joan Galeatius, founder of the Cathedral of Milan 1386. Rev. View of the Cathedral. Bronze ; artistic medal by *Broggi*, perfect. 30.

O 2174 Bust of Gaisruchius, archbishop. Rev. Cathedral of Milan. Bronze; fine. 28.

O 2175 Duplicate; same condition.

O 2176 Cathedral of Milan. Exterior and interior views. Bronze gilt; fine. 30.

O 2177 Busts jugata of Ferdinand I and Maria Anna of Austria crowned for Lombardy at Milan 1838. Rev. View of the cathedral. Bronze; perfect. 26.

S 2178 Exterior and interior views of the church of St. Ouen at Rouen, begun 1318, completed 1850. Bronze; fine. 37.

S 2179 Cathedral of Notre Dame, Paris. Exterior view; rev. interior plan and dimensions. Bronze; fine. 36.

O 2180 Cathedral of Chartres. Exterior view and inscription. Bronze; very fine. 30.

S 2181 Cathedral of Strasburg. Exterior view; rev. inscription. Silver; fine. 34.

O 2182 St. Stephen's Church, Ouen. Exterior and interior views. Bronze; very fine. 38.

O 2183 Bust of the duke of Orleans. Rev. Exterior view of St. Ferdinand memorial chapel, erected to his memory, 1843. Bronze; very fine. 32.

S 2184 Cathedral of Reims. Medalets. Varieties; cop. and brass. Fine. 15.   2 pcs

S 2185 Bust of Napoleon I. Rev. St. Stephen's Cathedral, Vienna, where thanksgivings for peace were offered, 1805. Bronze; very fine. 25.

S 2186 Cathedral at Cologne. Without and with spires. Bronze; very fine. 37.

S 2187 The same. Similar views. W. m.; proof. 28 and 32.   2 pcs

S 2188 St. Peter's Church, Hamburg. Exterior and interior views. Bronze; fine. 38.

S 2189 German Reformed Church, Hamburg. Exterior view and arms. Bronze; very fine. 26.

J 2190 Bust of E. G. Sonnin. Rev. Church of St. Michael, Hamburg. Bronze; very fine. 27.

O 2191 View of Church, 1342-1516. Rev. The same in ruins, 1842. On edge (German, *stamped from the copper of St. Peter's tower, Hamburg*). Very fine. 28.

2192 Busts jugata of Frederic William, Elector, and of Frederic William, King of Prussia. 1835. Rev. 150 ANNIVERSAIRE DE LA FONDATION DE L'ÉGLISE FRANÇAISE RÉFUGIÉE DE BERLIN in pentagon surrounded by 5 edifices. Bronze ; perfect. 26.

2193 Canterbury Cathedral. Exterior and interior views. Very fine bronze medal by *Davis.* 38.

2194 Ely Cathedral. Exterior and interior views. Very fine bronze medal by *Davis.* 38.

2195 Interior view of Oxford Cathedral. Rev. The martyr's memorial. Bronze ; very fine. 38.

2196 Gloucester penny token, 1797. Rev. View of the Cathedral and of St. Nicholas Church. Uncir.
2 pcs

2197 Penny token. View of St. Paul's Cathedral, London. 1794. Rev. " H. Young, dealer in coins," etc. Uncir.

2198 Western Congregational Church, Montreal. Exterior view and inscription, 1874. W. m., silvered ; proof. 28.

2199 Y. M. C. A. building, Montreal. Rev. Inscription. Bronze ; very fine. 28.

2200 Cathedral of St. Peter and St. Paul, Philadelphia. Exterior and interior views. 1864. W. m. Fine. 50.

2201 St. Peter and St. Paul, Phila. Rev. Harp, IN HONOR OF THE GRAND PARADE MARCH 18 1878 ; another with view of St. Patrick's Cathedral, N. Y. W. m. proof ; pierced. 18 and 20.
2 pcs

NUMISMATIC MEDALS.

2202 Bust laureate of Louis XV by *Roettiers* Rev. The royal mint. Paris, 1770. Bronze restrike ; nearly proof. 40.

2203 Large head to right by *Veyrat.* Rev. LES NUMISMATES À LEUR ILLUSTRE MAITRE J. LELEWEL, NÉ À VARSOVIE EN 1786. Bronze ; perfect, a rare medal. 32.

2204 Bust to left of Antoine Bovy, the Genevese diesinker by his son Hugues ; the names of his principal medals on reverse Bronze proof. 32.

2205 Bust of Pope VII by *Droz.* Rev. Cabinet of medals visited January 1805. Bronze ; very fine 26.

2206 The same ; silvered. Cast (?)

2207 Bust of queen Hortense to right, Greek style and inscription. Commemorates visit at the mint cabinet. Bronze ; a gem of medallic art. 14.

2208 Bust of Frederic William III, King of Prussia. Rev. Inscription commemorative of his visit at the French mint cabinet 1814. Bronze ; very fine. 25.

2209 Bust of Francis I, emperor of Austria. Rev. His visit to French mint cabinet 1814. Yellow bronze; very fine. 26.

2210 Busts jugata. Visit at the French mint by the king and queen of Bavaria. 1810. Bronze ; perfect. 25.

2211 Charles Philip of France, brother of Louis XVIII. Bust to left. Rev. Visit at French mint 1818. Yellow bronze ; fine. 82.

2212 Other medal, struck on the same occasion. Copper ; very fine. 24.

2213 Arms of Sicily crowned. Visit of the King and Queen of Two Sicilies at French mint. 1830. Bronze ; fine. 23.

2214 A monetary press between female figures and crowned arms of Portugal. Visit of Don Miguel of Portugal at French mint cabinet. 1824. Bronze ; perfect. 26.

2215 Bust of Louis Philippe. Visit at the Rouen mint. 1831. Copper ; fine, edge lettered as on 5 franc piece. 24.

2216 Similar obv. Rev. TONNELIER ATTELE DE LA PRESSE MONETAIRE 1833. Edge lettered. Copper ; fine. 24.

2217 Napoleon III. Bust to left by *Dantzell.* Rev. Recoinage of copper coins. 1852. Moneta presetting a coin to Art, seated at a coin press, etc. Bronze ; a beautiful medal. 43.

2218 Bust of empress Eugenia. Rev. Industrial Palace, Paris, 1855, within which this medal was struck. W. m. ; fine. 31.

2219 British Archaeological Association. 1843. Hand pouring oil in lamp of antique model. Rev. Shields, arms, etc., commemorative of important events in the Society. Bronze ; perfect. 29.

4 prs.

ᒐ Ѳ 2220 Andrew Fountaine, English antiquary and numismatist, 1680–1753. Bust and inscription. Fine electrotype. 34.

ᵟ Ѳ 2221 John Bell, English antiquary and numismatist, 1736–1770. Urn on monument and arms, etc. *Silver;* very fine. 22.

ᒑ˗ 2222 Arms and inscription. Copper token, halfpenny size, of William Till, coin dealer, London, 1834. Very fine.   2 pcs.

ᒋ 2223 Lutwyches manufactory, Birmingham. A coin press, etc. Penny (?) and farthing tokens. Fine. 2 pcs.

/. /Ѳ 2224 D. Uhlhorn's coining press, exhibited at London Exposition, 1851. Copper; fine 24.

// 2225 English numismatic medal. W. m.; fine. 28.

ᒑᒑ 2226 Coin press and arms. Seville mint visited by the King of Portugal. 1856. Varieties; copper, uncir. 23.   2 pcs.

/ᒋ˗ 2227 Medalet with bust of Melgarebo for introduction of steam press at Potosi, 1869. Copper; fine. 14.

/.2 2228 Members' medal of the American Numismatic and Archæol. Society, N. Y. W. m., fine. Rare. 26.

ᒑ˖Ѳ 2229 Bust of Jonn Allan, antiquary and numismatist. BORN 1777. Rev. The Antiquary, 1859. *Silver;* fine. 20.

/ Ѳ 2230 Same rev., muled with "Great Eastern" obv. Copper; fine. 20.

ᒉ 2231 Old man riding a broom. WE ALL HAVE OUR HOBBIES. Rev. DEDICATED TO COIN AND MEDAL COLLECTORS 1860, in wreath, etc. Copper, brass (3) and w. m. Very fine, 4 varieties. 18.   5 pcs.

ᒉ 2232 Robert Lovett, die sinker. Philadelphia. GOLD AND SILVER MEDALS, etc., and another Copper; fine. 9 and 20 (2).   3 pcs.

/ Ѳ 2233 W. D. Grimshaw, 15 Gold St., N. Y. Coin press and inscription. W m., fine. 24.

ᵟ Ѳ 2234 Numismatic and Archæological Society, Montreal, Canada. Society medal, 1870 Bronze; very fine. 27.

/ ᵟ 2235 Vienna Numismatic Society, 1880. Bust and inscription. Copper; fine, but name scratched in the field. 22.

2236 Old Jetons. Head of Sol, spitting out coins (the golden morning hour); Moneta with scales and cornucopia filled with coins, and token of the Berlin Numismatic Club, 1876. Copper; fine. 16.
3 pcs.

MEDALS OF AUTHORS, REFORMERS, ARTISTS, ETC.

2237 William Shakespeare. Bust to right, by *Westwood*. Rev. JUBILEE AT STRATFORD IN HONOR AND TO THE MEMORY OF SHAKESPEARE SEPT 1769. *Silver*; fine and rare, pierced near edge. 29.

2238 The same. Copper; fine. 26.

2239 Bust nearly facing. Rev. Mountain scenery, with ABOVE RULE OR ART. NAT 1564. Bronze; perfect. 26.

2240 Bust to hip facing. Rev. Birthplace of Shakespeare, as it appeared in 1842. Bronze; very fine. 24.

2241 Bust to left by *H. Brown*. Rev. Birthplace of Shakespeare as restored in 1864. Bronze; fine but pierced. 26.

2242 Bust to left by *Davis*. Rev. The house in which Shakespeare was born, etc. W. m. proof. 27.

2243 Bust to left by *Wyon*. Rev. MCGILL COLLEGE MONTREAL, SHAKSPERE TERCENTENARY 1864. Bronze; perfect. 28.

2244 Bust facing by *Ottley*. Rev. Birthplace of Shakespeare, etc. Struck for the tercentenary celebration 1864. W. m., fine. 32.

2245 Another. Bust to left and house. W. m., pierced. 19.

2245*a* Bust to left. Rev. Birthplace of Shakespeare. Copper; uncir. 14.

2246 Brass shell. Bust to left, in high relief. 2x3 in.; also silk badge, bust of Shakespeare in colors, issued on tercentenary celebration. Both very fine. 2 pcs.

2247 Benjamin West. Bust to left. Rev. Different inscriptions. Bronze; fine. 26. 2 pcs.

2248 Martinus Folkes. Rev. Pyramid. Bronze; fine. 24.

2249 Thomas Snelling. Bust to right by *Pingo*. Rev. OBIIT MDCCLXXIII, etc. Bronze; very fine. 25.

2250 C. J. Fox. *Series numismatica.* Bronze; very fine. 26.

2251 Bust to right. Rev. FRANCIS HENRY EGERTON EARL OF BRIDGEWATER. Bronze ; fine. 26.

2252 Gioachino Rosini. Bust in high relief to left by *Bovy.* Rev. NÉ LE 29 FÉVRIER 1792. Bronze proof. 38.

2253 Giovanni Belzoni. Bust to left by Wells. Rev. A pyramid. OPENED BY G BELZONI, MARCH 2ND 1818. Bronze ; very fine. 33.

2254 Rembrandt Hermansz Van Ryn. Portrait bust to left. Rev. His celebrated painting, " La Ronde de Nuit." ~~Bronzed electrotype equal in appearance to an original.~~ 68.

2255 J. J. Rousseau. Seated figure from his statue at Geneva. Rev. Mortuary inscription. Very fine bronze medal by *Bovy.* 38.

2256 The same. Bust to left. Rev. Extract from one of his works. Bronze; fine. 22.

2257 Merle d'Aubigné. Portrait bust to right by *Bovy* Rev. Extracts in German, French and English, from the works or sayings of three great reformers, Luther, Calvin and Knox. A beautiful medal; bronze proof. 38.

2258 John Calvin. Bust with old features to left. Rev. Inscription in Gothic portico. Another masterpiece by *Bovy.* Bronze proof. 38.

2259 J. Wolfgang Goethe. Bust in high relief to right by *Bovy.* Rev. Janus' head, old and young features, surmounted by an eagle; a lion's head below, a cornucopia on each side. Bronze proof. 26.

2260 The same obv. Rev. Flying eagle bearing a wreath. Bronze proof. 26.

2261 Ludwig Beethoven. Large portrait bust, in high relief, nearly facing. Rev. Mortuary inscription. Fine bronze proof medal by *Bovy.* 38.

2262 Richard Wagner. Head to right by *Wiener.* Rev. Group of personages from one of his compositions. Bronze; very fine. 44.

2263 Isaac Pitman. Short-hand inventor and writer. Bust nearly facing. Rev. Short-hand inscription in wreath. 1837. Tin; fine. 28.

2264 Naked bust of Aphrodite by *Bovy*. Rev. Cupid seated on a shell, grasping a butterfly. Bronze proof. 28.

2265 Mr. and Mrs. Florence. Rev. "100th night of of the Mighty Dollar." W. m., very fine. 27.

2266 The same. Rev. SOUVENIR. THE MIGHTY DOLLAR. *Silver* ; fine, dollar size.

MEDALS OF PHYSICIANS, SCIENTISTS, ETC.

2267 William Cheselden. English surgeon and anatomist 1688–1752. Bust. Rev. Body prepared for dissection. s THOMAS HOSPITAL in exergue. Bronzed electro; very fine. 46.

2268 Sir Benj. C. Brodie. English surgeon 1783–1862. Bust to left. Rev. Naked female in chemical laboratory. Bronzed electro ; very fine. 46.

2269 Robert Liston. English surgeon, 1784–1847. Bust and inscription. Bronze ; perfect. 27.

2270 A. Fothergill. English physician. Rev. Health feeding a serpent entwined around a burning altar. Fine bronze medal of the London Medical Society. 28.

2271 Bust of Queen Charlotte to left. Rev. Health feeding a serpent : similar to last. Bronze; fine. 26

2272 Bust to left of George Heriot. Rev. PRESENTED BY THE GOVERNORS OF GEORGE HERIOT'S HOSPITAL: etc; name of recipient and date, 1842, engraved. *Silver*; very fine. 28.

2273 Award medal of the Pharmaceutic Society of London, 1841, bust of Galen on obverse. Bronze; perfect. 28.

2274 Bust of J. C. Saunders, founder of the Royal London Ophthalmic Hospital, 1804. Greek inscription on reverse. Bronze proof. 21.

2275 Bust of Henry Quinn, M.D. Rev. Blank. Bronze; very fine. 25.

2276 Bust of Richard Carmichael. School of Anatomy, etc. award medal. Electrotype; fine. 44.

2277 Sir William Browne, Physician and Writer, 1692–1774. Bust to left. Rev. Inscription commemorative of his election as a fellow of the London Medical Colleges, etc. Bronze, very fine. 22.

1. o-o 2278 Peter Clare, English surgeon. Bust. Rev. ARTEM MEMENDI REMED : ORE ABSORPT INV ET DIVLG A: D: 1779. Very fine bronze medalet, by *Holloway*. 20.

6 0 2279 Edward Jenner, discoverer of vaccination. 1749–1823. Bust; rev. Allegorical representation of safety against disease by vaccination. Fine bronze medal by *Loos;* German inscriptions. 17.

1. o-o 2279a Albert Isaiah Coffin. Founder of the system of Medical Botany in England. Bust facing. Rev. Inscription in wreath. 1849. Bronze; very fine. 30.

3 0 2279b Bust of James Cook, English navigator. Rev. Brittania leaning on oar and capstan. English Royal Society medal. Bronze ; fine. 27.

3 0 2280 Orphan Asylum at Wanstead. Rev. INSTITUTED 1827, etc. Bronze; very fine. 30.

1. o-o 2281 Madras Medical School. Johnstone Award medal. 1848. Copper; very fine. 24.

y o 2282 School of Medicine, London Hospital. Award medal. Bronze ; very fine. 24.

7 o 2283 Medical College, Madras. English arms. Rev. GOVERNMENT MEDAL 2ND DRESSERS PRIZE ESSAY. Copper ; very fine. 20.

2 2 2284 Token. VAUXHALL SICK SOCIETY FOUNDRY Rev. Blank. Copper; good. 22.

1 2 2285 Montrose halfpenny, 1799. Rev. View of the Montrose Lunatic Hospital. 1781. Good.

3 2286 Bust of Spolasko, "the friend of the afflicted," etc., 1838. Brass tokens, farthing size. Fine. 2 pcs

3 2287 Duplicate ; also Prof. Holloway's token. Fine. 2 pcs

1. o-o 2288 George Cuvier. French naturalist. 1769–1832. Bust in high relief to left by *Bory* Rev. Inscription. Bronze ; very fine. 42.

6 5 2289 Allegorical representation of Medicine relieving sickness. Rev. Inscription. Fine bronze medal in honor of the 5 French physicians who lost their lives in Barcelona, during the prevalence of the pestilence, 1821. 30.

5 5 2290 Æsculapius with wand protecting a naked female, a cow in the field ; LA VACCINE MDCCCIV. Rev. Name of recipient engraved in wreath. Bronze ; fine. 25.

2291 Snake wound around a chemical retort AU SOU-
LAGEMENT DE L'HUMANITÉ. Rev. Wreath of
medical plants. Bronze; very fine. 24.

2292 Ambroise Paré. French surgeon. 1517-1590. *Gallerie métallique;* bronze, fine. 26.

2293 Jean Fernel. French mathem. and phys. 1497-
1558. Bronze; fine. 26.

2294 J. I. Guillotin. French physician and inventor.
1738-1814. Bust and inscription. Bronze medalet; fine. 18.

2295 Edm. Cl. Bourru. French physician. Bust by
Duvivier and inscription. Copper; fine. 18.

2296 J. Car. Hen. Salin Grayaeus. French physician.
Bust by *Duvivier* and crowned arms. 1784-1785.
Copper; fine. 18.

2297 Head to right. XAVIER BICHAT. Rev Wand of
Æsculapius. SOCIÉTÉ MÉDICALE. etc. 1807.
Bronze; very fine. 17.

2298 Brass jetons of Mayence "médecin dentiste" and
——"artiste pédicure." Fine. 12 and 14. 2 pcs

2299 Head of Æsculapius. Rev. SOCIÉTÉ DE MÉDE-
CINE. etc., 1808. Tin; good. 14.

2300 Bust of Galen. Rev. Minerva feeding a serpent.
SOCIÉTÉ DE PHARMACIE DE LYON. 1806. *Silver ;*
very fine. 20.

2301 Silver token of the Pharmaceutic Society of the
Seine. 1824. Octagonal; very fine. 20.

2302 Bernard de Jussieu. French botanist. 1699-1777.
Gallerie métallique. Bronze; very fine. 26.

2303 Head to left. C. L. J. L. Bonaparte. 1803-1857.
Rev A CHARLES BONAPARTE LES AMIS DE LA
SCIENCE in wreath. Bronze; very fine. 32.

2304 John Caspar Lavater. Swiss physiognomist. 1741
-1801. *Swiss numismatica.* Bronze; very fine.
26.

2305 Bust of Charles Ferdinand. Grand-son of Louis
XIII. by *Gayrard.* Rev. Beautifully executed
naked male figure leaning against a funeral monument. SOCIETAS ARTIBUS AMICA PATRONO. etc.
Bronze; fine and artistic medal. 31.

2306 Simon Labin. Belgian physician. Large bust to
right. Rev Inscription. 1845. Bronze; perfect.
31

6 0 2307 Charles Rogier. Belgian Minister of State. Large
bust to right by *Wiener*. Rev. Allegorical representation of the promotion of public health in
Belgium, 1852. Bronze ; very fine. 42.

2 5 2308 Academy of Medicine of Belgium. Female seated
and inscription. Bronze ; very fine. 26.

4 5 2309 Full figure of Æsculapius with wand. Rev. Arms
of Amsterdam on label engraved *Petras Louren-
tius* ; Latin legends. Old bronze medal ; cast.
Very fine and rare. 30.

4 5 2310 Cupid with gardener's tools protecting a tree from
Boreas' furious attack. Rev. I. S. B in mono-
gram. LA NATURE ET L'AMITIÉ AU TALENT 1821.
Bronze ; very fine. 31.

9 0 2311 Aug. Hermann Niemeyer. Austrian physician,
and author of a work on phthisis. 1754-1827.
Bust by *Loos* and allegorical figures. Bronze ;
fine. 30.

1. 2 0 2312 Arms of Austria, crowned. Rev. Disabled soldier
at the foot of a trophy, and distant view of the
Invalids' Home. PROVIDENTIA AVGVSTAE and
MILES EMERITUS CONDIGNE NUTRITUS MDCCL.
Medal in honor of the military hospital founded
by Maria Theresa. *Silver*, gilt ; fine. 38.

6 5 2313 Medical Lyceum of the ancient town of Ladera now
Zera in Dalmatia, issued during the occupation of
the town by the French in 1809. LYCAEUM LADE-
RENSE in wreath, MDCCCIX. Rev. The wand or
caduceus of Æsculapius. NAPOLEONE MAGNE
IMPERANTE. Copper, silvered ; fine and very rare.
29.

9 0 2314 Joannes Freind. Member of the London Medical
College, etc. Naked bust to left, with flowing
hair. Rev. Two figures, representing old and
new medical schools, grasping hands. Fine old
bronze medal. 36.

0 0 2315 Adolph Occo. German physician and numismatist.
1524-1605. Rev. IACTA CVRAM TVAM IN DOMINO,
etc. Lead : fine. 40.

2 0 2316 Karl von Rotteck. German historian and jurist.
1775-1840. Rev. LICHT UND RECHT in wreath.
Bronze ; fine. 21.

2317 View of Hospital Buildings. NASOCOMIVM above. Rev. Draped figure dissecting a human body in a grove of trees. SEXCENTOS EXSECVIT VT NATVRAM SCEVTARETVR. Bronze; very fine and old award medal. 31.

2318 Christian W. Huffeland. German physician. 1762–1836. Bust to right. Rev. Allegorical representation of the relief of sickness. *Silver*; very fine. 26.

2319 Thirty-second Congress of German scientists and physicians at Vienna, 1856. Elaborate design; bronze. Very fine. 44.

2320 Johann Wendt. German philosopher and physician. 1783–1836. Bust to left by *Loos*. Rev. A snake twined about a wand drinks from an urn an altar ornamented with small head of Hippocrates, an owl to right. (German) "The greatest wisdom is to be a true man." Bronze proof. 26.

2321 Henry Meyer. German physician. Bust by *Loos*. Rev. Similar to last; the inscription commemorates the artist's thankfulness for successful medical treatment by Meyer, in 1819. Bronze; very fine. 25.

2322 D. E. Gunther. German physician. Draped bust to left by *Loos*, and inscriptions. 1822. *Silver*; very fine. 26.

2323 Van Hende. Dutch physician. 1738–1819. Head to left, Æsculapius' wand behind it. Rev. Inscription in wreath. Tin; fine. 26.

2324 J. Ar. Jos. Buettner. Assist. medical director of cavalry, Prussian army. Rev. Emblematical of continued services for 25 years. 1835. Bronze; perfect. 30.

2325 Head of Jo. Wm. de Wiebel. Medical director of cavalry, Prussian army. Rev. Æsculapius inscribing a monument, trophy to left, etc. 25 years' services, 1834. Bronze; perfect. 50.

2326 J. C. J. Lohmeyer. Medical director, etc., Prussian army. Bust to right. Rev. Æsculapius seated pointing to a soldier in classical garb, an inscribed tablet above. "25 years' service," etc. 1850. Bronze; very fine. 30.

2327 Jo. Stieglitz. German physician, etc. 1767–1820. Bust and inscription. Rev. Æsculapius hanging a wreath inscribed STIEGLITZ to temple of fame. Bronze; perfect. 30.

6 0 2328 Christopher Knape. German physician and jurist.
1747–1823. Head to left. Rev. Justice and Æsculapius at an altar, etc. Bronze; perfect. 26.

/ /5⁻ 2329 Samuel Hahnemann, German homœopathist. 1755–
1843. Fine portrait bust to right by *Rogat*. Rev.
SIMILIA SIMILIBUS CURENTUR, and inscription in
French commemorating his visit in Paris, 1835.
Bronze; perfect. 32.

6 0 2340 The same. Head to left and shield with monogram ;
English and Latin inscriptions. Fine bronze
medal, struck in England, 1842. 26.

5⁻0 2341 The same. Bust to left. Award medal of the Hahneman Medical College, Philadelphia. Bronze,
very fine. 28.

/2 2342 Another ; from the same dies as last. W. m.;
proof. 28.

// 2343 Same obv. Rev. Blank. W. m.; fine. 28.

/.2 0 2344 Alexander von Humboldt. Head to right, by
Brandt. Rev. The sun driving a quadriga over 6
signs of the zodiac, allegorical figures below. Berlin, 1828. Bronze; perfect. 40.

5⁻ 2345 The same. Head to left. Rev. Inscription in 7
lines within wreath of oak. Bronze; perfect. 36.

2.0-0 2346 The same. Bust to left by *Loos*. Rev. Humboldt
seated, looking at a map of the Western continent.
NOVI ORBIS DEMOCRITUS. Struck on the occasion
of his return from explorations in America. 1805.
Silver ; fine. 24.

/5⁻ 2347 The same. Large head to right by *Paquet*. Rev.
EARTH AND HEAVEN HE EXPLORED, etc. W. m.
bronzed; fine. 32.

/. 0-0 2348 Henry Meyer, German physician. Bust to left.
Rev. A snake forming a circle, within which AN
DENKEN AN DANIEL LOOS BERLIN 1819. *Silver ;*
very fine. 25.

6 0 2349 Bust to right. ANDREAS LIBER BARON STIFFT.
Rev. Heavy wreath of oak and laurel and inscription commemorative of his 50th anniversary as a
practicing physician. 1824. Bronze; perfect. 32.

/. 2 0 2350 Christian Daniel Beck. German antiq. and historian. 1757–1832. Bust to left and inscription.
Silver ; very fine. 24.

/ 25⁻ 2351 Draped bust to right. JOANNIS BARTHOL. TROMMS
DORFII. In exergue SEMISECVLARIA PHARMACEV
TICA 1834. Rev. Pharmaceutist and pupils at
work in laboratory, etc. *Silver ;* very fine. 27.

2352 Bust to right. MAXIMIL. HI. BOIOR. DUX EL.ECT.
Rev. SAT 1727 INSTITUTO REI METALLICAE COL-
LEGIO, etc. Tin ; fine. 24.

2353 Charles Linnaeus, Swedish naturalist. 1707–1778.
Bust to right and inscription. Rev. ILLUSTRAT in
radiant sun over 3 crowns. *Silver* ; very fine impression. 24.

2354 The same. *Series numismatica.* Bronze ; fine. 26.

2355 C. L. Giesecke. Naturalist. Bust to right. Rev.
Arctic scenery and inscription commemorative of
his prolonged sojourn in high latitudes. 1817.
Bronze ; fine. 26.

2356 Aloysius Sacco. Italian physician. Bust to left.
Rev. Inscription in heavy wreath of oak : a snake
coiled around the stems at the bottom. Bronze ;
very fine. 35.

2357 Duplicate. Same metal and condition. 35.

2358 I. B. Morgagnus, Italian physician. 1682–1771. Bust
in robes by *Luckner*. Rev. Æsculapius with wand
between a childish figure and an owl on human
head. PROXIMOS OCCVPAVIT HONORES. Fine
bronze medal of characteristic workmanship.
1771. 32.

2359 Same obverse. Rev. Figures of Pallas & Æsculapius. 1770. Lead ; good. 32.

2360 Marcellus Malpighius, Italian anatomist. 1628–
1694. Bust to left. Rev. Female reclining on a
monument. TVTISSIMO. LVMINE. EXHIBITO.
Bronze ; very fine. 22.

2361 Same obv. Rev. Bust of Hieronymus Sbaralba,
and inscription. Bronze ; very fine. 22.

2362 Bust and inscription as in last reverse. Rev. Prun-
ing knife suspended to tree. INVTILES AMPVTANS.
Bronze ; very fine. 22.

2363 J. Baglivus. Italian physician and anatomist. 1668–
1707. Bust to right and inscription. Rev. VNAM
FACIEMVS VERAMQVE. Bronze ; very fine. 25.

2364 The same obv. Rev. Bust of Marcellus Malpighius
and inscription. Bronze ; very fine. 25.

2365 Vincenzo Chio. Italian homœopathic physician,
died 1846. Bust and inscription in wreath.
Bronze ; very fine. 27.

2366 Hospital at Pisa, restored, 1830. Benevolence
tending a cripple, view of the buildings in the distance. Rev. Piety, etc. Bronze ; fine. 35.

*3 S -*2367 River-god crowning a turreted female. VINDOBONA
PHYSIOLOGIS. 1832. Rev. XAIPEIN in wreath.
Bronze ; fine. 26.

4 0 2368 Bust of W. N. Boylston to left. Rev. Blank.
Award medal, medical school. Harvard University. Bronze ; very fine. 28.

1. 3 0 2369 Joseph Pancoast. American anatomist, born 1805.
Bust in high relief to left by *Barber*. Rev. Inscription in heavy wreath of oak and olive. Very
fine bronze medal. 48.

J U- 2370 Portrait bust, head turned to right. PROF. C. P.
BRONSON, A. M. M. D. Rev. Inscription in 14 lines
beginning with THIS MEDAL IS PRESENTED TO PRO-
FESSOR C. P. BRONSON M. D. BY HIS EYE PATIENTS,
etc. Bronze ; fine medal by *Wright*. 36.

1. 2 S- 2371 Bust to left. BENJAMIN RUSH M: D: OF PHILADEL-
PHIA. Rev. Landscape, etc. MDCCCVIII. Fine
bronze medal by *Furst*. 26.

1. 2 S- 2372 Same obv. Rev. Book on an altar. SYDENHAM
MDCCCVIII. Red bronze ; fine. *Furst*. 20.

1 S 2373 Head to right. DAVID HOSACK M. D. Rev. ARTS
AND SCIENCE. Bronze ; very fine. 21.

3 0 2374 Award medal of the Medical department, University of New York, founded 1856. Bust of Dr.
Valentine Mott and inscription. W. m., fine.
22.

1. 0 S- 2375 Bust of Hippocrates (?). *S. Schmidt f. N. O.* s.
M—C. L. Rev SOCIETAS MEDICO-CHIRURGICAE
LUDOVICENSIS. *Silver ;* fine. 20.

J 2376 Eagle in a circle of stars. Rev. ROYAL PREVENTA-
TIVE. Cast. 14.

3 0 2377 Robert S. Newton, M. D., Professor of surgery
1876. Rev. Eclectic Medical College, etc. Bronze ;
very fine. 24.

S-0 2378 Award medal of the Alumni Association, College
of Pharmacy, City of New York, instituted 1871.
Hand pouring oil into a lamp of antique model
and inscription. Bronze proof. 32.

MISCELLANEOUS.

2379 George III. 1819. Pistrucci crown ; uncirculated.

2380 Bust to right of William Ellery Channing, D.D. Rev. "Rejected design for prize medal of University of Glasgow ; dies purchased by and 25 impressions struck for Henry W. Holland, Esq., of Boston, Mass. Pres. by him to Isaac F. Wood of N. Y.," *engraved. Silver ;* proof. 28.

2381 View of Capitol, 33 stars in curving lines above. CITY OF WASHINGTON 1860. UNION. Trial impression on thin lead planchet. 30.

2382 Bust of Martha Washington. Trial impression on large lead pl. of the 1876 centennial reception, N. Y.

2383 Radiant star filled with minute stars. "Struck in the Centennial building in the one hundredth year of American Independence, 1876." Lead planchet ; unique. 24.

2384 Head of Liberty to left. JUSTITIA AMERICANA 1874. Lead pl. 22.

2385 Trial and incuse impressions of rare medals, chiefly American. Cop., lead, etc. 7 pcs

2386 Medalet with bust of Carl Ekeberg, Swedish oriental traveler 1716-1784. Tin ; thick and fine. 14.

2387 Trophy before landscape, a fort to right. HOSTIS HISP. AN. PROFLIGAT. Rev. Dedicatory inscription in 13 lines to Christoph Artishau. SOCIETAS AMERICANA 1637. Tin, cast. 40.

2388 Building. SOCIETAS ALUMNORUM SCHOLÆ DUMHERENSIS 1822. Rev. CREDE UT POSSE UT POTES. Lead. 23.

2389 Washington, Wesley, Louis Philip, etc. Profile busts ; copper shells. Fine. 30 to 58 in length. 6 pcs

2390 Washington on horseback ; Liberty bell. Rev. "That old State House Bell is silent," etc., Centennial 1876. Compressed wood ; square. 44x64. 2 pcs

2391 Centennial plates. Busts of Lincoln and Washington (2 colors) ; alphabet on border. Diam. 7 in. 3 plates.

2392 Academic medal of Bewick, Maine. Bust to left.
EX DONO GULIEMI LAMBERT COGSWELL. Rev:
Arms in wreath, above which a radiant star and
a hand in cloud reaching a burning torch to an
extended hand; below the wreath a label inscribed DEI TIMOR INITIUM SAPIENTIAE. Bronze:
very fine and I believe unpublished. Oval.
23x28.

2393 Engraved medal. A hound at the foot of crowned
harp. "Honor to whom honor is due." Rev.
"Presented to John Leahy by the members of
the Mathewite sons, etc. 1854. *Silver;* raised
border, loop. Fine. 45.

2394 Ship in a gale. TAYLEUR FUND FOR THE SUCCOUR
OF SHIPWRECKED STRANGERS. Rev. Blank.
Bronze; fine. 28.

2395 1871. Annual assay medal. Bronze proof. 21.

2396 John Adams. Peace medal. 1797. Bronze; fine.
32.

COIN AND MEDAL CABINETS.

2397 Medal cabinet. Solid black walnut, polished ornamental frame; exterior dimensions 32 in. high, 40
wide, 24 deep. Contains 18 drawers, cloth lined,
each partitioned in the centre, movable slats, and
of sufficient depth for the thickest medals; double
door with sliding hinge and lock. In perfect
order, and a valuable cabinet for a large collection
or for dealer's stock.

2398 Coin cabinet. Solid black walnut. 25 in. high, 19
wide, and 15 deep. Contains 18 drawers, velvet-
lined, with and without fixed partitions. The
top is movable, on hinges. Double door, in perfect order.

2399 Coin and medal cabinet. Solid black walnut frame,
in four sections, three below, and one above in the
centre, each section with double door. Total
length 45 in., height 30 in., depth 17½ in. The
three lower sections contain each 20 drawers, the
upper one 16, all with movable partitions and
double porcelain knobs. The cabinet rests on a
solid black walnut table 20 in. high, and of suitable width and depth. In perfect condition.

2400 Hard wood spool case, suitable for a small medallic
collection. Height 12 in., width 15 and depth
21. 5 drawers, porcelain knobs, no lock.

2400*a*. Military bust in high relief to right ; *Halliday's.*
under the shoulder. GEORGE WASHINGTON PRESI-
DENT OF THE UNITED STATES. Rev. Draped altar,
the American shield embossed on one end. A
sword, the fasces and a wreath above. COMMISSION
RESIGNED : PRESIDENCY RELINQUISHED. 1797.
Silver; a splendid and excessively rare medal, obtained in Europe some three years ago. 35.

The only other *silver* specimen known was sold by Mr. Hamilton
in the Crosby sale. It was then considered to be unique and catalogued as such. Limited at $100 —— and the only piece in the
entire catalogue not the property of Mr. Wood.

NUMISMATIC LIBRARY.

—

1.40 2401 **A**BBOTT, C. C. Stone Age in New Jersey. 223
figures. 8vo, half morocco   Wash. 1877

4√‑ 2402 ADAM, A. Roman Antiquities, including Money.
8vo, sheep   N. Y. 1814

2.62 2403 AKERMAN, J. Y. Descriptive Catalogue of rare
and unedited Roman Coins. Numerous plates
from the originals. 2 vols, 8vo   Lond. 1834

60 2404 ——— Guide to Study of Greek, Roman and
English Coins. 1st edition. Plate from originals.
16mo, cloth   Lond. 1832

1.80 2405 ——— Observations on Coinage of the Ancient
Britons. 21 pp. (2 plates inserted.) 4to. half
morocco   Lond. 1837

3.5√‑ 2406 ——— Ancient Coins of Cities and Princes; His-
pania, Gallia, Britania. 24 plates. 8vo
    Lond. 1846

2.30 2407 ——— Numismatic Manual. 17 plates. 8vo
    Lond. 1840

2.10 2408 ——— Tradesmen's Tokens, current in London and
its vicinity between 1648 and 1672. 8 plates. 8vo
    Lond. 1849

8√‑ 2409 ——— List of Tokens issued by Wiltshire Tradesmen. Plate. 8vo, half roan   Lond. 1846

4.5‑0 2410 ——— Numismatic Journal. Plates and woodcuts.
2 vols. 8vo, half roan   Scarce   Lond. 1836-8

30 2411 ——— Numismatic Chronicle. Nos. 64 and 66, '7,
'8, '9 and 70 (1854-55); also, The Chronicle, Nos.
65 and 66, 1877. Together, 8 Nos.   Lond.

2/3 2412 ——— Numismatic Illustrations of the Narrative
Portions of the New Testament. 58 woodcuts
8vo, cloth   Lond. 1846

2413 American Antiquarian. By C. De F. Burns. 9
Nos. 1870–74

2414 —— Antiquarian Society Proceedings; Special
Meeting, March 16, 1866, &c. Article on Paper
Money of Massachusetts, &c. 8vo, half morocco

2415 —— Journal of Numismatics. Vol. 11 complete. Nos. 2, 3 and 4 of Vol. 12; Nos. 2, 3 and
4 of Vol. 13; Vol. 14 complete; Nos. 1, 2 and 3
of Vol. 15; and No. 1 of Vol. 16. Together 18
Nos.

2416 Ainslie (General). Illustrations of the Anglo-
French Coinage. With Supplement. Also Sale
Catalogue of Gen. Ainslie's Cabinet, in one vol.,
9 plates, 4to, cloth Lond. 1830–47

2417 —— Another copy. In 2 vols. 4to 1830–47

2418 Anglo-Saxon Coins. Catalogus Nummorum
Antiquorum. A *manuscript copy* from Hicksii
Thesaurus. Thin folio, paper

2419 Ansell, G. F. The Royal Mint; its Working,
Conduct and Operations fully and practically
explained. With engravings. 4, cl. Lond. 1871

2420 Axmon, C. E. "The Gloriam Regni," or Silver
Louis of 15 sous, and of 5 sous. 8 pp. 8vo, paper

2421 Appleton, W. S. Description of Medals of Washington. Royal 8vo, half morocco Bost. 1873

2422 Arbuthnot, Chas. Tables of Ancient Coins,
Weights and Measures explained and exemplify'd.
4to, vellum Lond. 1727

2423 Archæological Institute Meeting at Winchester,
1845. 8vo (Broken copy)

2424 Arthur, Wm. The Antiquarian. Vol. 3. 8vo.
Rare Lansingburgh, N. Y., 1847.

2425 Armistead, W. Anthony Benezet from the Original Memoir. Plate of Indian Medal, 1757. 16mo
Lond. 1850

2426 Aurelii Victoris Historiæ Romanæ Breviarum;
also Viræ Imperatorum. Numerous portraits from
gems, &c. 8vo, old calf 1770

2427 Axford, J. Explanation of Coins, Money,
Weights, &c., of the Bible. 16mo, paper 1773

2428 **BARGAGLIUS.** Dell' Imprese di Scipion Bara-
gagli alla prima Parte, la Seconda e la Terza
nuouamente aggiunte. Numerous fine and curious
copper-plate engravings of *emblems*. Small 4to,
half turkey   In Venetia, 1594

2429 BARINGIUS, D. E. Clavis Diplomatica, Specimina
Veterum Scripturarum tradens, alphabeta nimirum
varia, medii ævi compendia scribendi, etc., singula
Fabulis æneis expressa. 4to, old calf
                                        Hanoveræ, 1754
Valuable volume, comprising explanations of the old manner of
writing, with plates.

2430 BARTHELEMY. Manuel de Numismatique Moderne.
Atlas of 12 folded plates. Small oblong sheep.

2431 BAYERIUS, FR. P. De Numis Hebræo-Samaritanis.
Plates of coins, alphabets, &c., and other illustra-
tions, including a superbly engraved portrait of
Charles III. of Spain. 4to, blue mor. Valentia, 1781

2432 BECKER, W. G. Zweihundert seltene Munzen des
Mittelalters, mit historischen Erläuterungen. 7
plates. 4to, half calf   Dresden, 1813

2433 BEGER, L. Thesaurus. Electoralis Brandenbur-
gicus selectus. 3 vols in 2. Folio, vellum
                                        Coloniæ. 1696
Description of the valuable collection of the Bradenburg Electors.
Gems and Coins. Numerous copper-plate illustrations. Rare.

2434 BELGIUM. Revue de la Numismatique Belge. 4
vols, 8vo, half turkey. 1842-48

2435 BELLORI, GIO. P. L'Historia Augusta da Gulio
Cesare a Constantino il Magno. Illustrata con la
verita dell' Antiche Medaglie. Numerous plates,
several leaves slightly damaged. Folio, boards
                                        In Roma, 1685

2436 BETHAM, SIR WM. Etruscan Literature and Antiquities investigated. Illustrations, including over
30 plates of coins. 2 vols, 8vo, half turkey
                                        Dublin, 1842

2437 BIBLIOTHECA LITERARIA: being a Collection of Inscriptions, Medals, Dissertations, &c. 10 Nos. in
1 vol. Small 4to, vellum   Lond. 1822-24

2438 BIZOT. Histoire Metallique de la République de
Hollande. Engraved title and numerous fine copper-plate representations of medals. Folio, half
morocco   Paris, 1687

2439 BLAKE, WM. P. The Production of the Precious
Metals. With a chapter on the Unification of
Gold and Silver Coinage. 8vo. N. Y. 1869

2440 BLOCHMANN, H. Contributions to the Geog. and
Hist. of Bengal (Muhammadan Period 1203-1538).
6 plates and 2 woodcuts (of coins, &c.) 8vo, half
morocco. Calcutta, 1873

2441 BOLZENTHAL, H. Skizzen zur Kunstgeschichte
der modernen Medaillen—Arbeit (1429-1840.) 30
copper-plates. 8vo, boards Berlin, 1840

2442 BOMPOIS, F. Restitution à Pergame de quelques
monnaies attribuées à Mytilene. 8vo, half morocco 1863

2443 ——— Lettre sur Deux Médailles Grecques Iné-
dites. 8vo, half morocco 1863

2444 ——— Remarques sur les Monnaies d'Argent de
l'Ile de Rhodes. 8vo, half morocco 1864

2445 ——— Des Médailles restituées à Lyncus, ou Hér-
chée de Lyncestide. 8vo, half morocco 1867

2446 ——— Etude Historique et Critique des Portraits
attribués à Cleomène III, Roi de Lacedemone. 8vo,
half morocco 1870

2447 ——— Notice sur un Dépot de Monnaies Carlovin-
giennes découvert aux environs du Venillin. 8vo,
half morocco 1871

2448 ——— Les Types Monétaires de la Guerre Sociale.
Etude Numismatique. 4to, half morocco 1873

2449 BONNEVILLE, P.-F. Traité des Monnaies d'Or et
d'Argent qui circulent chez les différens peuples.
Copper-plates representing a large number of
European Coins. Folio, sheep Paris, 1806

2450 BOWRING, JOHN. The Decimal System. 120
engravings of Coins. 12mo, cloth Lond. 1854

2451 BOYD, A. A Lincoln Bibliography. Books, Ser-
mons, Portraits, *Medals*. &c. Portrait and facsimile. 8vo, half calf Albany, 1870

2452 BOYNE, WM. Tokens issued in the Seventeenth
Century in England, Wales and Ireland. 42 plates.
8vo, half calf Lond. 1858

2453 ——— Tokens issued in Yorkshire in 17th. 18th
and 19th Centuries. 6 plates. Square 8vo, cloth
Headingley, 1858

2454 ——— Silver Tokens of Great Britain and Ireland,
Colonies, &c. 7 plates. Square 8vo, cloth
Lond. 1866

/. 6 2 2455 BRANDSENBURG, F. I. Nederlandsche Gedenk-Penningen. 10 plates. Small 4to, boards. Utrecht

/ 7.5' 2456 BREEK, S. Historical Sketch of Continental Paper Money. 8vo, half roan   Phil. 1863

/.2 J-0 2457 BURKE, B. The Book of Orders of Knighthood and Decorations of Honour of All Nations. With facsimile coloured illustrations. 8vo, cloth, gilt
        Lond. 1858

2. J 0 2458 BURN, J. H. A Descriptive Catalogue of the London Traders, Tavern and Coffee-House Tokens current in the 17th Century (the Beaufoy Cabinet). 4 plates of Portraits, &c. *2d edition.* 8vo, half calf   1853

/. 6 0 2459 ——— Do. do. 1st edition. 8vo, half calf   1853

4. 2 J' 2460 BUSHNELL, C. I. An Arrangement of Tradesmen's Cards, Political Tokens, Election Medals, &c. With engravings. 8vo, russia, gilt   N. Y. 1858

/. / 2 2461 ——— Historical Account of the First Three Business Tokens issued in N. Y. City. Plate. 12mo, half roan   1859

J-0 2462 ——— Do. do. Another copy, in paper cover

3. 0-0 2463 **CAMDEN, WM.** Britannia, newly translated, with large additions. Folio, old calf. Portrait, maps and plates of Roman, old British and Saxon coins. (Binding broken)   Lond. 1695

2. J-0 2464 CANADIAN Antiquarian and Numismatic Journal. Vols. 1, 2 and 3, half calf, and Vol. 4 in Nos. 4 vols. 1872–75

3 0 2465 ——— Nos. 2, 3, and 4 of Vol. 5. Nos. 3 and 4 of Vol. 7. No. 1. of Vol. 9. 6 Nos.

/. 3 7 2466 ——— Vols. 6 and 8, in Nos. 1877 and 1879

/. 0-0 2467 CARDONNEL ADAM DE. Numismata Scotiæ, or a Series of the Scottish Coinage. (14 plates, several missing and other leaves torn and soiled.) 4to, half morocco   Edinburgh, 1786

J 0 2468 CARDWELL, ED. Lectures on Coinage of Greeks and Romans. 8vo   Oxford, 1832

8. 0 0 2469 CARTER, THOS. Medals of the British Army, and how they were won. *Colored plates.* 8vo, cloth, gilt   Lond. 1861

4 0 2470 CATALOGUS Nummorum Veteris Aevi Monumentorum ac Gemmarum (Museum Meadianum). Plate. In same vol., Catalogue of the Library of Richard Mead. 8vo, half calf   Lond. 1755

' ' 2471 ——— Nummorum. *Plate.* 8vo, half tky. 1755

2472 Catalogue of Books, Prints, Pictures, *Coins,*
  Medals, &c., of William Stevenson. Small 4to,
  half morocco Lond. 1821

2473 —— des Poincons, Coins et Médailles du Musée
  Monetaire. 8vo, half calf. Paris, 1843

2474 —— of Collection of Greek and Roman Coins,
  sold at auction. 8vo, half roan Lond. 1833

2475 ——. Do. Greek and Roman Coins of Rev. G.
  F. Notthold. 8vo, half roan. *Priced and named*
  Lond. 1842

2476 —— Do. of Coins of Rev. Fr. Blick. 8vo,
  half morocco. *Priced and named* Lond. 1843

2477 Catalogue of Greek and Roman Coins, Cabinet of
  the Cavaliere Campana of Rome. Sold Lond.
  1846. 8vo, half calf. *Priced and named.*

2478 ——. Anglo-Saxon, English, Scotch and Irish
  Coins. Cabinet of Rev. J. W. Martin. 8vo, half
  roan. *Priced and named* Lond. 1859

2479 ——. Anglo-Saxon and other Antiquities. Gibbs'
  Collection. 8vo, half morocco Lond. 1871

2480 —— des Medailles Romaines. Collection de
  Mon. de Moustier. Sold 1872, Paris. 8vo, half
  morocco

2481 —— of Cabinet of Coins of Robert St. John, Esq.
  17 pages in manuscript, with a few rude drawings.
  Folio, boards

2482 —— of Books, Autographs, Engravings, Coins
  and Miscellaneous Articles. Collection of John
  Allan. N. Y. 1864. Royal 8vo, morocco. *Large
  paper copy, priced.* With Autograph Letter of
  Allan inserted.

2483 —— The Allan Silver Cabinet. *Photos.*
  N. Y. 1870

2484 —— of Collection of M. L. Mackenzie. *Photos.*
  8vo, half morocco N. Y. 1869

2485 ——. American Coins, &c. Collection of Charles
  Clay *Photos.* 8vo, hf. mor. N. Y. 1871

2486 —— of the Seavey Collection of American Coins.
  Photos. 8vo, half morocco Bost. 1873

2487 - —— Another copy in paper cover

2488 —— of Ed. Cogan's Collection of U. S. Coins.
  Sold by private biddings. 8vo, half morocco
  Phil. 1858

The following Catalogues (lots 2489 to 2513) are *priced* and
neatly bound in half morocco or half roan—all in good condition.

8 7 2489 Cogan's Sale of American Coins and Medals.
March, 1862. 4to. Printed prices

5-0 2490 ———. Same sale. 8*vo* catalogue. Printed prices

5-0 2491 ——— American and Foreign. March 26, 1862.
8vo, lead pencil

1. 1 2 2492 Woodward's Sale of the McCoy Collection. 1864.
8vo

2 5- 2493 Cogan's Coins, Numismatic Books, &c. N. Y.
1862. 4to

2. 1 3 2494 Woodward's Sale of the Mickley Collection. 1867.
8vo

6 0 2495 Cogan's Sale. 1869. N. Y. 8vo

5-5- 2496 Maguire's Collection of Coins and Autographs.
N. Y. 1870. 8vo

1. 0-0 2497 Cogan's Sale of the Packer Collection. N. Y. 1871.
8vo

6 5- 2498 Leveridge's Sale. N. Y. 1873. 8vo. *Only one
day's sale priced*

6 5- 2499 Macallister's Cabinet. N. Y. 1873. Photo plate

6 5- 2500 Haseltine's Sale of John Campbell's Collection.
Phila. 1874. 8vo

1. 0-0 2501 Woodward's Eighteenth Sale. 1874. 8vo

6 5- 2502 Cogan's Sale of Jas. Parker's Collection. N. Y.
1874. 8vo

6 5- 2503 Coins and Bric-a-Brac Collection of C. D. Lathrop.
N. Y. 1874. 8vo

6 5- 2504 Cogan's Sale. (two days.) Dec. 1874. 8vo
N. Y. 1874

7 5- 2505 Haseltine's Sale. (Collection of a widow of Boston.) N. Y. 1875. 8vo

6 5- 2506 ———. Two days. Phil. 1875. 8vo

6 5- 2507 Cogan's Sales. March and May, 1875. 2 vols, 8vo

6 5- 2508 Strobridge's Catalogue of Collection of Jos. E.
Gay. N. Y 1875. 8vo

6 5- 2509 Cogan's Sales. Jan., Oct. and Dec. 1876. N. Y.
3 vols, 8vo

6 5- 2510 Haseltine's Coins and Curiosities. March and
Sept. 1876. 2 vols, 8vo

1. 0 5- 2511 Strobridge's Havana and Parmelee Collections.
1876. 2 vols

2512 COGAN'S Sales. Feb., April, May, June, Sept.,
Nov. and Dec. 1877. 6 vols

2513 ANDERSON, Strunz, &c.; Randall, Haines, Harzfeld,
Cogniat and Scott's Sales. 1877 7 vols

2514 CATALOGUES. Nine in one volume. Curtis' Priced
Catalogue, 1862; Groh's Sale, 1860; Gallagher's,
1860; also Satterlee's Arrangement of Presidential Medals, &c. 8vo, half morocco

2515 ———. By J. K. Curtis, 1858, printed; Whitmore's
Collection, 1859; also Bushnell's Arrangement of
Tradesmen's Cards, &c., 1858. 1 vol, 8vo, hf. mor.

2516 ———. Coins and Medals from Collection of Jas. L.
Hill, Esq. 8vo, half mor. Madison, Wis. 1874

2517 ——— of Roman and Greek Coins, with marked
prices. By N. Ponce De Leon. 2 parts. 12mo,
paper N. Y 1877

2518 ——— of English Coins and Medals. By Lincoln
& Son and J. Henry. 6 vols. 12mo, paper
Lond. 1861-76.

2519 ——— of Rare American and English Coins, with
prices. By J. C. Vail, Washington Market, N. Y.
4 pp, 12mo. *Rare.*

2520 ——— *with plates* (five priced), including Chaff-
man, Chubbuck, Snow, Redlich, &c. 13 in all

2521 (25) ——— Miscellaneous. Priced

2522 (25) Do. Another lot

2523 (30) — Do. Another lot

2524 (66) ——— Miscellaneous. *Unpriced.* 1855 and
other early dates

2525 (100) ——— Miscellaneous. *Unpriced*

2526 (100) ——— Do. *Unpriced*

2527 (100) ——— Do. *Unpriced*

2528 (122) Do. *Unpriced*

2529 ——— Fragment of Fonrobert's Catalogue, &c. A
lot. *Plates.*

2530 (42) ——— Coin Chart Manuals, Circulars, Book
Catalogues

2531 Colonial, Continental and Confederate Currency, by Scott & Co.; Taylor's Coin Examiner.
5 pamphlets

2532 CHOUL, G. DU. Discours de la Religion des Anciens Romains; de la Castramentation, &c. Illustré *de medailles et figures.* 4to, vellum. (Title damaged) A Lyon, 1567

2533 ———. Another copy. Later ed. 4to, vell. 1685

2534 CHRONICON PRECIOSUM; or, Account of English Money; Price of Corn, &c., for 600 years. 12mo, sheep Lond. 1707

2535 CLARKE, F. W. Weights, Measures and Money of all Nations. 12mo, half roan N. Y. 1875

2536 CLARK, H. Concise History of Knighthood. 82 copper-plates. 2 vols, 8vo, half calf Lond. 1784

2537 ———. Introduction to Heraldry. 11th edition. 48 engravings. 16mo, half calf Lond. 1829

2538 CLAVIGERO, FR. S. Storia Antica del Messico; corredata di carte geog. et di *varie figure.* 2 vols, 4to, calf In Cesena, 1780

2539 COIN CHART MANUALS by Brown & Co., and Thompson. 6 pamphlets

2540 COIN COLLECTOR'S JOURNAL, 1876-80. Vols. 1 and 2 in half morocco; Vols. 3, 4 and 5 in Nos. Sold as 5 vols N. Y.

2541 ———. 7 odd Nos. of Vol. 6. 1881

2542 COIN AND STAMP JOURNAL. Vol. 1. 1875. 4to, half morocco Kansas City

2543 COLDEN, CADWALLADER D. Memoir at the Celebration of the Completion of the N. Y. Canals. Portraits, Maps, Charts, Views and other plates. 4to, calf. *Scarce* N. Y. 1825

2544 COLEMAN'S Masonic Calendar. 8vo, paper Louisville, 1879

2545 COLLECTOR'S Rate-List of Amer. Store Cards. By Phil. Num. Soc. 4to, half roan

2546 COLOMIE. La Bibliotheque Choisie de M. Colomie's; Notes de Bourdelot; etc. 12mo, calf Paris, 1731

2547 COMBES, CHAS. Index Nummorum Omnium Imperatorun Augustarum, et Cæsarum a I. Cæsare asque ad Postumum. 4to, half calf Lond. 1773

2548 CONDER, JOSIAH. Arrangement of Provincial Coins, Tokens and Medalets issued in Great Britain, Ireland and the Colonies within the last twenty years. Plate. 12mo, hf. cf. Ipswich, 1798

2549 CONFEDERATE GREAT SEAL. Some Account of it. 8vo, half roan Wash. 1873

2550 CORK, NATH. Statistics of Australasian Banking.
8vo, half morocco   Lond. 1874

2551 CROSBY, S. S. The Early Coins of America, and
the Laws governing their issue. Illustrated. 4to,
half morocco, gilt top   Bost. 1875

2552 ——. Another copy. 4to, half calf, gilt top

2553 CROSS, J. L. The Templar's Chart. Illustrated.
12mo   N. Y. 1845

2554 CURIOSITY CABINET. Vol. 1. 1870-71. 8vo, half
roan   N. Y.

2555 CURIOSITY HUNTER. Nos. 1 to 12, except 8 and 9.
10 Nos. 1872-3

2556 CUSTOMS, Tariff, Legislation. &c. : Duties on Coins ;
&c. 8vo   1871

2557 CREVIER. History of the Roman Emperors.
Illustrated with Maps, Medals, Gems and other
copper-plates. 10 vols, 8vo, calf   Lond. 1755

2558 DARIER, H. Tableau du titre, Poids et Valeur
des differentes Monnaies d'or et d'argent,
qui circulent dans le Commerce. 32 *plates*. 4to,
half roan   Geneve. 1807

2559 DAVIS, W J. Catalogue of his Library. Large
Paper Copy. 4to   N. Y. 1895

2560 DAVIS, J. FR. H. The Chinese : a Description.
Illustrated. 12mo   Lond. 1840

2561 DECIMAL COINAGE. Report thereon from select
Committee of House of Commons. 1853. Folio,
half morocco

2562 DECORAH NUMISMATIC JOURNAL. Vol 1. (4 Nos.)
12mo, half morocco   1878

2563 DE PEYSTER, J. WATTS. The History of Carausius,
the Dutch Augustus. 8vo, half morocco
Poughkeepsie. 1858

2564 DERBY, E. H. History of Paper Money in Massachusetts before the Revolution. 8vo, half roan
1874

2565 DE VINNE, THEO, L. The Invention of Printing.
A Collection of Facts and Opinions. Illustrated
with facsimiles of early types and woodcuts.
Small 4to, half morocco, gilt top   N. Y. 1876

2566 DICKESON, M. W. The American Numismatic Manual. Illustrated with 25 plates of facsimiles. 3d edition. 4to, cloth   Phil. 1865

2567 —— Do., do. 2d ed. 4to, cloth   Phil. 1860

2568 —— Do., do. 1st ed. 4to, cloth   Phil. 1859

2569 DONALDSON, T. L. Archictectura Numismatica ; or Architectural Medals of Classic Antiquity illustrated and explained. 100 lithographs and woodcuts. Royal 8vo, cloth   Lond. 1859

2570 DONATUS, ALEX. Roma Vetus ac Recens, utriusque Ædificiis illustrata. Beautiful copperplates. Small 4to, vellum   Amstel. 1694

2571 DRAKE, S. A. Old Landmarks and Historic Personages of Boston. Profusely illustrated. 12mo   Bost. 1874

2572 DRAPIER. Letters to the People of Ireland concerning Mr. Wood's Brass Half-Pence. 8vo, calf   Lond. 1730

2573 DYER, T. H. Ancient Rome. Map and numerous illustrations. 8vo   Lond. 1864

2574 ECKFELDT & DUBOIS. Manual of Gold and Silver Coins of all Nations struck within the past century, with corrections to 1851. (No plates.) 4to, half roan   Phil.

2575 —— New Varieties of Coins, Counterfeits and Bullion. 8vo. (2 copies)   N. Y. 1852

2576 —— Do. 2d edition. 8vo   1851

2577 —— Do. 1850. edition. 12mo, boards. With colored plates, &c.

2578 ECKHEL. Lezioni Elementari di Numismatica Antica. 6 plates of figures. 4to, half calf. Roma, 1808

2579 EGGERS, AUG. Coin-Map of the World. 16mo, boards   Lond. 1879

2580 EGYPT. The Antiquities of Egypt, with particular notice of those that illustrate the Sacred Scriptures. Numerous engravings. 8vo   Lond. 1841

2581 —— Numi Ægyptii Imperatorii prostantes in Museo Borgiano. Adjectis præterea quotquot reliqua huius classis numismata ex variis Museis atque libris colligere obligit. 22 *plates*. 4to, vellum   Romæ, 1787

2582 ELDER, W Biography of E. K. Kane. Illus. 8vo   1858

2583 ELMER, L. Q. C. History of Early Settlement and Progress of Cumberland Co., N. J., and of the Currency. 8vo Bridgeton, 1869

2584 ENGLAND. Twelve plates of Engl. Silver Coins from the Conquest to Henry VIII., with values, &c. 4to, boards Lond. 1756

2585 —— A View of the Silver Coin and Coinage of England from the Conquest. 14 plates. 4to, boards Lond. 1762

2586 —— The Medallic History of England to the Revolution. With 40 plates. 4to, half morocco, gilt top Lond. 1790

2587 EVANS, JOHN. The Coins of the Ancient Britons. Plates engraved by Fairholt. 8vo Lond. 1864

2588 EVELYN, J. A Discourse of Medals, Antient and Modern, together with some Account of Heads and Effigies of Illustrious and Famous Persons of whom we have no medals extant. Numerous illustrations. Folio, half calf Lond. 1797

2589 EXCHANGE MARKET; the Swappers' Journal. 23 Nos. 1873-4. N. Y.

2590 FALKENER, ED. Description of some important Theatres and other Remains in Crete. Illustrations of coins, &c. Thin 8vo. Lond. 1854

2591 FAWCETT, W. L. Gold and Debt; an American Hand-book of Finance. 12mo Chicago, 1877

2592 FEUCHTWANGER, L. Treatise on Gems. 8vo N. Y. 1838

2593 FELLOWS, CHAS. Coins of Ancient Syria before the reign of Alexander. Map and 19 plates. Royal 8vo, half roan Lond. 1855

2594 —— Do. Another copy in cloth

2595 FELT, JOS. B. Historical Account of Massachusetts Currency. 8vo, half morocco Bost. 1839

2596 FLEMING, GEO. Horse-Shoes and Horse-Shoeing, their origin, history, uses and abuses. 210 illustrations. 8vo Lond. 1869

2597 FOLKES, M. English Coinage; Silver and Gold, faithfully copied from the originals, 67 plates, with 1208 coins and their reverses. 4to, half morocco

2598 FOSTER, M. F. Pre-Historic Man; Darwinism and Deity. The Mound Builders. 8vo, half morocco Cinn. 1873

1. 7 ʃ⁻ 2599 FORTIS, ALBERT. Travels into Dalmatia; Observations on Natural History; Manners, Customs.
Copper-plates. 4to, calf (broken)   Lond. 1778

4. ᴏ⁻o 2600 FRANCE. Souvenirs Numismatiques de la Revolution de 1848; recueil complet des Medailles, Monnaies et Jetons. 60 plates. 4to, half mor. Paris

1. 6 0 2601 GATTERERS, J. C. Abritz der Heraldik. 8
copper-plates. 8vo, half shp. Gottingen, 1792

1. 1 0 2602 GERHARDT, J. H. Gold and Silber-Munzen. (Tables
of values). 8vo   Berlin, 1818

4. ᴏ⁻ð 2603 GEMS, selected from the Antique, with illustrations. Fine plates. 4to, half morocco Lond. 1804

ʃ 0 2604 GILBART, J. W. Elements of Banking. Portrait.
12mo   Lond. 1855

1 7ʃ⁻ 2605 GILPIN, WM. Observations on the Highlands of
Scotland. Numerous tinted plates—one of the
Newark Shilling. 8vo, vellum   Lond. 1808

2. 6 0 2606 GOLTZIUS, HUBERT. De Re Nummaria Antiqua
Opera, quae extant universa: a numismatic study
of Roman life, government and governors. Illustrated with a great number of copper-plates. 5 vols,
folio, old calf   Antwerp, 1708

1. 7 0 2607 GORHAM, G. C. Gleanings of a few scattered ears
during the period of the Reformation in England.
With engravings of seals, &c. 8vo, cloth
Lond. 1857

2. 7ʃ⁻ 2608 GOSMOND, A. Les Campagnes de Louis XV. Representees par des Figures Allegoriques. 45 copperplate vignettes with descriptions. 4to russia,
stained   1751

1. ᴏ⁻● 2609 GOUGE, WM. M. A Short History of Paper Money
and·Banking. 8vo, half roan   N. Y. 1835

1. 1 0 2610 —— Journal of Banking, July, 1841, to July,
1842. 8vo, half sheep   Phil.

3. 7ʃ⁻ 2611 GREECE. Veterum Populorum et Regum Numi
qui in Museo Britannico adservantur. 15 plates
containing representations of many coins. 4to,
sprinkled calf, red edges.   Lond. 1814
Edited by Taylor Combe. Fine copy

2 ʃ⁻0 2612 GUTHRIE, M. Tour in the Taurida, or Crimea; the
once powerful republic of Tauric Cherson. With a
map and engravings of a great number of *Ancient
Coins, Medals, Inscriptions, &c.* 4to, boards
Lond. 1802

2613 **H**AIGH, D. H. Essay on Numismatic History of the Ancient Kingdom of the East Angles. 5 plates. Royal 8vo, half morocco Leeds, 1845

2614 HARDUIN, J. Nummi Antiqui Populorum Urbium Illustrati. 4to, old calf Paris, 1684

2615 (HARRIS.) An Essay upon Money and Coins. Two parts in one vol. 8vo, half morocco Lond. 1757
Privately printed, and scarce.

2616 (HART.) History of the Issues of Paper-Money in the American Colonies. 8vo, half roan
St. Louis, 1851

2617 HART, C. H. Remarks on Tabasco, Mexico. 8vo, half morocco Phil. 1867

2618 HARZFELD, S. K. Old Coins and their Values: On the Falsifications of Ancient Coins. 2 pamphlets

2619 HARWOOD, ED. Populorum et Urbium, Selecta Numismata Graeca ex aere descripta et figuris illustrata. 7 plates. 4to, half morocco. Lond. 1812

2620 HASELTINE, J. W. Description of Continental and Colonial Paper Money. 4to, half mor. Phil. 1872

2621 ——— Type Table Catalogue. 8vo, paper 1881

2622 HAWKINS, ED. The Silver Coins of England, arranged and described. 47 plates. 8vo, half roan
Lond. 1841

2623 ——— Another. *Large Paper Copy.* Royal 8vo, half roan 1841

2624 HAYES, A. H. Science of Life. Plate of a Medal. 16mo Bost.

2625 HAYM, N. FR. Del Tesoro Britannico. Parte Prima overo Il Museo Numnario. Numerous illustrations of Ancient Greek and Roman Coins. 2 vols, 4to, old calf Lond. 1719

2626 HEARNE, THOS. Collection of Curious Discourses by Eminent Antiquaries—and many by Hearne including articles on numismatic subjects. 2 vols, 8vo, calf, broken Lond. 1771

2627 HEATH'S greatly improved Counterfeit Detector. Engraving from the original plates of paper money. 4to, cloth Bost.

2628 ——— Another copy.

2629 HENFREY, H. W. A Guide to the Study and arrangement of English Coins. Illustrated. 12mo
Lond. 1870

7. o~o 2630 HERAEUS, C. G. Bildnisse der Regierenden Fürsten und Beruhmter Manner vom vierzehnten bis zum achtzehnten Jahrhunderte in einer Folgereihe von Schaumunzen. 62 plates, containing a vast number of portraits from medals. Royal folio. half morocco   Vienna, 1828

2. 5~0 2631 HERBERT, A. An Argument to disprove supposed antiquity of the Stonehenge and other Megalithic Erections. 8vo   Lond. 1849

4. 2 0 2632 HICKCOX, J. H. An Historical Account of American Coinage. 5 plates. 8vo, hf. mor. Alb. 1858

1. / 3 2633 ————. History of the Bills of Credit or Paper Money issued by New York, 1709 to 1789. 8vo, half morocco   Albany, 1866

1. 9 0 2634 HIRSCH, JOH. CH. Bibliotheca Numismatica Exhibeus Catalogum Auctorum qui de re monetaria et numis scripaere. Folio, bds. Noeimbergæ, 1760

1. 3 0 2635 HISTORY of England. 32 copper-plates. 12mo, sheep 1790

2. 3 0 2636 HOBLER, FR. Records of Roman History as Exhibited on the Roman Coins. Woodcuts. 2 vols, 4to, cloth   Westminster, 1860

3. 2 5 2637 HOE, R. M. The Literature of Printing. 16mo, cloth   Lond.: Privately printed, 1877

/ 0 2638 HOMANS. The Banker's Almanac. 1869, '73, '74, '82. 4 vols, 8vo

8 0 2639 ————. The Coin Book. Illustrated. 8vo. Phil. 1872

1. 2 0 2640 HONE, WM. Ancient Mysteries described. Illustrated. 8vo, cloth   Lond.

5. 25 2641 HOUGH, F. B. Washingtoniana: or, Memorials of the Death of George Washington ; account of Funeral Honors ; List of Tracts and Volumes, and Catalogue of Medals commemorating the event. 2 vols, 4to, half morocco   Roxbury, Mass. 1865

3. 2 5 2642 HUMPHREYS, H. N. Ancient Coins and Medals ; an historical sketch of coining money in Greece and her Colonies, in Rome, &c. Numerous illustrations in facsimile in actual relief and in the metals of the respective coins. 8vo, embossed cover (loose in binding)   Lond. 1850

2. 5 2) 2643 ————. The Gold, Silver and Copper Coins of England, in a series of facsimiles ; printed in gold, silver and copper. 12mo, fancy binding   1849

5 0 2644 Humphreys, H. N. The coinage of the British
Empire. Illustrated by facsimiles of the coins of
each period. 8vo, cloth   Lond. 1854

2 5 2645 ———. Do. A new edition, greatly enlarged. 8vo,
half morocco   Lond. 1861

2 0 2646 ———. The Coin Collector's Manual. Over 150 illustrations. 2 vols, 12mo   Lond. 1883

3 7 2647 ———. Stories by an Archaeologist and His Friends.
2 vols, 12mo   Lond. 1856

1 2 2648 Hughan, W. J. A Numerical and Numismatical
Register of Lodges which formed the United
Grand Lodge of England. 5 *plates*. Crown 4to,
cloth   Lond. 1878

1 5 2649 ILLUSTRATIONS OF POPERY. 12mo
N. Y. 1838

5 5 2650 International Statistical Congress Report. 1872.
8vo

6 2651 Irving, W. Rip Van Winkle. *Illustrated.* 8vo,
paper

5 0 2652 JENNINGS, D. Introduction to the knowledge
of medals. 12mo, calf   Birmingham. 1775

1 0 2653 ———Do. Another copy   Birmingham. 1775

7 0 2654 Jennings, H. One of the Thirty: a Strange History. *Illustrated.* 12mo, cloth   Lond.

5 0 2655 Jewett, L. Hand-Book of English Coins. *Illustrated.* 24mo, cloth   1840

1 0 2656 ———. Do. do. 11 colored plates. 24mo, cloth, gt.

1 0 2657 Johnston, E. B. Visit to the Cabinet of the U. S.
Mint. 12mo, cloth   1876

5 0 2658 ———. Another copy

5 0 2659 (Johnson, Chas.) Chrysal: or The Adventures of
a Guinea: With Curious and Interesting Anec-
dotes. 2 vols, 12mo, half vellum   Lond. 1783

2 0 2660 Jones, G. F. Coin Collector's Manual. 8vo, half
roan   Phil.

1 0 2661 Journal of the Liverpool Numismatic Society.
Vol. 1, 1873. Plates. 8vo, half morocco

1 0 2662 Judson, L. C. The Sages and Heroes of the American Revolution. 8vo   Phil. 1854

2663 **K**ING, C. W. The Gnostics and their Remains,
Ancient and Mediæval. 13 plates. 8vo,
cloth   Lond. 1864

2664 ———. Early Christian Numismatics, and other
Antiquarian Tracts. Plates. 8vo, cloth   1873

2665 ———. Natural History of Gems and Decorative
Stones. 8vo, cloth   Lond. 1867

2666 **L**ABRE, P. Bibliotheca Bibliothecarum; accedit
Bibliotheca Nummaria.   12mo, half morocco
1678

2667 LANKTREE, J. Synopsis of Roman Antiquities.
16mo, cloth   ·   Lond. 1857

2668 LEAKE, W. M. Supplement to Numismata Hellen-
ica; a catalogue of Greek Coins.   4to, cloth
Lond. 1859

2669 ———. Brief Memoir of.   4to, cloth   1864

2670 LEE, J. ED.   Roman Imperial Photographs; a
selection of forty enlarged Photos. of Roman Coins.
Royal 8vo, cloth   Lond. 1874

2671 LEITZMANN, J. Bibliotheca Numaria. 1800–1866.
8vo, half morocco   Weissensee, 1867

2672 LIESVILLE, A. R. DE. Histoire Numismatique de
la Revolution de 1848.   Plates. Parts 4 to 7.   4
parts, 4to   1880

2673 LINDERMAN, H. R.   Money and Legal Tender in
the U. S.   12mo, cloth   N. Y. 1877

2674 LIRUTI, G.   Della Moneta della Decadurza del'
Imperio Romano sino al Secolo XV.   10 plates.
4to, boards   Venice, 1749

2675 LOUIS LE GRAND. Historie du Roy par les Medailles, Emblemes, Devises, Jettons, &c., recueillis
par C.-Fr. Menestrier   64 plates.   Folio, old calf
Paris, 1693

2676 (LOWNDES, WM.)   A Report containing an essay
for the Amendment of the Silver Coins.   12mo,
half morocco   Lond. 1695

2677 LUTHER. Dos Guldene un Silberne Ehren-Bedächt-
niz.   D. Martini Lutheri.   Portraits and plates.
8vo, vellum   Franckfurt, 1706

2678 ———. Martin Luther's Andenken in Munzen. Von
H. G. Kreuszler.   41 plates of medals and 5 plates
of portraits. 8vo, boards   Leipzig, 1828

2679 ———. Do. Another fine copy. Uncut edges. 8vo,
half green morocco

2680 **MADDEN**, F. W. Hand-Book of Roman Numismatics. 16mo, cloth   Lond. 1861

2681 ———. History of Jewish Coinage and of Money in the Old and New Testament. 254 woodcuts and a plate of Alphabets. Royal 8vo, half roan
Lond. 1864

2682 MAFFEI, S. A Compleat History of the Ancient Ampitheatres, particular of Verona. Illustrated. 12mo, half morocco   Lond.

2683 MANBY, CAPT. G. W. Anastatic Drawings of Gold and Silver Medals presented to Him. Portrait and 12 plates. 8vo, cloth   Yarmouth, 1851

2684 MANCHESTER Numismatic Society Proceedings. 10 Parts, 1864-73. Photo-plates. 4to

2685 MARGOLIOUTH, M. Vestiges of the Historic Anglo-Hebrews in East Anglia. Plate. 8vo, cloth
Lond. 1870

2686 MARIS, ED. Varieties of the Copper Issues of the U. S. Mint in 1794. 12mo, half roan   Phil. 1869

2687 MARTIALIS Numismatibus illustratus. 22 pages of figures of Roman coins interleaved with blotting-paper, one cut cut out. 12mo, half calf

2688 MARVIN, W. T. R. The Carrara Medals. With Notices of the Dukes of Padua. Photos of 6 medals. 8vo, paper   Bost. 1880

2689 MASON's Coin Magazine. 1867-72. 6 vols. bound in 5. 8vo, half roan   Phil.

2690 ——— Vols. 1 to 4 in one vol. half sheep, and Vol. 5 in half roan. 2 vols

2691 MASSACHUSETTS Historical Soc. Proceedings, 1862-3. Illustration of an old paper note, 1690, &c. 8vo, cloth

2692 MATHEWS, GEO. D. The Coinages of the World, Ancient and Modern. Illustrated. 8vo, cloth
N. Y. 1876

2694 MEDALLIC HISTORY OF ENGLAND. Illustrated by 40 plates. 4to, half morocco   Lond. 1862

2695 MÉDAILLES sur les Principaux Evenements du Regne de Louis le Grand, avec des explications historiques. A great number of vignettes. 4to, half morocco   Paris, 1702

2696 MEDAILLE. Oratio Anniversaria Haweiana, 1724, adjecta est Dissertatio de Nummis quibusdam a Smyrnæis in Medicorum Nonorem percussis. In same volume : Explication de Quelques Medailles de Peuples, de Villes et de Rois Grecques et Pheniciennes par M. Le Dutens. Illustrated. 4to, half calf. (Cracked)   Lond. 1773

2697 MEDAGLIE DEL MUSEO FARNESE ; or, I. Cesari raccolti nel Farnese Museo, composto dal Padre Paolo Pedrusi. Illustrated with a great number of copper-plates.   10 vols, folio, old calf
                              In Parma, 1694

2698 MEREWETHER, J.   Examination of the Barrows and other Earthworks on the Downs of Wilts. Illustrated. 8vo   Lond. 1851

2699 MILLINGEN, JAS.   Ancient Coins of Greek Cities and Kings from various collections. 5 plates. Also Sylloge of Ancient Unedited Greek Coins. 4 plates. 1 vol, 4to, half morocco   Lond. 1831-37

2700 MINER, CHAS.   History of Wyoming. Maps, &c. 8vo   Phil. 1845

2701 MISCELLANY.   Lettre a Fr. Salvolini sur les Monumens Egyptiens, with 32 plates ; Precis du Systeme Hieroglyphique des Anciens Egpytiens, par M. Champollion, with plates ; also, Specimen alterum Inscriptionum Coemeterii Bononierias. 1 vol, 8vo, half roan

2702 MONELL, J. J.   Washington's Headquarters, Newburgh, N. Y.   Illustrated. 12mo, half morocco
                              Newburgh, 1872

2703 MORELL.   Thesaurus Morellianus sive Familiarum Romanarum Numismata Omnia ; accedunt Nummi Miscellanei, Urbis Romæ, Hispanici, &c.   Edidit et Commentario perpetuo illustravit S. Havercampus.   Nearly 200 plates of figures of Roman coins. Folio, vellum.   (Front two pages of text missing)
                              Amsterdam, 1734

2704 MORRIS, ROBT.   The Twelve Cæsars, Illustrated by Readings of 217 of their Coins and Medals. Plates. 4to, half morocco.   La Grange, Ky., 1877

2705 —— Masonic Odes and Poems. 12mo, cloth
                              Chicago, 1876

2706 MORTILLARO, M. V.   Il Medagliere Arabo-Siculo della Biblioteca Comunale di Palermo.   Plate. 8vo, half morocco   Palermo, 1861

2707 MORLE, THOS. Heraldry of Fish: Notices of the principal Families bearing Fish in their Arms. Illustrated. 8vo, half morocco Lond. 1842

2708 MUDIE. Historical and Critical Account of the Grand Series of National Medals. Published under direction of Jas. Mudie. With outlines of the series. 4to, half morocco Lond. 1820

2709 MULLER, L. Numismatique d' Alexandre le Grand. With atlas of 29 plates. 2 vols. 8vo and 4to, half calf Copenhagen, 1855

2710 MURRAY, J. The Truth of Revelation Demonstrated by an Appeal to Monuments, Gems, Coins, &c. 8vo, cloth Lond. 1840

2711 NUMISMATA (Ærea Selectiora Maximi Moduli e Museo Pisano olim Corrario. 92 fine copper-plates (one damaged). Folio, obl cf. Venice
Medals of the Greek and Roman rulers and others.

2712 NAPLES : National Museum. Collection of the Most Remarkable Monuments of the. Published by R. Gargiulo, Controller. 240 fine outline engravings. 4 vols. in 2. 4to, hf. mor. Naples, 1872
This interesting work is thus classed : Marble Sculptures, 60 plates : Bronze Sculptures, 40 plates : Engraved Stones, objects in Gold and Silver, Mural Paintings and Mosaics, 30 plates ; Terra Cotta Sculptures, and Painted Italo-Greek Vases, 60 plates.

2713 NAPOLEONIDE di Stefano E. Petroni. 100 Odes, each with a vignette illustration. 4to, half morocco Napoli, 1810

2714 NAPOLEON. A Description of the Series of Medals struck at the National Medal Mint by order of Napoleon, commemorating the Most Remarkable Battles and Events during his Dynasty. By Capt. J. C. Laskey. Portrait and woodcut. LARGE PAPER. Royal 8vo, half morocco Lond. 1818

2715 — Histoire Metallique de Napoleon ; ou Recueil des Medailles et des Monnaies qui ont été frappées depuis la première Campagne jusqu'à son Abdication. 74 plates. 4to, mottled half, gilt. *Fine copy* Lond. 1819

2716 Napoleon. Medallic History of Napoleon: a Collection of all the Medals, Coins and Jettons relating to his Actions and Reign, from 1796 to 1815. With Supplement. Together, 74 plates. 2 vols, 4to, morocco and half morocco   Lond 1819-21

2717 —— The Napoleon Medals : a complete series of the Medals struck in France, Italy, Great Britain and Germany, from 1804 to 1815. Engraved by A. Collas. With Historical and Biographical Notices. 40 plates. Edited by Ed. Edwards. Royal folio, half morocco   Lond. 1837

2718 —— Medallic History of Napoleon the First. By Fred. J. Jeffery. 7 plates. 4to, half morocco   Liverpool, 1864

2719 Neuste Munzkunde. Abbildung und Beschreibung der jeszt courfirenden Gold-und Silbermünzen, &c. 90 Tafeln Münzabbildungen. 2 vols, 8vo, half sheep   Leipzig, 1853

2720 New Haven Colony Historical Society Papers. Vol. 1. With account of Connecticut Currency. 8vo, cloth   1865

2721 New York Documentary History, Vol. 3 ; Civil List, 1858. 2 vols

2722 —— State Library Catalogue of Maps, Medals, &c. 1856. 8vo, half morocco

2723 —— Catalogue of Coins and Medals in Library. 8vo, paper   1853

2724 —— State History. By Yates & Moulton. Vol. 1, Part 1. 8vo, boards, uncut   1824

2725 —— City Directory Register, 1818-19. 12mo, bds.

2726 —— Do. Common Council Manual, 1869. 8vo

2727 —— Daily Graphic. 13 bundles of nos.

2728 Nicolson, W. The English Historical Library. 2d edition. Folio, old calf   Lond. 1714

2729 Nicolas, N. H. History of the Orders of Knighthood of the British Empire ; of the Order of the Guelphs of Hanover, and of the Medals, Clasps and Crosses conferred for Naval and Military Services. Illustrated with colored plates and woodcuts. 4 vols, royal 4to, half morocco Lond. 1842

2730 Nieupoort, G. H. Rituum qui olim apud Romanos obtinuerunt succincta explicatio conscripta; accedunt Gesneri prolusio de Tribunali Praetoris. Plates. 12mo, boards   Berolini, 1767

2731 NOBLE, M. Two Dissertations upon the Mint and Coins of the Episcopal-Palatines of Durham. With plates of Coins, Coats-of-Arms, &c. 4to, half morocco. Birmingham, 1780

2732 NORTH, O. The Practical Assayer. Illustrated. 12mo, cloth Lond. 1874

2733 NORTHERN ARCHÆOLOGY, a Guide: by the Royal Society of Northern Antiquaries. Edited by the Earl of Ellesmere. Woodcuts. 8vo, cloth Lond. 1848

2734 NORTON, C. B. Norton's Literary Letter, comprising American Papers of Interest and Catalogue of Books. Small 4to, half morocco N. Y. 1857–60

2735 NORTON, Eu. National Finance and Currency. 12mo, cloth Lond. 1873

2736 NUMISMATA COLLEGII de Gonvile et Caius nuper J. Burrough et J. Smith. The Donor's Catalogue. Edited by Rev. J. J. Smith. 4to, half morocco Camb. 1846

2737 NYSTROM, J. W. Project of a New System of Arithmetic, Weight, Measure and Coins. 8vo Phil. 1862

2738 **O**DERICUS, G. A. De Argenteo Orcitirigis Numo Coniecturæ. Illustrated. 4to, half morocco Roma. 1767

2739 OROSIUS, P. Historiarum libri septem, ut et Apologeticus contra Pelagium de Arbitrii Libertate. Edidit S. Havercampus. Illustrated with cuts of Roman Coins. 4to, old calf Lugduni. 1738

2740 OXFORD SAUSAGE, or Select Poetical Pieces, by Celebrated Wits. Portrait and vignettes by Thomas Bewick. 12°, hf. roan, uncut. Lond. 1815

2741 **P**AINE, N. Remarks on the Early Paper Currency of Massachusetts. 8vo, half morocco Camb. 1856

2742 PANVINIUS, O. Fasti et Triumphi Roma a Romulo Rege usque ad Carolum V. Cæs. Aug. additum sunt suis locis Impp. and orientalium and occidentalium verissimæ icones. Numerous woodcuts of medals and coins. Folio, vellum. Venice. 1557

2743 PARUTA. La Sicilia di Filippo Paruta descritta con Medaglie e Ristampata con Aggiunta da Leonardo Agostini. About 150 plates. Folio, old red morocco, gilt In Lione, 1697

2744 PATINUS, C. Introductio ad Historiam Numismatum. 16mo, vellum Amster. 1683

2745 PEGGE, SAML. A Series of Dissertations on some Elegant and very Valuable Anglo-Saxon Remains; Gold and Silver Coins, &c. With a plate. 4to, half sheep Lond. 1756

2746 —— An Essay on the Coins of Cunobelin, &c. 4to, half calf Lond. 1776

2747 PENNSYLVANIA HISTORICAL SOCIETY MEMOIRS. Vol. 6. Plate of the Penn Treaty Wampum Belt. 8vo, cloth 1858

2748 PERROT, A. M. Collection Historique des Ordres de Chevalerie Civils et Militaires. 39 plates of numerous figures, colored. 4to, hf. cf. Paris, 1846

2749 PERRY, FR. A Series of English Medals. No. 1. 3 fine plates of figures. Thin 4to, boards 1772

2750 PETTIGREW, T. J. On Superstitions connected with Medicine and Surgery. 12mo, cloth Phil. 1844

2751 ——— Notes on the Seals of the Endowed Grammar Schools in England and Wales. 22 plates. 8vo, cloth Lond. 1859

2752 PETIT, PIERRE. Traite Historique sur les Amazones. Engravings of *Medals*, &c. 2 vols, 12mo, old calf A Leide, 1718

2753 PHELPS, F. A. History of the Copper Mines and Newgate Prison, at Granby Ct. 8vo, half morocco Hartford, 1845

2754 PHELPS, R. H. History of Newgate of Connecticut, its Insurrections and Massacres. Portrait. Small 4to, half morocco Albany, 1860
Contains account of the "Granby Coppers."

2755 PHILADELPHIA NUMISMATIC Soc. Proceedings, 1866, and on Mar. 20, 1879. 2 vols, paper

2756 PHILLIPS (Jr.), H. Historical Sketch of Paper Money of Pennsylvania. 8vo, half roan 1862

2757 - —— Catalogue of New Jersey Bills of Credit. 8vo, half roan 1863

2758 ——— Historical Sketches of the Paper Currency of the American Colonies and Continental Paper Money. Two series in one vol. 4to, half morocco Roxbury, Mass. 1865-66

2759 ——— The same. In two vols, 4to, half morocco

PIDGEON, WM. Traditions of De-Coo-Dah and Antiquarian Researches in America. 70 engravings. 8vo, cloth N. Y. 1858

PINKERTON, JOHN An Essay on Medals. 1st edition. 12mo, half calf Lond. 1784

Do. 2nd edition. Corrected, enlarged and illustrated with plates. 2 vols, 12mo, calf, gilt Lond. 1789

Do. 3rd edition, with Corrections and Additions. 2 vols, 8vo, half russia Lond. 1808

POINTER, J. Britannia Triumphans: or Naval Victories. Thin 8vo, boards 1743

POSTE, BEALE. Celtic Inscriptions on Gaulish and British Coins. With Glossary of Archaic Words. 14 plates of coins. Also a Vindication of the Celtic Inscriptions. With woodcuts. 2 vols, 8vo, cloth Lond. 1861-62

POWNALL, G. Notices and Descriptions of Antiquities of the Provincia Romana of Gaul, and Appendix on Roman Baths. Plates. 4to, cloth N. Y. 1788

PRIEST, Jos. American Antiquities and Discoveries in the West. 3d edition. Maps. 8vo, sheep Albany. 1833

PRIME, W. C. Coins, Medals and Seals Illustrated and Described. 114 plates. Square 8vo, cloth N. Y. 1861

QUEEN DAGMAR CROSS. Facsimile in gold and colors. With Introductory Remarks by Prof. G. Stephens. Royal 8vo, half morocco Lond. 1863

RAPIN. The History of England; translated from the French by N. Tindal. 2nd edition. Illustrated with maps, a series of beautifully engraved portraits, cuts of *coins*, &c. 2 vols, large folio, calf Lond. 1732

RAEDORA Maximi Moduli Numismata Selecta; ex Bibliotheca Casp. Carpegna. Illustrations of Roman Medals. 16mo, old calf Amstel. 1683

RAUTHMEL, R. The Roman Antiquities of Overborough, including a medal of Vespasian. 5 plates. 8vo, half calf *Kirkby Lonsdale.* 1824

3. o-o 2773 ROBERTSON, J. D. A Hand-Book to the Coinage of
Scotland from Alex. I. to Anne. Woodcuts.
Small 4to, half morocco   Lond. 1878

6. J 0 2774 Rocco, SHA. The Masculine Cross and Ancient
Sex Worship. 12mo   N. Y. 1874

1. 7 J ⁻ 2775 ROME. Series Augustarum, Cæsarum, et Tyran-
norum Omnium ad Carolum VI. Auctore L. Pat-
arol. Numerous cuts of *coins.* 8vo, half vellum.
Rare.   Venice 1722

2. o-o 2776 ⸺ A Treatise of the Revenue and False Money
of the Romans; with a treatise on the manner of
distinguishing Antique Medals from Counterfeits.
8vo, calf   Lond. 1741

2 J⁻ 2776a. ⸺⸺ Roman Antiquities. (No title-page.)
Many plates of coins, &c. 8vo, half sheep

8 0 2777 ⸺ Tableau de la Rarete et du Prix des
Medailles Romaines par Le Baron Leon d'Heerey.
Thin 8vo, half calf   1849

1. 0 J⁻ 2778 ⸺ A Manual of Roman Coins. 21 plates. 8vo,
cloth   Lond. 1865

J.⁻2 0 2779 ⸺ Roman Medallions in the British Museum.
By H. A. Grueber. Edited by R. S. Poole. 66 auto-
type plates. 4to, cloth   Lond. 1874

9 2 J⁻ 2780 ⸺ Joannis Rosini Antiquitatum Romanarum
corpus absolutissimum, cum notis. Fine copper
plates of coins, &c. 4to, vellum   Lugduni, 1663

6. J⁻0 2781 RUDING, REV. R. Annals of the Coinage of Great
Britain and its Dependencies from the earliest
period of authentic history to the reign of Victoria. 3rd edition corrected and enlarged and continued. (One vol. of plates.) 3 vols. 4to, cloth
Lond. 1840

8 J⁻ 2782 RUGGLES. S. B. Report to Department of State on
International Coinage. 8vo, half mor. N. Y. 1870

J.J⁻0 2783 RUTTENBER, E. M. Catalogue of MSS. and Relics
in Washington's Headquarters, Newburgh, N. Y.
8vo, half morocco   1874

6 2 2784 SALLUST. Histoire de la Republique Romaine;
en partie traduite du latin; en partie rétablie
et composée sur les fragmens qui sont restés de
ses Livres perdus. Maps and plates of coins, &c.
3 vols, 4to, calf, gilt   A Dijon, 1777

2785 SAMSON, L. Recherches sur les Monnaies de la presqu'ile Italique depuis leur origine jusqu'a la Bataille d'Actium. 24 plates. 4to, half morocco
Naples, 1870

2786 SANDHAM, A. Coins, Tokens and Medals of Canada. 150 facsimiles. With Supplement. 2 vols, 8vo, cloth and paper 1869–72

2787 —— Sketches of Montreal, Past and Present. Numerous engravings. 8vo, cloth 1870

2788 —— McGill College and its Medals. Illustrated with photographs. 8vo, boards 1872

2789 SATTERLEE, A. H. An Arrangement of Medals and Tokens, struck in honor of the Presidents of the United States. *Interleaved copy.* 8vo, half morocco N Y 1862

2790 SAVARIN. Gastronomy as a Fine Art. 12mo, cloth Lond. 1877

2791 SCHLUMBERGER, G. Les Principautés Franques du Levant. Woodcuts. 8vo, paper Paris 1877

2792 SCHUBERT, T. F. DE. Monnayes Russes des derniers trois siecles, 1547–1855. Text in 4to, half morocco. 37 plates in colors in oblong folio cloth box, as 2 vols. Leipsic, 1857
Perfect copy. Very rare.

2793 SCOTTISH. Della Rarita delle Medaglie Antiche. 12mo, half morocco Roma, 1838

2794 SCOTT, J. W. Postage Stamp Catalogue. 8vo, paper 1895

2795 SESTINI, A. Museo Sestiniano ; collezione di Monete antiche. A manuscript of over 1,000 pages. 3 vols, small 4to, vellum 1784

2796 SEYD, E. Suggestions in reference to the Metallic Currency of the United States. 8vo, boards Lond. 1871

2797 —— The Bank of England. Note Issue and its Error. 8vo, cloth 1874

2798 SHARPE, S. Texts from the Holy Bible, explained by the Help of Ancient Monuments. With Plans and Views (including coins). 12mo, cloth Lond. 1869

2799 SHORTT, W. T. P. Sylva Antiqua Iscana. Numismatica, &c., or, Roman and other Antiquities of Exeter. Description and Elucidation of Ancient Coins, &c. 10 plates. 8vo, cloth Exeter

2800 SIMON, JAS. An Essay towards an Historical Account of Irish Coins and of the Currency of Foreign Monies in Ireland. 8 plates with Horace Walpole's bookplate. 4to, half calf   Dublin, 1749

2801 _____ Another copy with Mr. Snelling's Supplement and an additional plate of 19 coins. 4to, boards   Dublin, 1810

2802 SLAFTER, ED. F. The Vermont Coinage. 2 plates. 8vo, cloth (Only 50 copies printed.)
                              Montpelier, 1870

2803 _____ The Copper Coinage of the Earl of Stirling, 1632. Woodcuts.   Small 4to, paper
                Boston: Privately printed, 1874

2804 SMITH, J. T. Observations on the Duties and Responsibilities involved in the Management of Mints. 8vo, boards   Madras, 1848

2805 SMITH, A. M. Prices of Old Rare Coins. 16mo, boards   Phil.

2806 SMYTH, CAPT. WM. H. Descriptive Catalogue of a Cabinet of Roman Imperial Large Brass Medals. 4to, half calf   Bedford, 1834

2807 _____ REAR-ADMIRAL, WM. H. Descriptive Catalogue of a Cabinet of Roman Family Coins belonging to His Grace the Duke of Northumberland. 4to, cl.   Printed for private circulation, 1856

2808 SNELLING, T. A View of the Silver Coin and Coinage of England, from the Norman Conquest; also view of the Gold Coins and Copper Coins; also the Silver Coins of Scotland, and Miscellaneous Views of the Coins struck by English Princes in France; Counterfeit Sterlings, &c. Illustrated with numerous plates; all in one volume. 4to, calf   1762-69

2809 _____ View of the Silver Coin and Coinage of Scotland. Plates. 4to, half roan   Lond. 1774

2810 _____ Thirty-three Plates of English Medals. 33 plates. 4to, half morocco   Lond. 1776

2811 _____ The Doctrine of Gold and Silver Computations; in which is included that of the Par of Money, the proportion in value between Gold and Silver, &c. Numerous plates. 8vo, boards
                                  Lond. 1766

2812 SNOWDEN, J. R. A Description of Ancient and Modern Coins in the Mint Cabinet of United States. 27 plates in colors. Interleaved copy. 8vo, half morocco   Phil. 1860

2813 SNOWDEN, J. R. A Description of the Medals of Washington; of National and Miscellaneous Medals and other objects of interest in the Museum of the Mint. 79 facsimile engravings. 4to, cloth Phil. 1861

2814 ———— The Coins of the Bible and its Money Terms. Cuts. 16mo, cloth Phil.

2815 STEVENS, ED. T. Flint Chips, a Guide to Pre-Historic Archæology. Illustrated. 8vo, cloth Lond. 1870

2816 STONE, ED. M. The Architect and Monetarian: a Brief Memoir of Thos. Alex. Tefft. Thin 8vo, half roan Prov. 1869

2817 STRADA, J. DE. Epitome du Thresor des Antiquitez, c'est a dire, Pourtraits des vrayes Medailles des Empp. tant d'Orient que d'Occident. Numerous small engraved portraits. 4to, old calf A Lyon, 1553

2818 STUKELY, WM. The Medallic History of Marcus Aurelius Valerius Carausius, Emperor in Britain. Plates. 4to, old calf Lond. 1757

2819 Symbola Diuina A Humana Pontificum Imperatorum Regum: accessit breuis and facilis Isagoge Iac-Typotii. 60 plates. Folio, old cf. Pragæ. 1601

2820 **TARIF GENERAL.** Monnaies de Pays-Bas. Brabant, France, etc. 12mo, bds. 1820

2821 TATE, WM. The Modern Cambist: a Manual of Foreign Exchanges. 8vo, hf. mor. Lond. 1834

2822 TAYLOR'S Gold and Silver Coin Examiner. Thompson's Coin Chart Manual. Harzfeld's Circular, 1877. Mason's Magazine, Dec., 1868, and April, 1872, &c. 11 pamphlets

2823 THOMAS, ED. A Collection of some of the Miscellaneous Essays on Oriental Subjects. 12 in number — on coins. 1 vol. 8vo, hf. cf., gilt Lond.

2824 ———— Sassanian Coins. Plates and woodcuts. 8vo, cloth Lond. 1873

2825 ———— Early Sassanian Inscriptions, Seals and Coins. Illustrated. 8vo, cloth Lond. 1868

2826 THOMASON, SIR ED. Memoirs during Half a Century. Numerous illustrations of works of art in metal and pottery. 2 vols, 8vo, cloth Lond. 1845

2827 THOMPSON's Coin Chart Manual. Numerous woodcuts. 8vo Lond. 1891

2828 TILL, WM. An essay on the Roman Denarius and English Silver Penny, showing their derivation from the Greek Drachma ; with a list of English and Scotch Pennies, &c. Plate. Small 12mo, half calf Lond. 1837

2829 —— Another copy in bds., *uncut* Lond. 1837

2830 —— Descriptive Particulars of English Coronation Medals from Edward VI. to Victoria. 12mo, cloth Lond. 1838

2831 TILESTON, ED. G. Hand-Book of the Administrations of the U. S. Photo-plate. 16mo, cloth 1871

2832 TRIFET, F. The American Stamp Mercury. 1867–70. 3 vols. bound in 2. 8vo, half roan Bost. All ever published.

2833 TRIP of the Steamer Oceanus to Fort Sumter and Charleston, S. C., 1865. 8vo, paper Brooklyn

2834 TRUBNER'S American and Oriental Literary Record. 14 Nos. 1871–3

2835 ♎NITED STATES Report on the Finances for 1874. 8vo, cloth

2836 —— Statutes in reference to Coins, 1792 to 1876. 8vo. paper

2837 ♎AILLANT, J. Numismata Imperatorum Romanorum a Julio Cæsare ad Postumum usque Numerous copper-plate illustrations. 3 vols, 4to, half vellum Romæ, 1743

2838 —— Series Nummorum Antiquorum Familiarum ac Imperatorum. Interleaved. 16mo, vellum Venetiis, 1768

2839 VAN LOON, G. Histoire Metallique des XVII. Provinces des Pays-Bas. Profusely illustrated. 5 vols, folio, calf À la Haye, 1732

2840 VELASQUEZ, L. J. Ensayo sobre los Alphabetos las Letras desconidas, que se encuentran en las mas antiquas Medallas, y Monumentos de Espana. 20 plates. 4to, vellum Madrid, 1752

2841 VENUTI, R. Numismata Romanorum Pontificum. Many illustrations. 4to, old calf Romæ, 1744

2842 VILLARESTAN, C. DE. Catalogo de las Monedas Arabigo-Espanolas. 8vo, hf. mor. Madrid, 1861

2843 VOLCKAMERS, Jon. G. Rariora Magnae Graeciae
Numismata cum enumerationi Sanctorum, Pontificum, Imperatorum, Regnum, Ducem, etc. ex Calabria, Sicilia, &c. originem suam trahentium. 29
plates of coins and 5 maps. Folio, calf 1683

2844 VALLAVINE, P. Observations on the Present Condition of the Current Coin of this Kingdom. 8vo,
half morocco Lond. 1742

2845 **W**ALLEN, WM. History and Antiquities of
the Round Church at Little Maplestead,
Essex, formerly belonging to the Knights Hospitallers. Illustrated. 8vo, cloth Lond. 1836

2846 WALSH, R. An Essay on Ancient Coins, Medals
and Gems, illustrating the Progress of Christianity. 3d edition. Illustrated. 12mo, half morocco
Lond. 1830

2847 —— Do., do. 2d edition. 12mo, cloth 1828

2848 WARREN, A. H. Arms of the Episcopates of Great
Britain and Ireland, emblazoned and ornamented
12mo, cloth, gilt Lond. 1868

2849 WELLS, A. The Pedigree and History of Washington, derived from Odin, the Founder of Scandinavia. B. C. 70. Illustrated. 8vo, cloth, gilt
N. Y. 1879

2850 WESTROPP, H. M. Pre-Historic Phases; or Introductory Essays on Pre-Historic Archaeology. Illustrated. 8vo, cloth Lond. 1872

2851 WHARTON, Jas. Memorandum concerning Small
Money and Nickel Alloy. 8vo, paper

2852 WHELAN, P. The Numismatic Atlas—mounted
and folded. 8vo, cloth Lond. 1864

2853 WHITEHEAD, W. A. East Jersey under the Proprietary Governments. Maps &c. 8vo, cloth
N. Y. 1846

2854 —— Contributions to the Early History of Perth
Amboy and adjoining Country. Maps and engravings. 8vo, cloth N. Y. 1856

2855 WILLIAM III. OF ENGLAND. His Life, Account of
his Family, his Will, Death and Funeral. Illustrated with cuts, medals, &c. 8vo, old calf
Lond. 1703

$\mathcal{8}7$ 2856 WILLIS, THOS. Doctrine, &c., of the Quakers.
16mo, sheep　　　　N. Y.: *Saml.* Wood, 1812

$/.\,05$ 2857 WILLIS'S CURRENT NOTES : a Series of Articles on
Antiquities, Biography, Heraldry, History, Language, Natural History, &c. 7 vols, small 4to,
cloth　　　　Lond. 1851–57

$/7.\,00$ 2858 WILSON, H. H. A Descriptive Account of the Antiquities and Coins of Afghanistan. With a Memoir on the Buildings called Topes. 22 plates of
coins besides other plates. 4to, cloth　　Lond. 1841

$4.\,50$ 2859 WOOD, J. T. Discoveries at Ephesus, including the
Site and Remains of the Great Temple of Diana.
With numerous illustrations from original drawings and photographs. Sq. 8vo, cloth. Bost. 1877

$3.\,25$ 2860 WOODWARD, W. ELLIOT. A List of Washington
Memorial Medals　　　　1865
Privately printed. Only 30 copies in quarto, of which this is No.
5. Elegantly bound in green morocco, gilt.

$2.\,62$ 2861 —— Another copy. No. 2 of Drawing Paper
copies. 4to, half calf

$2.\,50$ 2862 —— Catalogue of Selected Specimens from the
Finotti Collection. Printed *prices* interleaved.
4to, half morocco　　　　1862

$/.\,50$ 2863 —— Catalogue of American Coins, Medals, &c.
Interleaved copy　Sale of March, 1865. 4to, half
morocco　　　　N Y.

60 2864 WOODWORTH, J. Reminiscences of Troy from
1790 to 1807. 2d edition. With Notes. Small 4to,
cloth　　　　Albany, 1860

$\checkmark 0$ 2865 —— Another copy. Cloth, uncut

$4.\,25$ 2866 WYATT, THOS. Memoirs of the Generals, Commodores and other Commanders of American Army
and Navy during the Revolution and War of 1812
who were presented with medals. 82 engravings
on steel of the medals. 8vo, half calf　Phil. 1848

$,.\,25$ 2867 WYTTENBACH'S, PROF. Guide to the Roman Antiquities of the City of Treves, edited by Dawson
Turner With plates from unpublished drawings
and other illustrations. 8vo, cloth　Lond. 1839

2868 **Z**ABRISKIE, A. C. Descriptive Catalogue of
Lincoln Memorial and Political Medals.
Photo-plate. 8vo, half morocco   N. Y. 1873
Only 75 copies printed.

2869   Another copy. 8vo paper. (No plate)

2870 ZACHARIAS, ERNST. Numotheca Numismatica
Latomiorum. 7 parts in one vol. With cuts. 4to,
half roan   Dresden

2871 ZAIDIN. FR. C. Y. Errores de Varios Numismati
cos Extranjeros al tratar de las Monedas Arabigo-
Espanolas. 8vo, half morocco   Madrid. 1874